The Radiant Heart

HEALING THE HEART
HEALING THE SOUL

SHARON J. WENDT, PH.D.

Radiant Heart Press

Munster, IN

The Radiant Heart

HEALING THE HEART
HEALING THE SOUL

BY SHARON J. WENDT, PH.D.

Published by
Radiant Heart Press
520 Ridge Road
Munster, IN 46321

Printed in the United States of America

First Edition

ISBN: 0-9647663-0-2

Cover Illustration by Milli Maria Oden
Book Design by The Green Edge
Editing by Patsey Kahmann

DEDICATION

To my father:

His love is the light of my life.

*My father's death and the loss of his love
became the inspiration for me to begin a
transformational journey inward to my heart. It
has been a journey of discovery to reclaim my
own radiant heart.*

ACKNOWLEDGMENTS

There are so many teachers who have given me love and encouragement as they guided me on my transformational journey. I am deeply grateful to each of them for their guidance and inspiration.

My first teacher was my mother, who instilled in me a love for learning and values about higher education. She also gave me two very significant permissions that allowed me to go exploring in the world. She said, "You can do anything you set your mind to," and "You are different, and you don't have to be one of the crowd." She and my father believed in me and taught me to believe in myself.

I have been guided by many psychotherapists, trainers, and spiritual teachers over the years. Each of them helped me see who I was in the moment and who I could become.

My most important teachers have been my clients, who have enriched my life as they opened their hearts and bared their souls to me. They trusted me with their feelings, which is the most precious part of themselves.

This book has evolved with the assistance of many people. Numerous professional friends have given me feedback over the years including Ken Bentall, Dr. Valerie Hunt, Walter Weston, Catherine Reidel, and Dr. Stewart Wong. I have also incorporated improvements from numerous editors including Dr. Teri Mahaney, Julianne Stein, Donna Cunningham, Gerry White, and Elaine Born. I wish to thank each of them for their contributions to this project.

My deep appreciation to Patsey Kahmann, who has been the main editor for this book. She has been an incredible stabilizing force with her attention to detail and her ideas for restructuring the book. I am truly grateful for her assistance.

I also wish to give special heartfelt thanks to Dr. Daniel Benor and Rita Benor for their contributions to *The Radiant Heart*. Dan's professional expertise in spiritual healing and his editorial contribution to the manuscript have been important assets to this project. His professional support over the years has also given me many opportunities to teach Radiant Heart Therapy internationally. Rita's clairvoyant abilities have added a special gift to this book.

I extend my appreciation to Milli Maria Oden for creating the original artwork entitled *Temple*. Her beautiful painting hangs in my office and brings "the light" to the cover of the book.

I also extend my thanks to Kung Ha for his artistic contribution in designing the cover and illustrations. His talent is another gift for this project.

I also want to thank Collette Bargy-Campbell, my office manager, for her never-ending support as the book was in process. I could always count on her to lend a helping hand and go the extra mile in her efforts to assist in whatever way was needed.

My special thanks to my spiritual sister, Jill Miller, for her support and inspiration as I worked to define the Radiant Heart Therapy. Her persistent questioning was invaluable in helping me define the theory of the heartwork and clarify my thoughts about the deathwish and the issue of radiance.

I also wish to acknowledge the guidance I have received from my teachers in the spiritual dimension. This book is filled with words inspired by the whispering voices of those spirit beings who work with me from the other side of the veil. I feel their loving guidance as I do the heartwork, as I write these stories, and as I travel forward on my journey of transformation.

Special Note:

The names of clients in this book have been changed to protect their confidentiality.

The spiritual healing techniques outlined here are not intended to be used in place of standard medical treatment. All of my clients with physical illnesses were also being treated by their medical doctors.

TABLE OF CONTENTS

MEDITATION ON THE COVER PICTURE

The artwork on the cover of the book is entitled TEMPLE. The original hangs in my office as a symbol of the spiritual nature of the Radiant Heart work. It is my daily reminder of the purpose of this work which is to reconnect people to the energy of their souls. This helps people bridge the void between two levels of existence: the human level and the soul level.

Radiance is the beauty of the soul energy shining forth through the whole being of individuals who have a conscious connection to their spiritual nature. The soul energy infuses the entire aura making it bigger, brighter, and full of vibrant colors. The white light shines forth from the human heart radiating love to self and all other human beings.

The artist has captured the truth of our very existence. We are human and we are divine. We are both at the same time. We are connected through our soul to the universal energy which is divine love and our whole being is filled with this divine love. There is no need to strive to become divine. We already are divine and we radiate divine love.

This picture is a wonderful representation of who we really are at the spiritual level. We are an energy field filled with vibrant colors. We are dynamic. We are constantly vibrating and sending waves of energy into our aura. We are energy. We are white light. We are divine love. We are radiant.

THE RADIANT HEART:
THE BRIDGE BETWEEN THE HUMAN AND THE DIVINE

This book is a bridge. It is a bridge of light. It is a bridge of love. It is a bridge between physical and non-physical experience, between the human and the spiritual experience. It is a healing bridge between the mind and the heart, and the heart and the soul.

We live in a time of spiritual crisis. Many people live in the physical and material world and are disconnected from their spiritual nature. Growing numbers are feeling a need to reconnect to the energy of their souls. They seek a way to rise above the struggle of human existence to find true meaning for their human suffering as they live from day to day.

A paradigm shift is happening at this time. After centuries of focusing on intellectual understandings, we are being called to experience our feelings—to experience the knowingness that comes through the heart. This knowingness of the heart is very different from the knowingness of the mind. To experience it, we need to look beyond the volumes of books we have read and studied. It is not enough to read a book about what is in the world beyond the physical, we must also take the risk of having our own experiences. Beyond what is learned with the mind is the truth of experience that is learned with the heart.

A paradigm shift is also happening in the field of medicine. In traditional medicine physicians are trained to deal with the body like a machine. In such a model, the machine has various parts that can malfunction and need to be repaired. Traditional physicians are not trained to deal with the energy of the soul that flows through the body, with the role of the mind as it affects the body, nor with the role of emotions influencing the body.

A new kind of medicine called holistic medicine is emerging as part of the paradigm shift. In this model there is an emphasis on the mind-body connection, or how the mind influences the health or ill-health of the body. Some holistic practitioners believe the spiritual aspect of a person influences the health of the body.

Radiant Heart Therapy advances the paradigm shift even further to include the emotional heart. A more encompassing view of a human being is body, mind, heart, and spirit. The heart is the seat of the uplifting emotions: love, joy, peace, compassion, contentment, and harmony. These uplifting emotions have a definite positive influence on the health of the physical body. The heart is also the seat of painful emotions: sadness, loneliness, grief, and emptiness. These painful emotions also have a definite negative influence on the health of the physical body.

My contribution to holistic medicine is to shift the focus to the emotional heart and provide a method to reclaim the radiant heart. When the heart is radiant it becomes the bridge between the human and the divine—between body and soul. The radiant heart is the key to transforming the body, mind, and spirit of each of us. The radiant heart is the key to preventing physical illness. The radiant heart is the key to experiencing the energy of love. The radiant heart is the key to healing both psychological and physical illnesses using the energy of love.

I have written my own story as one individual who has been willing to risk exploring in the invisible world beyond the body. I offer it to you as a living metaphor of the possibilities for personal growth and the attainment of expanded consciousness. It is the story of how I built my own bridge and forged my own path as I went on an incredible journey of discovery in an exciting new world. I began the journey searching for answers to the questions concerning my human pain. I found some answers, but I found much more. I found my Higher Self in this invisible world beyond the body. I found my soul.

I discovered after building my bridge that it had spanned the deep chasm between my humanness and my soul. The discovery came when I made the connection—the connection to this invisible energy. Constructing my own bridge allowed me to heal the disconnection from my soul. I offer you my story from my heart to your heart with the hope that it will touch the deepest part of your psyche that is your soul.

"We are radiant beings filled with light and love."

–Louise Hay

CHAPTER 1

AWAKENING TO MY SOUL

RADIANCE: OUR NATURAL STATE OF BEING

n the beginning there was LIGHT.

This light is the radiant light of divine love. From the very beginning of our existence we are spiritual beings and we exist in the universe without a physical body. We are divine and we swim in a sea of divine love. We are radiant beings filled with light and love. We are radiant because we are filled with the energy of divine love. We have a glow about us that is blissful to experience and wondrous to see. We exist as a soul in this place of divine love, and radiance is our natural state of being.

THE LOSS OF RADIANCE

As souls we are on an endless journey of evolution through eternity. As part of that journey we come to the earth plane so that we might learn lessons and evolve to higher levels of consciousness. We leave our home of light and love to come to a strange place with very little light. It is such a difficult journey that only the most courageous souls will come. As courageous souls we enter the earth plane filled with curiosity, hopefulness, and a sense of adventure. Most often we experience a deep sense of disillusionment and incredible heartache at the loss of divine love.

As human beings on the earth plane we experience a sense of *disconnection from the divine*. We take on physical bodies that act like shrouds over the light of our souls. We must learn to use the five human senses, which seem very strange and inadequate compared to our keen spiritual senses. We lose touch with our souls and we forget the very purpose of our journey here to earth. We even forget we were once radiant beings and we experience a loss of radiance. We don't really lose our radiance; however, it seems like we do because we lose our *awareness* of our radiance. All of these experiences create a great chasm between the two parts of ourselves—the human and the divine.

The loss of divine love is so incredibly painful that we close off our hearts to deaden the pain. As we close our hearts we lose even more of our radiance. We don't lose our souls, but we lose our conscious connection to soul. We experience a disconnection from our souls and begin to believe we are merely human.

If we were born to parents who could provide unconditional love (the equivalent of divine love) we could keep our hearts open and keep our radiance. However, this is rarely the case. There are so few human beings who can manifest their radiance that most of us are born to parents with closed hearts. We are born to parents who, because they have lost their own sense of radiance, cannot transfer radiance to us. It seems to be part of the human condition. This is the way it is. And yet I ask: *Is this the way it has to be?*

RECLAIMING OUR RADIANCE

We are born with an innate drive to return to divine love. This innate drive becomes a motivation for us to find ways to reclaim our radiance after we become human beings. Reclaiming our radiance involves opening our heart, releasing the heartache of feeling so unloved, and forming a conscious connection back to soul. Then the energy of our soul can flow into our open heart and radiate forth from the very core of our being. The energy of divine love from our very own soul and from the universe once again flows through our whole being. When we accomplish this we become what we were meant to be: *human beings with radiant hearts.*

THE RADIANT HEART: THE BRIDGE BETWEEN THE HUMAN AND THE DIVINE

The radiant heart forms a bridge that spans the chasm between our two levels of consciousness—the human level and the spiritual level. This bridge allows the energy of divine love to flow from the spiritual realms to the earth realms and be experienced by human beings as we stay in our human bodies on the earth plane.

This energy of divine love flows through our radiant heart and heals our sense of disconnection from the divine. This energy carries with it the intuitive knowledge about our soul purpose and our lifeplan for this lifetime. This lifeplan contains all the spiritual lessons our soul chose to learn during our life here on earth. It was developed by the soul before coming to the earth plane. We lost our awareness of our lifeplan when we experienced our disconnection from the divine. *When we can reclaim our radiance we become a human being with a radiant heart who is consciously aware of the soul's purpose and feels empowered to complete the lifeplan.*

RADIANT HEART THERAPY FACILITATES TRANSFORMATION

"Unless I care for my soul, I will not have changed who I am."
— Adrianna Huffington, *The Fourth Instinct: The Call of the Soul*

Radiant Heart Therapy is a new model of spiritual psychology that provides people with a specific method for reclaiming their radiance. It is an integration of spiritual healing and psychotherapy. In the Greek language the word psychology means the study of the soul. Radiant Heart Therapy puts the heart and soul back into the practice of psychology. It rises above the personality level and focuses on healing at the spiritual level. Radiant Heart Therapy is a model of psychotherapy and healing based on the healing power of love.

Every treatment model has a few basic philosophical tenets. The key tenet of Radiant Heart Therapy is simple:

The root cause of both psychological and physical illness is the disconnection from soul.

True healing is teaching people to open their hearts and experience the spiritual energy of love. This heart opening forges the connection back to soul. This spiritual healing at the heart and soul level facilitates both psychological and physical healing at the human level.

Radiant Heart Therapy is a process that can be used to promote both personality transformation and spiritual transformation. It can be used for personal growth, psychotherapy, reversing physical diseases, and spiritual awakening. It is designed to facilitate transformation at all four levels of being: spiritual, mental, emotional, and physical.

Spiritual Level: The Radiant Heart exercises use specific visualizations to enhance the flow of spiritual energy through the physical body so ordinary human beings can perceive it and believe in its existence. This invites us to form a *conscious connection to our soul.*

Mental Level: The Radiant Heart process invites us to open our minds and allow important shifts in consciousness concerning our beliefs about ourselves, other human beings, life here on earth, and life in the spiritual world.

Emotional Level: The Radiant Heart process invites us to open our emotional heart to the energy of spiritual love. It also gives us a simple method for releasing the lower frequency emotions of fear, sadness, and anger while enhancing our ability to live in the higher frequency emotions of peace, joy, and love.

Physical Level: The Radiant Heart process gives us the tools to enhance our own natural healing abilities by using specific visualizations that bring radiant healing energy into the heart. This process strengthens the energy field and stimulates the thymus gland, the master gland that controls the immune system.

DEVELOPING RADIANT HEART THERAPY— MY TRANSFORMATIONAL JOURNEY

"Our life is meant to be a story that mysteriously writes itself and our work is the creative fruit of our lives."
— Marianne Williamson, *A Return to Love*

Over the past twenty years, following the wisdom of my heart, I created a new model of spiritual psychotherapy that I now call Radiant Heart Therapy. It evolved outside my conscious awareness for the first fifteen years. It was not something I planned to do. It just "sort of happened" while my conscious mind was busy focusing on important things like growing up, becoming a math teacher, getting married, raising two children, grieving my father's death, becoming a transactional analysis therapist, earning my doctorate in clinical psychology, getting divorced, creating and directing a holistic clinic, and exploring metaphysics and energy medicine.

I now know Radiant Heart Therapy is my life's work. It is a major part of my purpose in life. On a soul level it is the work I came here to do. It absolutely lights up my life and makes my own heart radiant. I work with my own heart open—sharing feelings—sharing love— sharing energy with my clients. When I'm in the process I usually feel connected back to soul and at peace with myself. As I finish a day at my clinic, I often think, "I'm in the right place at the right time. I'm doing what's right for me and I'm flowing with the process of life."

I didn't always know about my purpose in life. In fact, I spent most of my life not knowing. As I look back over my life, I can trace the unfolding of this model of therapy I call Radiant Heart Therapy. I can now see how it all evolved as if by a master plan. However, at the time I had no idea of the plan and no idea of where I was going. I felt like

I was meandering through life wishing that I could find some signposts saying, "This is the way to your path." I did not consciously know I was on my path. In fact, I was not tuned in spiritually, so I didn't even know I was supposed to be looking for a path.

Radiant Heart Therapy evolved out of experiences in my personal life and experiences in my professional training. Over the past twenty years I immersed myself in transactional analysis, Gestalt therapy, bioenergetics, prenatal psychology, MariEL Healing, subtle energy therapies, and the study of energy field medicine. I experienced all of these modalities first as the client and later as the psychotherapist. The insights I received from both of these roles have been invaluable in developing this new model of psychotherapy.

I know the development of Radiant Heart Therapy was closely guided. I often get inspired to say or write something that I've never considered with my logical mind. These bits of intuition or connection to higher mind have usually given me another key to the creation of this model. I always seem to be given the right teacher, the right book, or the right connection to evolve to the next level in the process. It's not always on my time schedule but I am given what I need. At times I don't even "get it" that I have what I need. Many times it has taken several years for my left brain (conscious logical mind) to understand what my right brain (unconscious intuitive mind) has already created. In other words, I *know* intuitively through the wisdom of my heart long before I understand with the intelligence of my mind.

CONNECTING TO EARTH AND SKY

It seems to me that I've always been connected to the earth and the sky. I grew up on a farm in northwest Indiana. I often worked with my dad out in the fields, walking the earth, sitting with my back against a huge oak tree and feeling the energy of the sun. I absolutely loved the sun. Even as a child, I called myself a sun worshipper. The only way I could ever relax was to lie in the sun getting a tan. I could do it for hours. I loved the feel of the sun warming my body. Since I did not understand the concepts of energy, I had no understanding that I was absorbing the earth energy and the radiance of the sun and re-energizing my whole being.

As a teenager I loved to go to a beautiful beach area at the southern tip of Lake Michigan called the Indiana Dunes. To this day, my favorite activity is to walk the beach barefoot and watch the sun glistening on the water. I can feel the earth energy as my feet touch the sand. I can feel the sun energy coming in the top of my head. I love it so much that I bought a beach home so I could spend time walking the beach before I go to work every day. I often spend an entire day on the beach. I never seem to tire of it. It's good for me at the heart level and it reconnects me to my soul. I feel rejuvenated—reborn—revitalized by the energy I receive from being connected to both the earth and the sky.

These seemingly mundane life experiences gave me the energetic experiences of being grounded to the earth and open to the spiritual energy of the sky. Of course, I didn't know this at the time. Neither did I know that this experience would become a cornerstone of my energy exercises for Radiant Heart Therapy. When I look back, I'm always intrigued that my heart already knew what my mind did not understand.

MY FATHER CONNECTION

Although I didn't know it had begun, my journey to connecting consciously with my soul purpose started on a September night in 1973 with my father's heart attack. At the time I was a retired math teacher raising my two children, John and Renee. I was looking for information to improve my parenting skills. Out of the blue, a friend handed me a newspaper clipping describing the book I'm OK—You're OK. It also announced that a therapist was starting a series of classes discussing transactional analysis therapy, the benefits of psychotherapy, and parenting techniques.

I was sitting in my first class at the very moment of my father's heart attack. I came home to a phone call from my mother. Her words are still embedded in my mind.

> Your father has had a massive heart attack. He's in intensive care and not expected to live through the night.

This event absolutely changed my whole life. I was so bonded to my father that I felt like the light went out of my life. My heart hurt so much I thought it would break. The only way I could deal with the pain was to shut it off and get depressed. Within a week I made a significant and very unusual choice. I chose to begin psychotherapy as a client to deal with my heartache and my depression. Again, at this time, I didn't know this choice was an opening to my life's work. I was only interested in healing my heartache.

My father spent two months in the hospital before he was released with the restriction of not returning to work. I spent a lot of time visiting with him. We never talked about the possibility of his death. I seemed to have this childlike belief that my father could never die.

We vacationed together in Florida where he and I would walk the beaches early in the morning before anyone else was up. On one of our walks, I shared with him how much I loved the personal growth process of psychotherapy. I told him what I was learning about transforming myself through working with my feelings. I also told him I loved it so much that I had decided to give up mathematics and go back to graduate school and become a psychotherapist. I'll always remember his response. His face lit up in a big smile as he said:

> That's my girl! I knew you couldn't stay home in the kitchen much longer. I could see you were getting restless.

My heart sang the rest of the day. I felt such joy in my inner child. I was so delighted to have his blessing about this major career change.

Two months after the Florida trip my father had his second heart attack and died. This tragedy happened only a week before I started the training for my life's work. I went through the funeral process in shock. I was not prepared for him to die, even though all the doctors had said he was living on borrowed time.

When he died, the light truly went out of my life. I had this longing to go and be with him on the other side. I had no interest in continuing my life here without him. In retrospect, I developed my own deathwish. I carried on with my regular routines of being a housewife and mother, keeping my longing to be with him a secret from friends and family.

My first week of training involved an experiential retreat which focused on releasing feelings. I decided to attend because I couldn't face staying home and being alone with my depression and my numbness. At the retreat I poured my heart out, breaking the barrier of shock and denial. It was a safe place to open my heart and release the pain. I raged, I screamed, I cried with the pain of my father's death. I opened my heart to the pain and released it. I was furious that he was gone. I was furious with God for taking him. I was furious with him for not taking care of himself. I felt the deep agony of my loss. I truly felt my heartache to the depths of my soul. This was the first step on my healing journey, the transformational journey inward to my soul.

THE NEXT TEN YEARS

After my father's death I continued my training to become a psychotherapist and at the same time I worked through my grief about his death. I threw myself into my training. It was the only thing that brought joy to my life. I loved the process of learning from both books and personal experiences. I seemed to have a passion for it like I had never experienced before in my life. I earned a master's degree in psychology and began working as a psychotherapist. I immediately enrolled in a doctoral program for clinical psychology and juggled my roles of therapist, student, wife, and mother. The massive amounts of reading and the training weekends were not work for me. They were a joy, and I felt my own creativity and personal power developing as I honed my skills to become a therapist.

My professional life was easy, while my personal life seemed to be filled with heartaches. In the six years after my father's death I coped with one painful event after another. First, my twin sister received a diagnosis of multiple sclerosis. As twins we were connected at a deep psychic level, so I felt much of her emotional pain. Then I filed for divorce and went through the pain and sadness of leaving a sixteen-year marriage. During this time my mother-in-law developed cancer. She was like a mother to me and my heart ached as I helped with the caretaking while she fought to regain her health. After fifteen months she made her transition to the other side.

At the human level all this emotional pain made very little sense to me. I kept asking myself, "What is the purpose of this pain? Why is this happening to me? Why is my life so filled with struggle and heartache?" And the little child part of me longed for a time with my father so I could feel protected again by his strength.

"I'VE COME TO SAY GOOD-BYE"

"The Spirit is both birthless and deathless.
The Principle of Life cannot know death."
— Earnest Holmes, *The Science of Mind*

I had a profound transformational experience in my own living room just two days after my mother-in-law's funeral. I had been trying to write a paper on meditation for my doctoral program. My creativity was totally blocked because I was trying to stifle my feelings. I did not want to feel the pain of my loss. I did not want to open my heart because it was too wounded. I was trying to stay in my mind and focus on completing my work.

My mother-in-law, Golda, had been a second mother to me. I had been married to her son for many years and she had helped raise our two children. She had always been available to give me a break when I needed it. She died after a brave battle against cancer that involved chemotherapy and months of being in and out of the hospital. Throughout her illness I was in the process of divorcing her son. It was a terrible time for all of us. We were all feeling the pain of separating and letting go.

Golda and I shared this deep love. I always thought it was rather unusual that we had such a strong love bond. I knew I had stayed in the marriage longer than was healthy because I didn't want to break her heart. She and I agreed to keep our relationship and not discuss the divorce. So I did a share of the caretaking during her illness and we carried on with our love for each other even though she disapproved greatly of my decision. I always thought she was a very wise woman to be able to rise above her own pain and keep the love. That was in 1980 and my heart still carries a tiny portion of the pain I felt then. I still deeply miss her presence on the physical level.

As I was sitting and trying to write about meditation, I kept getting the idea to lie down on my couch and actually do a meditation process. A part of me resisted; I felt that taking a break would be like giving up. This part told me I should keep on working. But I finally listened to the insistent voice inside my head and lay down with a meditation tape. I was able to relax quite easily and I drifted into a deep altered state of consciousness.

I remember the experience as if it were yesterday. I was suddenly aware that my dear Golda was right next to me. She appeared about six inches from my left shoulder. I could only see her head, shoulders, and upper torso, although that didn't seem strange at the time. I was amazed to see this beautiful light shining forth from her face. She looked absolutely radiant! She had lost her hair during chemotherapy but now it had grown back, and she looked thirty years younger than I remembered her. As I stared at her in shock she began to communicate without speaking aloud. I was hearing with my inner ear and the message was very clear, "I've come to say good-bye." She leaned forward and I felt something brush my cheek. It was the lightest kiss I've ever experienced, but I knew it was a kiss.

It all happened so fast that I didn't have time to think or feel. I only had time to experience. The moment she was gone I burst into tears. I cried from the depths of my being. I didn't even know why I was crying. I felt this burst of joy that she had come to me. I was so overjoyed to see her looking so radiant. I know I lost my fear of death in that moment. Who could be afraid when she looked so wonderful? On another level I was crying for my loss. I felt my human loss of not being able to be with her and talk to her on a physical level. There seemed to be nothing to do so I just let myself cry. The sadness and pain of my loss flowed out from my whole body. I still remember the physical aching in my chest as I released the pain from my heart.

It is very interesting to me that I didn't feel scared. In the moment there was no time to be scared. Afterwards, I only felt the joy and the sadness. I had always believed that seeing a spirit would be terribly frightening. My experience was very different from my belief.

Of course, afterwards I began to question my reality and my sanity. My left brain began to ask all the logical questions. Did this really happen? Was it only a dream? Did I just imagine it? Was she really here? Am I just making this up? Who could I tell this to? Who would believe me? Did I really hear what I thought I heard? Did I really feel a kiss on my cheek? How can this be? Am I going crazy? What is reality?

I questioned myself for days before I risked telling my experience to another human being. I finally decided to tell just one friend. Thank God she didn't laugh and she didn't pronounce me crazy. Instead she told me her husband's experience of seeing his dead brother appear in their bedroom just three days after the funeral. In retrospect, I can see that I intuitively picked a compassionate person. In that moment I needed a friend like her, for I wasn't strong enough in my beliefs to trust my own experience entirely. Also, I swore her to secrecy. I didn't want anyone to know for fear they might criticize. I felt too vulnerable to withstand any criticism.

Gradually, I risked telling more and more people. The response was almost always the same. Most people opened up and began to share their own experience or that of a friend. I soon learned that many people have had a loved one appear to them from the other side. Most people, like me, did not know what to think or feel. I was comforted to find my questioning was a fairly normal response to this rather abnormal experience.

Eventually, I learned to trust this experience and not question with my mind. My logical mind could never make any sense of it. I could never produce any proof that the doubting part of my brain would accept. It was impossible to prove anything about it.

Golda's appearance from the other side was a deep transformational experience for me. It produced numerous shifts of consciousness almost automatically. I truly became a different person because of those few seconds in time. I lost my fear of death without even thinking about it. Previously I had a belief that there was a God and a heaven where we all go after death. However, I was only believing what I was taught as a child. I had no experience to back it up. I didn't really know if it was the truth. Also I had heard about the "light," but had never seen it with my own eyes. I came out of the experience saying to myself, "Death can't be so bad. She looked so radiant, so joyful, so young, and so filled with light. She can still think and communicate. She's really dead but she's alive in a different way. She's still alive but she doesn't have a body, and she exists in a place I can't normally see."

Her appearance gave me great comfort. It helped me handle the grief process with much less pain. I still grieved my loss but I didn't feel the loss of hope I had felt when my father died eight years earlier. At his death I felt as if the light went out of my life. At her death I felt as if the light came into my life. I shall be forever grateful to her for giving me such a gift.

After this experience I continued on with my life, taking care of my children, completing my doctoral work, and facilitating psychotherapy sessions with my clients. I went about my daily life wondering about this mystical experience that so deeply changed my perspective on life. I wondered why was I given such a wonderful gift. How was I able to perceive my mother-in-law as a spirit? Why had I not had the same experience with my father? Was my father alive and radiant somewhere in the universe also? I longed to know and yet I received no signs or evidence that this was so.

AN ANGEL VISITATION

As part of my training in my doctoral program I went to California to learn a therapeutic process called Rebirthing. I had been reading about this method for several years and was excited to have my own personal experience with it. I knew it involved lying on a mat doing deep breathing to access an altered state of consciousness. From this state the person is able to open the unconscious mind and remember buried emotional trauma from the past. The goal is to release the repressed emotions of these traumas through the remembering. The method is called Rebirthing because many people often are able to remember their own birth trauma and release any negative effects from their birth experience. I left for California feeling as if I were going on an adventure. Little did I know how much of an adventure was in store for me.

I worked with the rebithing process each day for seven days, pulling up old emotional traumas and clearing them from my consciousness. It was a wonderful process, and I looked forward to the next day as I wrote my experiences in a journal each night. On the fifth day I had a very unexpected experience.

I had been doing the breathwork for almost an hour. I was in an altered state and was resting after a deep release of some old emotional hurts. I felt this wonderful sense of peace and bliss. It was like being asleep yet conscious at the same time. I remember everything was deep black on my inner screen of consciousness. Suddenly a beautiful white Pegasus horse floated into the blackness and startled me awake. It was majestic, and moved with an elegance that seemed unearthly. Within seconds I heard this deep booming voice say, "I am the Archangel Gabriel and I am always with you." Again I didn't hear it with my human ears. I heard it with my inner ears. The voice was so loud it filled my whole head and my whole being. It seemed to resonate over and over inside my head, like an echo. There was no doubt about the message. It was loud and clear.

Immediately, I became flooded with emotions. My heart opened and the tears flowed down my face. I felt so loved it was rather overwhelming. I felt as if my chest would burst with a pressure from the inside. I didn't have time to think. I could only feel. And the validity of my feelings could not be denied.

Later, when I had time to think I began to question the experience. I had many judgments and many questions. Did this really happen? Did I simply make it up? Is this a psychic experience or a psychotic experience? And how would I know the difference? Who am I to have such a powerful spirit being protecting and guiding my journey? How could this be? What does this mean about my life? Do I have to do anything different if I believe this to be true? How can I trust my own perceptions when they are so far from any reality that I know? I had so many questions and so few answers. And I wondered where to look for the answers. Certainly, I knew not to look in my psychology books from my doctoral program. I had never read any case studies that related to this kind of experience. I had no clue about where to find the answers.

I returned to my center and went about facilitating my usual individual and group therapy sessions. I told only a few trusted friends of my vision. They neither agreed nor disagreed with me about the validity of the experience. Frankly, they seemed just as puzzled as I was.

Eventually, I came to terms with this mystical experience. I came to trust and believe that it really happened. I came to believe that the Archangel Gabriel is always with me. I did not make this decision with my mind, for there was no proof. Instead, I felt the truth of it in my heart. I learned to trust the validity of my experience on pure faith. Part of my process was re-experiencing the echo of those words resounding inside my head. I could not deny that I truly heard the words. And I could not deny the rush of feelings those words produced. I held onto those feelings in spite of how much my left brain questioned and judged the experience.

It took months for me to integrate this angel experience into my consciousness. I began to read books about angels and found that many other ordinary human beings were having similar experiences with angels. It helped me immensely to read their stories. Later, I also found statistics from a 1991 Gallup Poll that reported sixty-nine percent of Americans believe in angels, and thirty-two percent of Americans feel they have had contact with an angel. These statistics helped me accept my own experience as "normal."

My own angel experience and these other stories confirmed my emerging belief that there is much more to life than our day-to-day existence. There is another dimension with spirit beings who are interacting with us humans. We can only touch into their dimension on occasion, but I believe they are always present. And their presence is confirmation that we as humans have a purpose to our lives that is much more than the material issues of paying the bills, having a career, and climbing the ladder to success.

This angel experience was a major event in my transformational journey. As I look back over my life it stands out like a huge signpost along my path. It came at a time when I was most discouraged. I had spent the months before feeling lost, lonely, and abandoned. I was truly wondering if I was going in the right direction. I was separated both physically and emotionally from my family after completing my divorce. My family of origin and my children had no understanding of my work or my inner process. I also knew they could not begin to deal with the new realities I was experiencing.

I kept these mystical experiences a secret, which only served to create more loneliness. I often felt like I was living a dual reality. I had one life I could talk about and share with my coworkers, friends, and family. I had another secret life of spiritual experiences that I held within my heart. I would often meditate on Gabriel's words, "I am always with you." They comforted me and eased the loneliness of being on a path that was so different from anything I had known. They soothed the fears I had about risking such experiences and being judged as crazy. They gave me strength when I felt like giving up. They gave me courage to begin sharing these experiences with more and more people. They allowed me to keep risking and creating more experiences for myself so that I could evolve to a higher level of consciousness. Those words nurtured me as I continued my journey of transformation.

ANOTHER MYSTICAL EXPERIENCE

By 1984 I had finished my doctoral work and opened a holistic clinic in northwest Indiana. I know this sounds rather strange, but I was not aware that I was a spiritual person. I organized a staff for treating the whole person—spiritual, mental, emotional, and physical. I hired physicians, massage therapists, and a nutritionist to attend to the body. With my doctorate in clinical psychology I felt competent to work with the mental and emotional aspects of the clients. And I hired two ministers who were also Reiki healers to work with the spiritual aspects of our clients. (Reiki is an ancient Japanese form of healing with spiritual energy.)

I certainly did not feel competent to deal with any spiritual issues and I did not believe I was a spiritual person. I had not even thought about the definition of a spiritual person. My self-image was that I was a doctor trained to deal with thoughts, feelings, and behaviors at the personality level. I thought of my clinic as a business rather than a place for spiritual transformation. Again, little did I know the true reality of what I was doing.

When I opened my holistic treatment center, I knew nothing about energy therapies, chakras, reincarnation, spirit guides, spirit communication, spiritual mediums, or trance channels. It wasn't that I disbelieved or disagreed philosophically with these types of practices. I simply knew nothing about them. I had been focused on my doctoral work for six years and was unaware of the growing metaphysical movement in the United States. Shirley McLaine had gone public with her book, Out On A Limb, but I had not read it. Metaphysically, I was in the dark.

A friend invited me to schedule a session with a trance channel from Chicago. I had no earthly idea what I was getting into when I said yes to her invitation. I had never heard of a channel or a trance channel. These were strange new words to me. I asked a few questions and it sounded like a fun experience. I did have misgivings about wasting my money on a charlatan, but my friend knew another person who had had a wonderful session with this channel, so I decided to risk it. To me the whole thing was just a lark—a new adventure that might break the routine, day-to-day monotony of life. I just wanted something fun and interesting to do on my day off from the clinic.

This one-hour session changed my life forever. It was a mindblowing experience that awakened me to a whole new dimension of reality. Two of my spirit guides "came through" and talked to me about my life. They seemed to know all about me from childhood to the present. They talked about events in my personal life and my career life and described my inner thoughts and feelings as well. They talked about things I had never shared with anyone. They also made predictions for my future that were amazing to me.

My guides explained to me that I had a natural ability for counseling people because I had done it many, many times before in past lives. They stated very clearly:

> Your work at your clinic is very good. Your clinic is part of your path. You were born to be the doctor. You were born to get your doctor's degree. You were born to develop a total scenario of energy work that will heal both physical and psychological illnesses. You are here to learn passion, to learn sensitivity.

> Your work is to help people to discover their worth, to realize their potential, and to place value on their heart chakra—the heart being the greater guide to inner sensitivity. You will be involved in research, writing books on word processors, and teaching others of this new way of helping people. Many will come to the work you are doing. You are here to be a forerunner and we are here with you to inspire you and smooth the way.

Imagine me, a former math teacher and a psychotherapist, trying to make sense of these foreign words like *path, past lives, total scenario of energy, heart chakra,* and *inner sensitivity.* I kept listening to the tape of my reading and trying to make sense of it. The vocabulary was so foreign I wondered briefly if they were speaking English. I could relate to their description of my childhood and my present life experiences, but I could not relate to their predictions for my future. I had just finished my doctoral research that took two years of my life. It was such a stressful process that I vowed I would never do research again. And I certainly didn't relate to anything about "energy" and "chakras." Nor did I see myself ever writing a book. I was computer illiterate and phobic of machines, so putting anything on word processors had to be a prediction for somebody else. I decided maybe they were correct about my past and the present, but they were definitely wrong about my future. In retrospect, this was my only defense against a feeling of being totally overwhelmed. If I dared to think that these predictions could possibly be true I felt a sense of panic that started to rise from the very core of my being.

I walked out of that session a different person. I experienced such a shift in consciousness that the whole world looked different to me. Even I looked different to me. I suddenly became aware of being more than a person struggling through life trying to make decisions about which direction to take. My guides talked about my purpose in life and being on my path. I had never considered these issues. I had never looked for my path or even wondered if I was on it. I felt as if someone had hit me over the head with a sledge hammer and opened up my mind. I was so stunned from the experience that I did my work in a bit of a daze for the next two weeks. I felt sorry for my clients because I wasn't fully there. My mind was still processing all this new information. And I continued processing this session for many months afterwards.

It is difficult to convey how profoundly my perspective about life shifted with this reading. I came to understand that my daily decisions were and still are part of a much bigger plan. The plan is mapped out on the spiritual level rather than on the human level. This plan filters down to the human level through intuition, gut-level feelings, and something called inspiration. I also came to understand that my guides are here to give me support and inspiration as I move along my path. I wondered quite often where the path was ultimately leading me. As I looked back over my life I could see the many forks in the road where I made significant choices. As I looked forward I couldn't even find the road. It seemed to disappear over a hill called "the future."

Actually life really wasn't any different. This had always been the case. The human reality and the spiritual reality existed simultaneously.

The only difference was that I was now aware of the spiritual reality. Believe me, it was a big difference. I awakened to the realization that my human experiences were somehow connected to a spiritual part of me. I awakened to a conscious connection to my soul.

*"Men often stumble over
the truth but most of them pick
themselves up and hurry off
as if nothing has happened."*

–Winston Churchill

CHAPTER 2

DISCOVERING A NEW
HEALING PROCESS

"Discovery is seeing what everyone else has seen and thinking what nobody else has thought."
— Albert Szini-Gyori

FIRST CLUE TO RADIANT HEART THERAPY

y first conscious awareness of a new healing process happened in the summer of 1985. I was working with a thirty-seven-year-old woman named Roxanne. She was suicidal and had multiple psychological and physical problems including depression, anxiety-panic disorder, PMS, migraines, and allergies. Her life was very stressful because she was divorced and raising three daughters who had various medical and psychological problems.

I had worked closely with Roxanne for several months. We had established a strong therapeutic bond and I felt a great deal of compassion for her. I was very concerned because she was threatening to act on her suicidal thoughts.

I had organized my holistic center around the idea that there is a significant synergistic effect when a client receives treatments in several different modalities at the same time. I knew these various treatment modalities needed to be directed toward the various levels of being—physical, mental, emotional, and spiritual. So I had organized a staff that included treatments for all these levels. I had physicians, massage therapists, and a nutritionist to work with the physical body, psychologists and psychotherapists to work with the mind and emotions, and two Reiki healers to work with the spiritual aspects of the person.

In an effort to gain the synergistic effect of the various treatment modalities, I scheduled Roxanne for a massage, a Reiki session, and then a psychotherapy session with me. My goal was to help her shift out of her suicidal state. Roxanne had finished her massage and was receiving her Reiki treatment. As fate would have it, several other clients cancelled so the second Reiki practitioner and I were both free. I looked at her and said, "Why don't you give me a Reiki healing session?" She agreed, and while I was receiving my Reiki treatment, Roxanne was receiving hers at the same time in another room.

Immediately after my Reiki treatment I walked into the room where Roxanne lay on her back on a massage table. I stood by the table and leaned over to give her a hug. As I held her close to me I asked, "How are you doing, Roxanne?" She responded, "My chest! My chest feels filled up for the first time in my life."

I couldn't make sense of what she was saying, so I didn't say anything. I continued to hold her, and in the next moment she started crying deeply, and spontaneously announced, "I want to live!"

This decision to live was a great surprise to me. This was a major shift in consciousness for Roxanne and it was accomplished within a few moments. With other clients, I had to work at great length to achieve this kind of shift. This time it seemed so effortless and so spontaneous that I could hardly believe what had just transpired. I couldn't make sense of it because it didn't fit into my current reality about facilitating a shift in consciousness with my clients.

I knew something very profound and very significant had just transpired. I had no words to explain it and it really mystified me. It took me four years and many kinds of experiences to understand the process that now appears so simple.

I had another unusual experience several months later while facilitating a women's weekly therapy group. The women were in treatment for depression, anxiety, and various other emotional issues. We sat on big pillows on the floor to elicit the inner child. As I talked with one woman across the room, another client named Susan lay down on her back on the floor beside me. After five or ten minutes I looked down to see my own hand placed firmly on the center of her chest. I had my attention focused on the other client so I had not noticed my hand moving towards Susan.

I asked her a benign question, "How are you doing?" Her response startled me, "How did you know to put your hand right there? I've been hurting there for days." She began to sob, releasing the deep emotional pain of being unloved and lonely in her marriage. Again, this experience did not fit the model of psychotherapy that I had been trained to do and I did not know what to make of it.

After these two experiences, I began to think about this place in the center of the chest. Something was happening that I didn't understand, because it went beyond my clinical training. I knew somehow it was very significant and I intuitively kept coming back to it.

I also knew my hands were wiser than my head. They seemed to have a wisdom all their own. Clients had always remarked that my hands ended up wherever they had pain. I would unconsciously touch their neck and they would say, "How did you know I hurt right there?" I never knew consciously but I let my hands lead the way. Over time, I realized my hands were often leading me to this place in the center of the chest but I didn't know why.

Month after month my clients continued to make me aware that this place in the center of the chest was very significant. Janet came in for help with her depression and a sense of loneliness. She was a bright young school teacher with no apparent reason for being depressed. She was single, with friends and family living nearby, but she felt disconnected from everyone at the emotional level. As she was telling me about her life she started to cry and said, "I feel so empty." And I noticed that her own hand went unconsciously to the center of her chest.

My heart went out to her as she cried about feeling so empty. As I sat with her I wondered to myself, "Empty of what?" I let it go because I didn't have an answer. Yet as I went about my work I kept seeing her sad eyes in my mind and I wondered, "Empty of what?" I kept pushing this thought out of my mind, but again and again I would hear this whispering voice inside my head asking, "Empty of what?"

Again, my clinical training had not prepared me to deal with a client having an empty feeling in her chest. I had just spent five years earning my doctorate in clinical psychology and none of my textbooks or professors had addressed this issue of emptiness.

Several months later a woman named Christine entered counseling for depression and marital distress. She was forty-five years old and considering a divorce. She described her problem as follows:

> I feel so empty. I have a dead spot right here (pointing to the center of her chest). I know something is wrong with my heart. I keep going to heart specialists and having more tests done, and these doctors keep saying nothing is wrong. But I know something is wrong because I can feel it.

Later in the interview I asked if she was in love with her husband.

She shook her head and said, "No, I've never been in love with anyone. I don't know what it feels like to be in love. We have a very distant emotional relationship."

So here was another client saying, "I feel so empty," and I still didn't have an answer for my question, "Empty of what?" And this woman was also describing a "dead spot" in the center of her chest. I honestly didn't know what to say to her regarding her emptiness or her dead spot. I felt confused and a bit helpless at not knowing how to identify the problem or facilitate a solution. Again, I felt frustrated that my clinical training had not prepared me to help this client. It all seemed like such a mystery and I didn't have a clue.

One day a teenager named David came in and reported feeling sensations in the center of his chest. This fifteen-year-old boy was a competitive swimmer who was very sensitive to his body and sensations of energy. He spontaneously described the movement of energy in his chest. I was amazed, particularly because we had never discussed these issues or anything about energy. He said to me:

> Sometimes I lose a race before I ever start. I just give up. I'm standing on the starting block and I can feel my heart sink and I know I'm going to lose the race. I can feel it drop—like it falls down in my chest. It takes a lot of energy to pull it back up.

Obviously David understood more about energy than I did and I wondered how he could be so wise at such a young age. His descriptions of the sensations in his chest deepened the sense of mystery.

FINDING THE KEY TO SOLVE THE MYSTERY

"Human beings are beings of energy."
— Dr. Richard Gerber, *Vibrational Medicine*

Four years after my experience with Roxanne I found the key I needed to solve the mystery. I "accidentally" found my way to a remarkable spiritual healer in Chicago named Ethel Lombardi. She was teaching a spiritual healing method that she had developed called MariEL. During this training she taught me to shift my focus from the human level to the spiritual level and sense the invisible energy field that exists beyond the physical body. She also explained that we all have seven major *chakras* or energy centers that are lined up along the midline of the body. She explained that the heart chakra is located in the center of the chest and is the chakra we use for processing the emotion of love. It is also the place where we feel the pain of being unloved. Sensitive people can perceive the energy of love moving through the heart chakra and they can sense the emptiness of being unloved.

As I listened to this new information about the heart chakra and the energy field, it suddenly dawned on me that my clients were describing their sensations about energy and the lack of energy in their own heart chakras. They didn't consciously know they were sensing energy and they didn't have the vocabulary to describe this spiritual dimension of themselves, but nevertheless they were telling me in whatever way they could about their sensations of energy.

During the sessions, I couldn't make sense of what they were saying because I was still focused on the human level—the level of the physical body and personality. I could only make sense of it if I shifted my focus to the spiritual level—the level of energies, chakras, and the human energy field that exists beyond the body.

Janet had said, "I feel so empty," and touched the center of her chest. Empty of what? Viewed at the human level there is no logical answer. Viewed at the spiritual level the answer is obvious. Janet was sensitive enough to feel that her chest was empty of energy—the energy of love. And the place that was empty was the invisible heart chakra in this invisible energy field.

However, it is only invisible if we stay focused at the human level relating to the world as five-sensory beings. We cannot perceive the heart chakra or the energy field with our ordinary physical senses. They both become apparent when we rise to the spiritual level and relate to the world as the multisensory beings that we really are. When we open our spiritual senses we can easily perceive the chakra and the field. This means sensing with our inner eyes, our inner ears, or our inner knowing. This ability to sense the energies is a skill. Some people have a gift or natural talent for sensing these energies. Others need to develop this skill through training.

Christine said, "I have a dead spot right here," and pointed to her heart chakra. Intuitively she knew her heart chakra felt dead. What she couldn't put into words was that her heart chakra was closed. It felt dead because she was closed to receiving the energy of love.

Christine was focused at the human level. She went to cardiologists looking in her physical body for the solution to her pain. The cardiologists could not find a solution there because her physical heart was not dead. It was quite healthy and doing its job of pumping her blood through her arteries. Both Christine and her doctors were operating at the human level in the five-sensory world.

Christine's problem was in the energy body rather than the physical body. Her heart pain was in her emotional heart or heart chakra. It was her spiritual heart that was dead or closed. Her heart chakra was blocked to the flow of spiritual love through her energy body. This was the root cause of her pain.

THE HEALING POWER OF LOVE

"If we can love enough . . . this is the touchstone. This is the key to the entire therapeutic program of the modern psychiatric hospital. . . Love is the medicine for the sickness of the world."
— Karl Menninger, M.D., *Love Against Hate*

Roxanne said, "My chest, my chest feels filled up for the first time in my life." Again, at the human level Roxanne's sentence does not make sense. However, it makes perfect sense if we shift our perception to the soul level—the level of the energy field beyond the physical body. As we hugged, our energy fields meshed, and our heart chakras aligned quite by accident. This set the stage for an energy transference to happen. The concern and compassion I had for Roxanne sent this loving energy out of my heart chakra. Her heart chakra was open from her massage and her Reiki treatment. She trusted me from the therapist-client bond we had established over several months. The energy of unconditional love went instantaneously from my heart chakra into her heart chakra. She was sensitive enough to feel it and announce, "My chest, my chest feels filled up for the first time in my life." She was describing the sensation of being filled with the energy of love.

Since her heart was open, she opened to her emotions and began sobbing. As she released her emotions she also opened at the mind level. She experienced a spontaneous shift in consciousness from "I want to kill myself" to "I want to live."

This scenario with Roxanne very clearly demonstrates the healing power of love. Roxanne went from depressed and suicidal to radiant and alive seemingly without effort from either of us. This transformation occurred because her chest was filled with the energy of love, making her heart radiant.

The transference of energy with Roxanne happened by "accident" rather than by any design generated from my conscious mind. At the time I had no knowledge of the possibility of such a transference of energy. Neither did I have any conscious knowledge about the transformative effects of such a transfer. This event was such a gift. It truly ignited my curiosity and motivated me to begin a long journey of discovery.

I have no proof but I believe in my heart that I was guided at the spiritual level in my process of discovery. So I continually thank the unseen forces of the universe who guided me on my journey of discovery. Now after ten years of working intuitively with the spiritual energies and the heart chakra, I have learned to facilitate this transference of energy by conscious design. I call this design Radiant Heart Therapy.

"*Someday, after we have mastered the winds, the waves, the tides, and gravity, we shall harness for God the energies of love. Then, for the second time in the history of the world man will have discovered fire.*"

– Teilhard de Chardin

CHAPTER 3

RADIANT HEART THERAPY

TEN YEARS OF RESEARCH

y father's death, my mother-in-law's appearance as a radiant light being, the message from the Archangel Gabriel, the trance channel reading, and my unusual energy experiences with my clients all motivated me to begin a journey of exploration to understand these experiences. I found myself doing research in the field of metaphysics. I began my investigations by reading books about life after death, spirit communication, reincarnation, spirit guides, the human energy field, the human chakra system, and spiritual healing. I also had numerous experiences of transforming my own energy field during hundreds of hours of working with spiritual healers to heal myself. Actually, I learned more from these personal experiences than from my reading.

Moving from clinical psychology to metaphysics was like going to a foreign country and not being able to speak the language. I found I had to learn a new vocabulary and change my perspective about human beings and how to facilitate growth and development. In retrospect, I shifted from seeing only the human perspective to seeing the spiritual perspective as well. During the ten years of working with these two perspectives I have developed a method that integrates both into a new model of spiritual psychology.

RADIANT HEART THERAPY: CONSCIOUS CONNECTION TO SOUL

Radiant Heart Therapy invites people to open their hearts and allow the light of the soul to radiate forth from the core of their being. It shows people how to stay grounded to the earth and integrate the spiritual energy of their souls into their daily existence. This process helps people to make a conscious choice to connect with the power of their soul. It is a choice that cannot be underestimated.

Radiant Heart Therapy was designed to facilitate transformation at both the human level and the soul level. It is based on the premise that each human being is a spirit incarnate in a human body.

At the human level, we are a human body and a personality with thoughts and feelings. Many people have not considered the possibility that they are more than human. They are unconscious of their spiritual nature.

At the soul level, we are energy that vibrates at various frequencies, forming an energy field called the "aura." This aura contains seven major energy centers called "chakras" from the base of the spine to the top of the head. The soul energy vibrates at such a high frequency that the aura and the chakras are invisible to the ordinary human eye. However, we can learn to perceive these higher frequencies by using psychic abilities that allow us to go beyond our ordinary five-sense reality.

There is a constant dynamic interaction between the human level and the soul level of being, even though most people are unaware of the existence of their soul energy and unconscious of its influence in their lives. In my own experience of undergoing psychotherapy, as well as in being a psychotherapist, I have found that people change more easily at the human level when they are willing to focus on the soul level.

RADIANCE: OUR NATURAL STATE OF BEING

The main purpose of Radiant Heart Therapy is to help people return to their natural state of radiance. Radiance is the beauty of the soul energy shining forth through their whole being when individuals awaken to a conscious connection to their souls. Radiance is the result of opening their human hearts and allowing divine love to pour forth from the spiritual realms. This process produces a human being with a radiant heart.

FEELING:

People with radiant hearts move through their daily lives with wide open hearts—loving and laughing, crying and releasing. They are passionate about feelings, allowing the energy of their feelings to flow easily through the body and be released out through the aura. They are alive and in love with life. Their heart chakras are filled with the emotions of peace, joy, and love.

LOVE:

People with radiant hearts are open to the energy of love: divine love from the spiritual realms; love from other human beings; and love of self. They are open to both giving and receiving the energy of love.

CONNECTION:

People with radiant hearts are conscious of their energetic connection to their own soul. They are also connected heart-to-heart to other human beings and they have a heart connection with their own inner child.

PURPOSE:

People with radiant hearts are consciously on their soul path, fulfilling their purpose in life. They are living their dreams as they follow their heart's desires.

INTEGRATION OF THE HUMAN AND DIVINE:

People with radiant hearts are aglow with the spiritual energy of divine love while still living in a human body on the earth plane. The real purpose in life is to achieve a blending of earth energy and spiritual energy. This blending of energies represents the integration of the human and the divine.

THE WORLD OF ENERGY

We live in a world of energy. Everything is composed of energy and everything is constantly vibrating at various frequencies. We live in frequency. We operate in frequency. We speak in frequency and we think in frequency. Frequencies are the patterns of the universe.

In his book, *After We Die What Then?*, George Meek explains that the form of all matter depends on the level of vibrational frequency. He uses water as an example of the changing form with the changing frequencies. Water changes from ice to liquid, to steam, to an invisible vapor as the temperature of the water changes. The vibrational frequency of the water is also changing as the form of the water changes. Ice, the densest form of water, has a very low frequency while the invisible vapor has a very high frequency. In fact, the "invisible" water vapor is vibrating at such a high frequency that the human eye can no longer perceive it.

As human beings we are beings of energy and we are constantly vibrating at various frequencies. Everything about us can be defined in terms of electrochemical and electromagnetic systems. Everything about us can also be defined in terms of vibrational frequencies. We each have a physical body that is composed of energy vibrating at a very low frequency, so it is dense like the block of ice. As ordinary five-sensory human beings, we can perceive this level of frequency, so we are able to see the human body with our own physical eyes. For most people, seeing is believing, so we believe our physical body exists.

Our thoughts and emotions are also composed of energy. This energy is vibrating at such a high frequency that we cannot perceive it as ordinary five-sensory human beings. The dog whistle is another example of energy vibrating at a very high frequency. We cannot hear it with our human ears but dogs can hear it because they can perceive sound at a much higher frequency.

There are many multisensory human beings who can perceive energy at much higher frequencies. These people are often called mystics, psychics, seers, or clairvoyants. These people can "tune in" to the higher vibrational frequencies of thoughts and emotions coming from others. They are then able to perceive these thoughts and emotions. We call this process telepathy, mind reading, or psychic phenomena.

For centuries, these mystics and clairvoyants have seen other energy bodies beyond the physical body of human beings. In the metaphysical literature they describe seven energy bodies beyond the physical body and seven chakras or energy centers along the midline of the body. Most people don't believe these exist because they do not have the ability to perceive these higher frequencies with their own eyes. Again for most people, seeing is believing.

For many, beliefs are changing because science is now developing the equipment to document the existence of energy at high frequencies. In the early 1940s a Russian scientist, Semyon Kirlian, developed a way to photograph these high frequencies. Now, through Kirlian photography, scientists are able to document the existence of energy beyond the body. They are producing pictures of various colored energy coming off the fingertips of human beings. They are able to show that the amount of the energy and the color of the energy changes as people change their thoughts and feelings. Scientists are able to show that each human being has his or her own unique, *energetic* fingerprint. This unique pattern maintains basic characteristics, although it changes with alterations in the mood, health, or the amount of drugs and alcohol in the person's system. Dr. Richard Gerber has successfully used Kirlian photography to determine the energetic patterns of cancer in the energy field. His results correlated with the diagnosis of cancer using traditional methods.

Through Kirlian photography scientists are able to see on photographic paper what the mystics have seen for centuries with their spiritual vision. This has opened the door for the possibility of scientific research with the human energy field. This new research is making evolutionary changes in our beliefs about how we function as human beings. It is creating new paradigms in the fields of metaphysics, science, medicine, psychology, and religion. This research is the cornerstone for the creation of a new field of medicine called vibrational medicine. It is a new model of the human being that takes into account the existence of spiritual energy, the energy bodies, and the chakras that exist beyond the physical body.

Beliefs are also changing because many more people are becoming multisensory human beings. Many more people are discovering they have the ability to perceive the higher frequencies. These higher frequencies are considered spiritual frequencies, so we call this process "seeing with our spiritual eyes" or "hearing with our spiritual ears." It is also called "seeing with our *inner eyes*" and "hearing with our *inner ears*." Spirit beings such as angels, spirit guides, our loved ones on the other side, all have spiritual bodies that vibrate at these higher frequencies. They do not have a physical body that vibrates at the lower frequencies. Consequently, only multisensory human beings can perceive the angels and the spirit beings.

In *The Seat of the Soul*, Gary Zukav defines this time in the history of evolution as a time of great change. He says:

> We are evolving from five-sensory humans into multisensory humans. Our five senses, together, form a single sensory system that is designed to perceive physical reality. The perceptions of a multisensory human extend beyond physical reality to the larger dynamical systems of which our physical reality is a part.

Zukav maintains that all of our great teachers have been, or are, multisensory humans. He cites William James, Carl Jung, Benjamin Lee

Whorf, Niels Bohr, and Albert Einstein as people who, in the depths of
their own thoughts, saw much too much to have been limited by the
five senses. Since they were not limited, their work contributes to the
evolution of their respective fields and the evolution of the human
race. Their ideas and inspiration came from beyond their personality.
They came from the soul.

Zukav proposes that at the turn of the century we are at a critical
time in terms of the evolution of the human race. We are moving from
an evolutionary phase when people have been five-sensory beings to a
new phase in which people are multisensory beings. These
multisensory beings have extraordinary abilities to perceive energy at
the higher vibrational frequencies. As more and more multisensory
beings populate the planet, what were once considered unusual
perceptions will become common and ordinary. Indeed, this is already
happening. More and more teenagers and adults are developing their
multisensory perceptions. More and more children are being born with
the ability to "see the invisible."

THE CHAKRA SYSTEM

A basic knowledge of the chakra system is essential to
understanding the process of Radiant Heart Therapy.

Dr. Richard Gerber has a very complete explanation of the chakra
system in his book, *Vibrational Medicine*. He explains that the chakras
are like energy transformers or stepdown units. They transform the
high frequency spiritual energy to a lower frequency so the physical
body can use it. So the chakras are the mechanism for integrating the
spiritual energy of the soul into the physical body. Clairvoyants can
actually see the soul energy coming in through the crown chakra and
moving down through the physical body via the chakra system.

The spiritual energy becomes like nutritional energy for our entire
organ system through several mechanisms. Each of the seven chakras
is connected to a major endocrine gland and the flow of spiritual
energy through each chakra affects the flow of hormones from the
corresponding gland. Changing the energy flow through the chakras
affects the flow of hormones from the glands. A minute change in the
quantity of these hormones can tremendously affect body function.
Therefore, a minute change in the flow of energy through the chakras
has a tremendous effect on the functioning of the physical body.

Dr. Gerber further explains that the chakras are involved in processing emotional energy or the energy of our feelings. When the chakras are not working properly, it is a reflection that we are not processing our emotional energy properly. So Dr. Gerber believes our inability to deal with emotions is the key issue that affects the chakras and the output of hormones. Thus our ability or inability to deal with our emotions is a key factor in maintaining a balance of hormones in the physical body, and in attaining and maintaining physical health.

Traditional physicians have long known this connection between emotions and physical health. They defined psychosomatic illnesses (ulcers, colitis, headaches) as illnesses related to emotional dysfunction. By understanding the chakra system we can understand how and why the emotions affect the physical body. We can also say that all physical illnesses are psychosomatic.

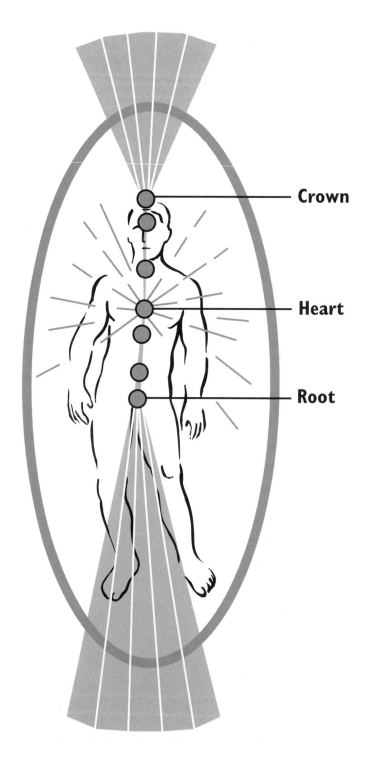

This list defines the psycho-spiritual issues for each chakra:

	Chakra	Gland	Functions
7	Crown	Pineal	Connects to the energies of the spiritual world
6	Brow	Pituitary	Controls psychic and intuitive abilities
5	Throat	Thyroid	Controls one's ability to communicate thoughts and feelings
4	Heart	Thymus	Controls the ability to express love
3	Solar plexus	Pancreas	Controls our sense of personal power
2	Spleen	Gonads	Controls sexuality and creativity
1	Root	Adrenals	Connects to the energy of the physical world. Controls the will to live

Over the past twenty years a new field of medicine has evolved called psychoneuroimmunology. It looks at the mind-body connection —or the interaction of the mind, the nervous system, and the immune system. Dr. Gerber believes there is something that affects the immune system even more than the mind, and that is the heart. He states, "Psychoneuroimmunology—mind/body medicine—left out *love* from the equation. Very innovative thinkers in vibrational medicine are starting to fill in this part of the equation."

Most experts in energy medicine agree that the heart chakra is the most important of the seven chakras. It is the chakra that deals with our ability to love. It is the bridge between the lower three chakras that relate to the physical aspects of a human being and the upper three chakras that relate to the spiritual aspects of a human being.

Other practitioners and researchers working with subtle energy have written about the heart chakra and the flow of energy through the heart. Dora Kunz is a healer with exceptional clairvoyant faculties. She can perceive both color and energy patterns in the human energy field, and specializes in making medical diagnosis using her clairvoyant abilities. She and Dr. Delores Krieger pioneered "therapeutic touch," which they have taught to thousands of nurses and health care practitioners. In her book, *The Chakras and the Human Energy Field*, Kunz makes these observations about the heart chakra:

> The heart chakra is located midway between the shoulder blades. It is approximately six centimeters in diameter.

> The heart chakra registers the quality and power of love in the individual's life.

> The heart chakra is a primary factor in spiritual transformation.

> Focusing on the heart chakra brings balance in the body. The heart chakra is the point of integration of the whole energy system. In the physical body, there is a relationship between the heart chakra, the thymus gland, and the immune system.

The spiritual energy of love moves through the heart chakra and influences the thymus gland, which is of major importance in the functioning of the immune system. This is the scientific explanation for the healing power of spiritual love. It is also a key to explaining some of the miraculous physical healings when people have a spiritual transformation. It is a key to explaining some of the healing effects of Radiant Heart Therapy as well.

RADIANT HEART THERAPY AND SPIRITUAL HEALING

The energy field is the blueprint for the physical body. Many people believe that the energy body is a reflection of what is happening in the physical body. Actually, it is the opposite. The physical body is a reflection of the energy body. Of the two, the energy body is the more important. It is the blueprint for whatever happens on all other levels. For significant change to occur at the level of body, mind, or emotions, we must invoke change in the energy field.

Spiritual healing involves working with the invisible energy field. To achieve true healing that will have permanence, we must learn to think of the human being as an energy field. People who are balanced and whole have a clear energy field into which spiritual energies and earth energies flow naturally, enhancing the person's own vital life force.

Spiritual healing is a process of working with the energy field to facilitate transformation and bring a person back to wholeness. The energy field is the energy of the soul. This means we are facilitating transformation at the soul level when practicing healing. Each of us is, first and foremost, a soul. We are an energy field. For a healer, working with the energy of the soul is the highest form of intervention. It is the most efficient way to identify and eliminate the root causes of both psychological and physical illnesses.

The key element in spiritual healing is raising the vibratory frequency of the person's energy field. At the emotional level this can be accomplished by releasing the lower frequency feelings of sadness, anger, and fear, and learning to live in the higher frequency feelings of peace, joy, and love. At the mental level this can be accomplished by releasing the lower frequency negative thought patterns and replacing these with higher frequency positive thought patterns. At the spiritual level this can be accomplished by using visualizations to bring more high frequency light (spiritual energy) into the energy field.

Raising the vibrational frequency is also defined as the process of evolution for the soul. Our Higher Self, our guides, and guardian angels all exist in the higher frequencies so raising the vibrational frequency of our energy field allows each of us to connect with these spiritual energies. As we connect with these higher frequency energies we draw more of our soul energy into ourselves and become more of the personality that we were meant to be in this lifetime. We open our hearts, form a conscious connection to soul, reclaim our radiance, and feel empowered to achieve our purpose for this lifetime. So the essence of spiritual healing is transformation at the soul level through transforming the vibratory frequency.

True healing that will be permanent must include these three ingredients:

1. Clear the energy field of energy blocks caused by negative thought patterns and stored emotional trauma.
2. Achieve permanent shifts in consciousness so the energy field will remain clear of blocks created by negative mental programming.
3. Achieve a healthy method for processing painful emotions so the energy field will remain clear of energy blocks caused by repressing negative emotions.

CONSCIOUSNESS AND THE HUMAN ENERGY FIELD

It is human consciousness that creates the energy field. In other words, the energy field is both created and influenced by our conscious and unconscious thoughts. Blocks in the energy field are caused by negative thought patterns. If a person works with a healer and removes an energy block, the vital life force will begin to flow properly. However, the person can immediately recreate the block by returning to the same negative thinking pattern. Therefore it is imperative to achieve permanent shifts in consciousness. Then and only then will people be able to keep their energy field clear after working with a healer to remove the energy blocks.

Here is an example of how consciousness interacts with the energy field. A person who has a conscious or unconscious belief of "I'm unlovable" will also have a heart chakra that is closed to receiving the energy of love. If the person changes the belief to "I am lovable," the heart chakra will open for receiving, in response to this shift in consciousness. Also, if we can create a loving experience that enables the person to sense the energy of love entering the heart chakra, a spontaneous shift in consciousness might then occur, giving rise to a redecision of "I am lovable." The consciousness and the energy field are interacting constantly, producing split-second changes that affect both the personality and the health of the physical body.

To achieve permanent shifts in consciousness I use Transactional Analysis (TA), a psychotherapy process developed by a Canadian psychiatrist, Dr. Eric Berne. Berne taught that each person makes script decisions in early childhood that determine his or her perceptions about self, other people, and life in general. The collection of various script decisions made by the inner child becomes the life script. This script often contains false messages about reality, but the inner child believes these messages because they were implanted by his or her parents. These harmful script decisions can be changed through Redecision Therapy. The main goal of transactional analysis therapy is to facilitate redecisions and achieve permanent shifts in consciousness.

Blocks are created in the energy field as people repress their painful emotions instead of allowing the normal process of releasing to occur. These blocks can be removed in healing sessions using imagery. However, the person can create new blocks by continuing to repress painful feelings in response to new life events and experiences.

It is essential to establish a healthy process of identifying painful feelings, moving the energy of the feeling through the body, and releasing the energy of the feeling out through the energy field. In my work I teach people to "own it, feel it, and release it." Such empowerment enables us to clear our own energy field of emotional blocks so that we do not need to keep working with a healer.

VISUALIZATION - THE PRIMARY TOOL OF RADIANT HEART THERAPY

THE POWER OF VISUALIZATION

Consciousness creates the energy field and consciousness can transform the energy field. The human mind is much more powerful than most people know. We can use the creative powers of the mind to create images that directly change the vibrational frequency in the energy field. We can use images to increase the amount of radiant light in our aura. When we use our imagination to "see" radiant healing energy pouring from the universe into the crown chakra and down through the heart chakra, there is a corresponding change in the amount of light present in these chakras and in the whole aura.

Below is a simple visualization to open the heart chakra:

- Relax your body and breathe deeply.
- Visualize a tiny rosebud in the center of your heart chakra.
- See the sun shining gently on the rosebud.
- Sense the warmth of the sun as it gently opens the rosebud to a beautiful rose.

Clairvoyants watching this process report that the heart chakra actually opens as people create these pictures in their imagination. Clairvoyants can see more white light flowing into and through the heart chakra immediately after this visualization process is completed. I don't *see* the energies. Instead I can *feel* the movement of my own energies in my body. As I do this simple visualization I can feel my heart chakra open and a gentle warmth fills the center of my chest. I can also tune into the energy fields of my clients and sense the warmth in the center of their chests.

REMOVING ENERGY BLOCKS
WITH VISUALIZATION

Emotions are composed of energy. When we do not release our painful emotions at the time of an emotional event we create energy blocks in our energy field. These blocks hold the painful memories and feelings locked into the energy field. They appear to clairvoyants as black, dark brown, or gray blobs of energy in the body or out in the aura. Sensitive energy therapists can also feel them as "hot spots" or "cold spots" as we move our hands through the person's aura. People can use imagery to remove these emotional energy blocks.

Below is a simple visualization for removing an emotional energy block:

- Give every cell in your chest permission to release the heartache about a particular event.
- Give the pain a color. (Any color will do.)
- See the color forming a geyser and flowing out of your heart chakra.
- Keep visualizing a stream of colored energy till it spontaneously changes colors and becomes clear. This is a signal from the unconscious mind that all the pain is released.
- Visualize a ball of radiant healing energy high in the universe and pull rays of this energy through your crown chakra and into your heart chakra.
- Use your imagination to send the radiant healing energy to every cell where you released the pain.

People who are sensitive to the higher frequencies can actually "see" or "feel" the energy of repressed painful emotions leaving the body, coming out into the aura, and floating up above the person. Often a small gray or black cloud of energy hangs in the air above the person for ten or fifteen minutes before it dissipates. Sensitive people can also "see" or "feel" the aura becoming bigger and brighter as the person imagines bringing in the radiant healing energy.

HOLDING TWO PERCEPTIONS
SIMULTANEOUSLY

At this time on the planet most people live their lives at the human level, being unconscious of their spiritual nature. Many who awaken to their spiritual nature believe it is important to disregard or "rise above" their human nature—particularly their painful emotions of anger, sadness, and fear. This is actually a "spiritual bypass," which leaves buried emotional trauma that can block energy flows. The key to fulfilling our purpose on the planet is to hold both our spiritual nature and our human nature in balance, valuing both equally. The energetic process for doing this is to stay grounded to the earth, bring in the spiritual energy from the universe, and blend the two in an open heart chakra.

Attaining this balance is quite a difficult task. This analogy shows how difficult it is to hold two perceptions at the same time. Look at the picture of the vase and the faces. Most people first see either the white vase or the black faces. Then as they become aware of the other figure they are able to switch back and forth perceiving either the vase or the faces. Most people cannot hold the perception of both the vase and the faces at the same time. However, with practice this is a skill that can be learned.

It is equally difficult for people to hold the perception of their human nature and their spiritual nature at the same time. Again, it is a skill that can be learned.

INTEGRATION OF THE HUMAN AND THE DIVINE

Radiant Heart Therapy facilitates the integration of the human and the divine, using imagery as the tool. The basic Radiant Heart visualization creates the energetic pathways for this integration to happen in the energy field. The process includes the following:

1. Opening the root chakra and bringing the earth energy into the body—the human element.
2. Opening the crown chakra and bringing the spiritual energy into the head—the spiritual element.
3. Opening the heart chakra and merging these two energies in the heart—the integration of the human and the divine.

RADIANT HEART VISUALIZATION

OPENING THE ROOT CHAKRA

- Sit on a chair.
- Visualize opening your root chakra at the base of your spine.
- Imagine sending four energy lines from your hips down into the earth.
- Send the first pair of lines from your hips out to your knees, down the center of your shin bones into the earth.
- Send the second pair of lines from your hips down into the earth.
- See the lines expand into big, thick roots.
- Send your roots through the layers of the earth—the rock, the sand, the gravel.
- Connect with an energy ball deep in the center of the earth. (This energy ball really exists and vibrates at 7.83 cycles per second.)
- See it as red energy.
- Bring the red energy up the four roots into your body.
- See it coming up the roots like a red line up a thermometer.
- Bring the earth energy up through your feet, legs, and into your root chakra.
- See a vibrant red energy at the base of your spine. Move this earth energy through your torso into your chest.
- See your heart chakra filled with the red earth energy.
- Begin repeating the affirmation:

    I am grounded to the earth.
    I am grounded to the earth.

- Feel the magnetic pull to the center of the earth.
- Invite all your cells to vibrate at the same frequency of the earth. (Your cells know how to do this. You just have to think the command.)
- Feel the earth energy gently fill your heart chakra.
- Allow this energy to open your heart from the inside.

OPENING THE CROWN CHAKRA

- Visualize a ball of radiant healing energy high in the universe.
- See it like the glistening energy when the sun shines on the water.

- See a limitless ball of this radiant energy. This energy was created by God and is still connected back to God. It is a spiritual energy with healing powers.
- Visualize opening your crown chakra on the top of your head.
- Create a funnel from your crown to the radiant ball of healing energy.
- Visualize the radiant energy flowing from the ball, down the funnel, into the top of your head.
- Channel the radiant energy along your spine.
- Direct it to open and balance all of your chakras.
- Send it into your heart chakra.
- Fill your heart chakra with this radiant light.
- Feel your chest expand and become warm from this radiant energy.

OPENING THE HEART CHAKRA

Merging the Two Energies in the Heart Chakra

- Visualize merging the red earth energy and the radiant healing energy in your heart chakra.
- See the red and the silver swirling together in the center of your chest.
- Send the red and silver mixture down your arms and into your hands.
- Rub your hands together to create a friction.
- Breathe deeply to enhance the flow of energy.
- Hold your hands about two inches apart.
- Feel the energy between your hands. (Most people feel heat, cold, tingling, or a magnetic pull between their hands.)
  This energy is your vital life force.
  This is what keeps you alive.
  This is your spark of life.
- Take time to thank God for this gift of life.

TO FEEL THE PRESENCE OF THE ENERGY IS TO FEEL THE PRESENCE OF THE DIVINE.

These Radiant Heart visualizations are designed to enhance our vital life force (spiritual energies) so the ordinary person can feel it, experience it, and believe in its existence. These visualizations are simple and yet they have profound effects. The process invites people to evolve to a higher level of consciousness. It affects the evolutionary process of the individual at the soul level.

These visualizations create a bridge between the physical dimension and the spiritual dimension—between body and soul. The heart chakra is the space where these two different frequencies can merge and be integrated. The heart chakra has to be open for the two energies to enter, make the connection, and merge. A closed heart chakra prevents any possibility of connecting body and soul.

Our life force is an energy and it is the physical manifestation of our soul. It is the tangible evidence that our soul is present in our physical body. The energy of the soul vibrates at such a high frequency that most people cannot perceive it because they are still operating in a five-sense reality. However, as we learn to "tune in" to the higher frequencies of our soul we are more able to connect with our Higher Self or the God-consciousness within. This is the key to the process of evolution.

"The heart chakra is the center through which we love. Through it flows the energy of connectedness with all life. The more open this center becomes, the greater our capacity to love an ever widening circle of life."

— Barbara Brennan,
Hands of Light

C H A P T E R   4

THE HEART CHAKRA:
CLOSED AND OPEN

ost souls who journey to the earth plane experience a disconnection from the divine and a loss of divine love. This experience is so painful they close off their hearts to deaden the emotional pain. Consequently, they become human beings with closed hearts, and they live out their lives on earth unaware of their loss of radiance. A small minority of souls learn to open their hearts and reclaim their radiance.

In exploring the concepts of the heart chakra, I have come to the following conclusions: Everyone has a heart chakra that has a basic position of open or closed. People who go through life with an open heart chakra have a very different experience than people who go through life with a closed heart chakra.

OPEN HEARTS

People with an open heart are sensitive to their own emotions and are emotionally expressive. These people have a passion or zest for life. They radiate a soft, loving energy from their heart center that others can sense. People feel unconsciously drawn to them because this loving vibration comes from their open heart.

People with a fully open heart can easily give and receive love. They are more likely to experience love in many different forms—compassion for others, motherly/fatherly love, love of friends, romantic love, and spiritual love. They bond energetically with others who also have an open heart. Therefore, they feel emotionally connected to other people and to God. The connecting bond is the energy of love moving through the heart chakra.

CLOSED HEARTS

People with a closed heart are out of touch with their own emotions and are therefore emotionally blocked. They do not usually experience passion or a zest for life. They do not experience the movement of energy in their own heart chakra and they do not send out energy to other people. Others can sense this lack of energy and may describe them as cold-hearted or having a heart of stone. These people might be described as empty, closed off, disconnected, loners, unable to love, and unable to connect emotionally with others. For them, love is an intellectual experience. They may think about love but do not have any energetic sensations of it in their chest cavity.

People with a closed heart also experience a spiritual disconnection from God. They often believe that God exists, but they have no personal experience of connecting in any way to a feeling of love from God. Life for people with a closed heart usually seems dull, empty, robotic, and often depressing. They frequently ask the question, *"What's it all about?"*

Most people with a closed heart have no conscious awareness that they are different from others who have an open heart. However, a few people with a closed heart have some vague awareness that others seem to be happier and have more love or better relationships, but don't understand why they themselves do not experience life the same way.

Tom, forty-four, came into therapy for depression. He was very intelligent and extremely successful in his career as a developer of apartment complexes, but he was not successful in relationships. He had many short-term relationships with women over the years, but could not maintain a healthy long-term relationship and had never married. Tom's heart chakra was very closed at the beginning of treatment. After about three months his heart opened and he began to have more emotional experiences in his life. Tom told me:

> I never understood what the women in my life were trying to tell me. They would be very loving to me and get totally frustrated when I couldn't respond emotionally. When they complained I was "closed off," I just didn't get it. I couldn't make sense of it. Now that I have opened my heart, I finally understand what they were saying.

The average person has no conscious knowledge about the heart chakra or open and closed hearts. They can only make these comparisons after learning about the chakras and feeling the different sensations in the heart chakra.

Robert, a truck driver, describes the vast difference in living with his heart closed and living with his heart open. He states:

Closed:

> When my heart was closed I was very selfish. I felt like I could not get enough of anything for myself—enough time with my wife, enough money, enough food, enough attention. I could never get satisfied so I always had this inner drive for more. I always felt empty but I didn't realize what I was missing. I did not know that I was missing love.

Open:

> Now that my heart is open I feel so much love. I can give and receive love from my kids. I now feel full as opposed to empty. I have a great deal of compassion for other people and their pain. I have stopped being judgmental and so critical. My kids know they can tell me their mistakes and I won't get mad. I'll just help them figure out how to fix the problem.

> My life is so different now. I care about other people and their feelings. I am more sensitive and yet I'm a stronger, more powerful person. I don't think I was ever powerful before—angry, yes, but not powerful.

Shoshanna, a critical care nurse, also learned to experience the difference in having her heart open and having her heart closed. She could only learn this from feeling experiences—experiences of the heart—not from intellectual discussions, which are experiences of the mind. She learned in her therapy process that she had her heart closed most of her life. She describes the difference for herself:

Closed:

> When my heart is closed I feel shut down—like I'm emotionally dead. I get real depressed and begin to think there is no hope or no way out. Whatever pain I'm in seems to be like a permanent condition and I can't get out of it. I can't laugh and everything seems so serious. In my mind I tell myself that I could get out of this but my heart doesn't believe it.

Open:

> When my heart is open I flow through my feelings, releasing them, and feeling alive. I release the negative ones and hold onto the positive ones. I feel connected to my soul and I feel connected to other people. I feel alive with all my emotions. I love to laugh and have fun.

Melinda, a sales representative for a chemical company, gave these descriptions of her heart after six months of therapy.

Closed:

> When my heart is closed I feel constrained and tense. Every little thing will set me off. I go through the motions of daily life without any emotions. I do my job, come home, and everything is monotone. There's no excitement, no feelings, no nothing. I have no passion about life.

Open:

> When my heart is open I feel relaxed instead of tense. I go through my day feeling so much emotion. I enjoy the little things in life like hearing a bird sing. I feel joy when a friend calls. I feel sad when I lose my favorite earring. I feel passionate about a lot of things. I like living with my heart open.

Beverly, a school teacher who came into therapy for depression, learned to distinguish between a closed heart and an open heart.

Closed:

> When my heart is closed I feel constrained and I lose all flexibility. I feel stiff. I feel like I'm going through life thinking about how tense I am. I feel like somebody else has got a hold on me and I can't do anything about it. I feel encased in a shell and I don't see beyond it. I don't appreciate that the sun is shining or that it is a beautiful day.

Open:

> When my heart is open I feel free and easy. I look at the
> world and I appreciate how beautiful it is. I get up in the
> morning and think, "What a beautiful day." I am able to
> laugh about a lot of things.

Olga, a nurse in her late thirties, gave these descriptions of her
personality and feelings as she moved between open heart and closed
heart.

Closed:

> When my heart is closed I feel self-critical and critical
> of others. It is easy to pass judgment on myself and
> others. I find it easy to think that a person is stupid for
> whatever reason. I also feel like I am walking around
> like a robot. I have a sense of being outside myself
> watching myself do it. Often I feel afraid and unable to
> trust the normal flow of life events.

Open:

> When my heart is open I accept people however they
> are. I believe that whatever is happening is part of the
> perfect design. I have a sense of surrendering to my
> Higher Power. I am more accepting, more trusting, and
> more intuitive. I feel as if I am in touch with some
> abstract intelligence. If I allow myself, I can do the
> things and be the things that are in harmony with my
> soul. I feel as if my life is flowing almost effortlessly.
> Knowledge comes to me almost effortlessly. The things
> I need appear in my life.

CLOSED HEART AND DEPRESSION

Ellen, a bank teller, came for help with severe depression. She had
closed off her heart as a young child to protect herself from her father
who was emotionally abusive. I explained to her that her depression
was due to the lack of energy which people experience when they
close off their heart chakras. Our conversation in her initial interview
was most revealing.

I asked her, "Would you like to get your energy back?" She answered, "Yes, but what are you supposed to do with it?" I said, "Whatever you want."

She looked at me, puzzled, and said, "I've always done what you are supposed to do. Life is about doing what you are supposed to do. My father was always real strict. We never had any choice about anything. All my life I have felt empty. I'm just there. I'm hollow inside."

Ellen had her heart closed and felt disconnected from her soul. She was living to please others outside herself rather than aligning her personality with her soul. She was also living her life with no love and no emotions. No wonder she was suffering from severe depression.

CLOSED HEART FOR PROTECTION

Bob and his wife came in for marriage counseling. They had been married only four years and were thinking about divorce.

One of my standard questions for new clients is, "Do you ever feel any sensations in your chest?" Most people answer, "No, I'm not aware of sensations there." I asked Bob and he said, "Yes, sometimes I feel like a quiver in my chest." I was surprised because he presented a macho image and wasn't expressing his emotions. He then said:

> I used to feel that quiver with my wife when we first fell in love. Somehow I lost it. Now I've closed off my heart to her. She's always angry and I don't want to get hurt so I put up a wall. I'm scared she'll leave me for another man. I guess I don't trust her and I'm protecting myself. I come off as cold and uncaring, but really I'm just scared to risk opening up my heart.

> I feel the quiver when I'm with my son, Joe, who is two years old. I just have to look at him sometimes and I feel this quiver in the center of my chest. When I lie down on the floor to watch TV he likes to come and lie on my chest. He'll fall asleep there often.

Obviously, Bob knew what it was like to open his heart and feel the sensations of energy moving in his chest. However, he presented this macho image to the world. He didn't want anyone to know he had such a soft, open heart. It took about eight individual sessions for him to even let me know about his soft heart. I was very shocked when I placed my hand on his chest and found this open and flowing energy. He smiled at my surprise and explained:

> People are out to get you. If you let people in they will hurt you. So I learned to pretend that I'm cold and distant.

His wife said in her own private session:

> The Bob I fell in love with has this soft little boy inside. I can't find that part of him any more. It went away somewhere. That's the part of him I love.

BASIC POSITIONS OF THE HEART CHAKRA

Loving is a process of both giving and receiving the energy of love. In observing myself and other people, I see these two separate processes—giving out the energy of love and taking in the energy of love. It is important to distinguish between these two opposite components of loving. The ideal is to have the ability to both give and receive love, keeping a healthy balance between the two processes.

Using this theory about giving and receiving the energy of love, four basic positions of the heart chakra may be defined:

THE GIVERS — OPEN TO GIVING
THE WITHHOLDERS — CLOSED TO GIVING
THE RECEIVERS — OPEN TO RECEIVING
THE BLOCKERS — CLOSED TO RECEIVING

These four basic positions describe the possibilities of how people deal with giving and receiving the energy of love in their heart chakra.

THE GIVERS — OPEN TO GIVING

Giving love is a wonderful exchange that blesses both the giver and the receiver. I was describing the heart chakra and the sensations of sending out the energy of love to a new client. As I explained being open to giving, Amy had a most unusual response. It was as if a light bulb went on and her whole face lit up in recognition. Amy began to cry softly as she explained:

> My granddaughter Melissa and I have always had this special bond. Whenever I think of her I start to cry and

I get this ache in my chest. I first noticed these sensations when she was diagnosed with leukemia at age two. I was one of her primary caretakers. I would rock her for hours at the hospital. She would just be very quiet against my chest as we rocked.

I never felt any of these sensations with my husband or even my own children. Actually, I still only feel it with Melissa.

This woman obviously had her heart open to giving love to her granddaughter. She had already sensed the energetic experience of giving out the energy of love, though she did not know how to define what was happening to her. Many people with open, giving hearts have described this same ache in their chest as they send love to another human being. They also describe this spontaneous urge to cry for no apparent reason. This crying is not out of sadness. It is a crying that comes from love. There is a natural welling up of tears that corresponds to the welling up of love energy in the heart chakra.

People who have their heart chakra open to giving love are often described as having *a heart of gold*. These people naturally send a warm energy out from the center of the chest as they interact with other people. Though others cannot see this energy, they respond to it intuitively and are very drawn to the person sending out love. Clairvoyants usually see this love energy as a soft, pink cloud in front of the person's chest.

Giving love to others is more than a mental process of thinking about love. It is an energetic process of allowing the heart chakra to be open and sending the energy of love out towards another person. We can use specific visualizations to enhance the process of sending love energy.

To open the heart chakra for giving, the person needs to have beliefs like:

People are lovable.
I have lots of love to give.
Love is infinite. It will never run out.
The more I give, the more I have available to give.

IT IS POSSIBLE TO BE TOO GIVING

Most of my clients have great difficulty comprehending that it is unhealthy to be too giving. Imagine you have a full water pitcher and people are constantly coming to you needing water. People hold up their empty glasses and you willingly fill them from your pitcher. You can only fill a certain number of glasses before your pitcher is empty. Then you must go to the faucet and refill the pitcher.

Those who choose not to refill the pitcher will have nothing left to give to others; neither will they have any water available to quench their own thirst. Refilling the water pitcher is the process of taking in love with a heart that is open to receiving. Those who are closed to receiving cannot possibly refill their pitcher. However, many of these people have gigantic pitchers and can give out for years before becoming depleted!

In my clinical experience people who are too giving are doing it to compensate for their own insecurities about feeling unlovable. They seem to adopt a style of giving and giving so that others will appreciate them and give them some love in return. They are basically afraid to trust that anyone will love them for just being themselves if they are not being a caretaker. Of course, this is happening on an unconscious level so the giver is usually unaware of this process.

Givers need to learn to fill themselves up with the energy of unconditional love from the spiritual realms. This spiritual love is the ultimate source of love energy for human beings. It is the water faucet or the well that fills the water pitcher of the healthy givers.

I teach people to use imagery to bring in the radiant universal energy through the crown chakra and send it out their heart chakra for other people. In the process of channeling this energy the sender also becomes filled up with divine love. People who do not use some method of filling themselves up with universal energy can easily become depleted when sending out their own energy.

Most giving people are unconscious of their energy fields and the transference of energy between two people. They do not know about bringing in universal energy, so they easily become depleted as they try to take care of other people using only their own energy.

As a healer I have learned the importance of pulling in radiant universal energy as I do energy work with my clients. I can do healing sessions for eight to ten hours a day as long as I remember to use my mind to pull in the energy and channel it through me. If I forget and use only my own energy I can work two to three hours and I'm exhausted. To pull in radiant energy I use the imagery of opening the crown chakra, erecting a funnel, and tapping into a radiant ball of healing energy.

THE WITHHOLDERS — CLOSED TO GIVING

People who are closed to giving have no love energy emanating from the center of their chests. They unconsciously put up an energetic wall across the front of their hearts that blocks the flow of love energy. These people might think about loving someone, but the outgoing energy of love is not transferred at the heart level. People who need love from a withholder feel frustrated, empty, and unloved.

These withholders seem to have tightened their muscular system to stop the flow of energy that would naturally move out from the heart chakra. Consequently, they appear physically rigid and rather stiff. They send out a silent but palpable message, *"I'm unapproachable."* Others intuitively respond by not coming close and not expecting to get a warm or generous response.

June, one of my women clients, knew exactly what I was talking about when I first introduced the idea of being closed to giving. She immediately responded:

> I know my husband has his heart closed real tight. He doesn't know it, but I can sense it. When I hug him, it is like hugging a dead tree. He is real stiff and I don't feel anything from him. I feel empty after I get a hug from him. He gets mad when I try to talk about it. He just doesn't even know what I am talking about. He doesn't have a clue.

Withholders not only withhold energy, they also withhold compliments and gifts. Behaviorally they appear stingy with their time, money, and emotional support for friends and family members.

Withholders have nothing to give because they are empty inside. They have been emotionally wounded in early childhood. They did not get unconditional love from their own parents, so their heart chakra is not filled up with the energy of love. There are two possibilities. One, the parents had wounded hearts and were not capable of sending love to the child. Two, the parents were sending love but the child blocked receiving it for some reason. Withholders must first learn to open their hearts and receive before they will have any love energy to give out to people in their relationships.

June's husband had no close emotional relationship with either of his parents during his childhood. His mother died of cancer when he was only four years old. He went to the funeral and didn't even cry. He described this event in a detached way:

> I didn't feel anything at the funeral. My mother had been sick for several years in and out of the hospital. I didn't even know her, really. She was like a stranger to me. My father raised us after that with the help of his mother. My grandmother was mean, so my brother and I stayed out of the house as much as possible. I only came home to sleep. I didn't even eat meals with the family. We had no family, really. Dad worked all the time and we just stayed out of Grandmother's way.

He told me all this without a hint of emotion. I felt as if I was listening to a robot giving out the facts. He had no idea that his denial of emotions and lack of emotional energy was a problem. In fact, he was rather proud of having handled it all so well, not getting upset and not upsetting others.

Listening to his history, I understood exactly why he had nothing to give to his wife energetically. His heart chakra was closed and empty. Since this was all unconscious to him, he felt very confused and angry when his wife tried to get through to him that her love needs were not being met. He simply could not understand what she was talking about. It was like a foreign language to him. He just couldn't "get it."

This man was insensitive to the movement of subtle energy and he was out of touch with his emotions. His wife was very sensitive, so she could feel things that he could not begin to feel. When she confronted him about her emotional needs he used a defense mechanism of blaming her for being "too sensitive" so he did not feel the need to change. He expected her to change and give up what he called "being too sensitive." He became very angry with me for not supporting him in this unhealthy solution of their relationship problem. Unfortunately, I see this pattern in many couples who come to me for marital counseling.

THE BLOCKERS — CLOSED TO RECEIVING

Most people have their hearts closed to receiving. I say this based on my own life experience and from observing several thousand clients over the past twenty years. Usually these people are living life in denial of their inability to receive. They have no awareness of it because they have no experience of truly receiving the energy of love.

People who have their heart chakra closed to receiving usually have been emotionally wounded at an earlier time in life. The wounding happened very early, perhaps at birth. Sometimes mothers do not have an open loving heart, so the infant does not learn to bond energetically with the mother. Babies who do not bond with their mother have a difficult time opening to receive love later in life.

Another possibility is that a person bonded with mother in infancy but was wounded later in life. The loss of a parent, grandparent, or other close relative could be the incident that triggers the decision to close off the heart. The person is essentially saying, "The pain of this loss is so great I don't want to risk hurting like this again. I won't let anyone in ever again."

Only a small percentage of people are born into an ideal family where both parents have open hearts and are aware enough to bond energetically with the infant. Consequently, most people experience some degree of difficulty in opening their heart and keeping it open to receive.

It appears to be part of the human condition for people of all ages in all cultures to struggle with getting their love needs met. I attribute this struggle to people trying to find love while their heart chakra is closed to receiving. If people could learn to open their heart to receive, they could be more successful in fulfilling this need for love. Radiant Heart Therapy assists people to open their hearts so they can experience receiving the energy of love.

In my therapy group and workshops I lead people through various structured exercises about giving and receiving the energy of love. At the end, I ask them if it seemed easier to give or to receive. The answer is always unanimous that it is easier to give. Most people report being very uncomfortable being the receiver. They say things like:

I feel too vulnerable.
I feel like I do not deserve it.
I feel more in control giving.
I feel scared receiving.
I can't take in the love.
I can't believe it.

For most people, being open to receive love is much more difficult than being open to give love. They experience a deep sense of vulnerability as they let down the protective wall that guards them from the possibility of being hurt or rejected.

One of the exercises I teach involves saying, "I need love" to another person. Looking into another person's eyes and asking directly for the love we each need brings up deep feelings of vulnerability, fear of rejection, and the pain of being unloved. Most people believe love is a universal need and that we each deserve to have our love needs met. Participating in this exercise and stating that need moves the person out of the mental and into the emotional aspect of this issue. At first, most people experience the repressed pain and sadness of not having felt loved in the past. After they release these feelings, they are open to the possibility of receiving love.

THE RECEIVERS — OPEN TO RECEIVING

Receiving love is not just a mental process of thinking about the concept of love. It is an energetic process of allowing the heart chakra to be open and sensing the energy of love as it moves within the chest cavity.

In Chapter Two, I reported Roxanne's description of sensing the energy of love. Her exact words were, "My chest, my chest feels filled up for the first time in my life." This is a very accurate description of what it feels like to truly receive love and consciously sense the energy.

We may have it all backwards about our traditional belief that it is better to give than to receive. For instance, Dannion Brinkley in his book, *Saved by the Light*, states:

> There is a power in learning to receive love. People have it all backwards. We think we came to earth to learn to give love. Actually we came to earth to learn to receive love. You can't give love until you have learned to receive because your heart is empty and has nothing to give.

To open the heart chakra to receive, the person needs to hold these script decisions both consciously and unconsciously:

I deserve love.
I am worthy to be loved.
I am lovable because I exist.
I deserve unconditional love without having to earn it.

RECEIVING THE ENERGY OF LOVE

I can put my hand on another person's chest and use imagery to send the energy of love from my heart chakra down my arm and out my hand. When I'm doing this, my hand gets very hot and energy pours out of my palm. The person always has the choice of whether to take in the energy or block it out. I cannot force another person to open his or her heart to receive. I can only provide a safe environment and invite the person to open his or her heart chakra to the experience of receiving.

Intuitively, I know if the person is blocking the energy or allowing it into the heart chakra. Think about spraying water from a hose against a solid wall. The water hits the wall and is repelled back. This is the impression I get when a person is closed to receiving energy. Now, think about spraying water against a screen door. The water goes easily through the screen with very little resistance. This is the impression I get when the person is open to receiving energy.

People who actually receive the energy look different from people who block the energy. Receivers brighten up. Their eyes light up, they spontaneously smile or laugh, and their faces get flushed. People who have the gift of clairvoyant sight report that the aura goes through many changes as people take in the energy of love. The aura expands, changes color, and becomes much brighter.

People who block the energy experience very little or no change. They appear bored and uncomfortable with the process. They usually have no idea they are blocking. Doing this work in groups helps the blockers because they can see the strongly positive experiences the receivers have and the blockers want to have the same experience.

THE HEART CHAKRA IN FLUX

The heart chakra is in constant energetic flux. Each person has a basic position, but that can change based on changes in the person's thoughts or feelings. Also the external environment can influence the state of the heart. People tend to open their hearts in a supportive, loving environment and close their hearts in a hostile environment. This is an excellent strategy of self-protection.

Generally, my heart is very open to giving, especially when I'm working with my clients. One day, I was involved in a conflict situation and I went to group therapy that night with the conflict unresolved. I was feeling uptight and angry, but I chose not to share this information with my clients. I said nothing about my feelings and proceeded as usual with the group.

We did the routine thirty minutes of energy exercises, which finished with all the group members exchanging hugs. I thought all went well. The next day, one of the group members came in for her individual session. She was a fairly new client so she often asked a lot of questions. She started this questioning very tentatively:

Carol: Do people sometimes change whether their hearts are open or closed?

Sher: Yes.

Carol: I think I could tell the difference with somebody in group last night. Is that possible?

Sher: Sure it's possible. Tell me what you noticed.

Carol: Well, usually when I hug this person at group I feel all this warmth from her heart. Last night she hugged me and there was no warmth. In fact, she felt very cold.

Sher: That's possible. You are getting very sensitive to be able to feel that. Who are you talking about?

Carol: You!

I was very embarrassed and I remember blushing immediately. I felt like I'd been caught doing something wrong. I wanted to deny it, but I also knew I needed to be honest so as not to deny her reality. It would be crazy-making to lie to her and deny the truth of her experience. So I explained to her that I had come to group therapy feeling angry about a conflict earlier in the day. I knew I was uptight, but I didn't realize I had closed off my heart.

The next week, I decided to share Carol's observations with the whole group. About half the group also knew I had closed off my heart. It was a wonderful learning experience for all of us. My clients gave me permission to be human saying, "It's okay, Sher. You're allowed to have a bad day, too."

THE MAN WITH LOCKS ON HIS HEART

Terri, one of my women clients, went through a divorce after twenty-six years of marriage and then reconnected with her high school sweetheart named Frank. They both opened their hearts, fell in love, and married with much joy and hope for a beautiful relationship. During the two-year courtship Frank had his heart wide open to giving. He was very affectionate, generous with time, energy, and gifts. He was also able to be emotionally close and spent time sharing feelings and having long heart-to-heart talks. Terri was thrilled to be in such an intimate, loving relationship.

Within a year after the wedding Frank closed off his heart and stopped being intimate. He changed his heart position from a Giver to a Withholder. He stopped being affectionate and became cold and aloof. He stopped sharing about feelings and went back to his familiar, workaholic pattern. Imagine Terri's surprise and ultimate frustration when she realized this big switch. At first she couldn't believe he could change so drastically. Finally, she confronted him with her perceptions. He did not realize he had shut off his heart. They came into marital therapy so he could open up again.

In his therapy I asked Frank to give me a symbol to represent his heart chakra. He answered, "I see double steel doors with a bar across the middle. There are five padlocks on the bar and they are all locked real tight. I don't see a key anywhere." I asked Frank if this image fit with what he knew about his heart. He replied:

> It fits. I'm protecting myself. Nobody can get in, so I'm safe. They can't hurt me anymore. It's strange but I was able to open up for awhile when I first fell in love with Terri. Now I don't feel safe again. I liked it better when my heart was open, but I can't get there anymore.

Frank's personality, his psychological profile, and his life experiences were all reflections of his closed heart chakra. He was not at all in touch with his feelings and he could not remember ever crying. His first marriage ended in divorce and his second marriage was in serious difficulty. His new wife complained he was closed off to her and she felt unloved and isolated in the relationship. He had been highly successful as a colonel in the marine corps and now as a CPA in civilian life. However, to achieve this he spent his whole life being a severe workaholic, working sixteen to eighteen hours a day.

Frank discovered in his therapy process that he had closed and padlocked his heart as a young boy in his family of origin. He felt a sense of emotional rejection from both parents and he bonded to no one in the family. He often described himself as the black sheep of the family. He had been a loner all his life and he was also severely depressed all his life. It took a year of therapy to break through his denial about this issue.

Frank's therapy focused on finding the key to unlock the five padlocks on his double steel doors. It was a difficult process for him but he slowly opened to his feelings and established a heart connection with his wife.

COMBINATIONS

The basic four positions of the heart chakra can occur in various combinations, depending on the person's personality and early childhood script decisions.

OPEN TO GIVING AND CLOSED TO RECEIVING
CLOSED TO GIVING AND OPEN TO RECEIVING
CLOSED TO GIVING AND CLOSED TO RECEIVING
OPEN TO GIVING AND OPEN TO RECEIVING

We can perhaps understand best by looking in detail at each combination.

THE MARTYRS — OPEN TO GIVING AND CLOSED TO RECEIVING

Some people have their heart chakra open to giving love but closed to receiving love. Actually, this is the combination that I see most often in people. People with this combination believe, "It is better to give than to receive." These people usually interpret taking in love as selfish.

Usually people with this combination are unaware of their own need for love or their own difficulties in receiving. They have no awareness of being out of balance. Most people who define themselves as loving are only thinking about giving love to others. These people are usually martyrs and people who love too much. They suffer from the psychological illness of co-dependency and easily become depleted energetically.

THE TAKERS — CLOSED TO GIVING AND OPEN TO RECEIVING

These people are willing to take in the energy of love. However, when it comes time to reciprocate they are incapable of giving anything in return. They usually establish relationships with people who are willing to do all the giving. As long as both people remain unconscious about this imbalance in energy flow, the relationship will remain unhealthy but stable. Usually the giver wakes up first and becomes very angry about being used. The taker rarely wakes up because he or she is in no pain about the imbalance.

THE STONES — CLOSED TO GIVING AND CLOSED TO RECEIVING

These people have the worst possible combination. They have no love energy flowing into their heart chakras and no love energy flowing out of their heart chakras. These people are emotionally blocked and go through life like a robot. They have no heart connections with people but they do not feel bad about this because they are not conscious of what they might be missing. They go through life without experiencing the feeling of love in any way— friendship love, brotherly or sisterly love, romantic love, or spiritual love. Other people can intuitively sense their closed hearts and will choose to stay away from them.

THE RADIANT BEINGS — OPEN TO GIVING AND OPEN TO RECEIVING

Some people are able to attain the ideal of establishing a healthy balance between giving and receiving love. These people are usually very well integrated and psychologically healthy. Most likely they had their love needs met when they were infants in psychologically healthy families. Consequently, they establish adult relationships which continue this pattern. They are able to sense and receive spiritual love from a higher source. They are also able to love their own inner child. Both of these abilities are prerequisites to establishing a balanced love relationship with another person.

Radiant beings are most likely human beings who were born to loving parents who knew how to open their hearts and bond energetically with the newborn infant. This bonding in love prevents the loss of radiance experienced by most people. Radiant beings can also be people who have reclaimed their radiance through various forms of spiritual awakening, healing, or intense psychotherapy.

"Through the gateway of feeling your weakness
lies your strength;
Through the gateway of feeling your pain
lies your pleasure and joy;
Through the gateway of feeling your fear
lies your security and safety;
Through the gateway of feeling your hate
lies your capacity to love."

– Pathwork Lecture #190

CHAPTER 5

HONOR YOUR HUMANNESS

s souls we come to planet earth for the very purpose of having a human experience. It is part of the divine plan that human beings are created with emotions. To honor our humanness we must honor our emotions. This is the key to becoming a human being with a radiant heart.

THE OPEN HEART IS THE DOORWAY TO THE SOUL

"The real self is found inside the pain."
– Arthur Janov, *The New Primal Scream*

The very process of becoming radiant requires human beings to open their hearts and release their emotional pain. A heart filled with pain has no room for the uplifting emotions of love, compassion, or joy. A heart filled with pain has no space left for bringing in the light.

As a psychotherapist, I often experience people coming to me feeling shattered. They are in a crisis of some sort: failing physical health, psychological problems of anxiety or depression, or life issues such as career or relationship problems. The process of putting them back together involves helping them open to the expression of their emotions. Their emotional pain is the spark that ignites their desire to take the journey inward to the heart. Their desire to heal the heartache of a wounded heart is usually the key motivation for beginning a healing journey.

The journey inward to the heart is the key to opening the doorway to the Soul Self. This journey is a pathway of discovery. It is the pathway of spiritual awakening and expanded consciousness. On this journey human beings find out who they really are at the soul level. They do this through discovering their emotional self. Through working with their emotions they start a process of expanding their personality to become who they intended to be when they decided to incarnate on this planet. This process of evolution through the emotions is our very purpose for incarnating. Blocking emotions also blocks this expansion of consciousness.

Many people on a spiritual path believe they are better human beings if they can rise above their normal human emotions of fear, anger, and sadness and learn to feel only spiritual love. They may also feel guilty, seeing it as unspiritual or inappropriate to express feelings, now that they are "spiritual." Again, nothing could be further from the truth. I call this process *spiritual bypassing* because these people are using spiritual teachings as a rationalization for bypassing normal human emotions. This process of denying or bypassing normal human emotions actually closes the doorway for connecting with the soul. Spiritual bypassing actually defeats the goal of becoming enlightened.

The process of healing the heart and reconnecting with the soul is one of working with the emotions. People need to identify, experience, and revel in their high frequency feelings of peace, joy, excitement, and love. They also need to identify, experience, and release their lower frequency feelings of fear, pain, sadness, and anger. I use the terms *own it, feel it,* and *release it* to teach people a healthy process of flowing through their lower frequency emotions. Then they are free to live in the higher frequencies and reclaim their radiance.

After the emotional energies are balanced, healing begins to occur. Healing can occur because the energies of the soul flow naturally through the body when the energy blocks of repressed emotions are removed. These energies from the soul have a healing effect at the mental, emotional, and physical levels. This is the cornerstone of the philosophy behind Radiant Heart Therapy. *Healing occurs at all levels of being when we realign the human being with the energy of his or her soul.*

The root cause of both psychological and physical illness is the disconnection from soul. The healing of illness can be accomplished by healing this disconnection from soul. And the key to healing this disconnection is found in the process of opening the wounded heart and releasing the repressed emotional pain. A closed heart becomes an insurmountable barrier to this healing process. An open heart becomes the doorway to the healing people are searching for on their inward journey of transformation.

HUMAN BEINGS CREATED WITH EMOTIONS

It is part of the divine plan that human beings are created with emotions. In *Embraced By The Light,* Betty Eadie presents the idea that as human beings we learn our life lessons through our emotions. She states, "Each person on earth experiences the pain and the joy that would help them progress."

An ancient tribe from Australia also believes we were created to deal with our emotions. Marlo Morgan, author of the best selling book, *Mutant Message Down Under*, is an American physician who lived with an ancient aboriginal tribe in the outback of Australia in 1991. She described her experience and her spiritual learnings from this ancient tribe in a speech presented in Orlando, Florida.

> The aborigines believe that we chose to come here. They believe that you as a forever spirit chose to have this human experience. You actually were aware of what color your skin was going to be and who your parents were going to be and what kind of genetic defects this body was going to have that you were coming into. You saw that as a golden opportunity in order to be the most enlightened being that you could be.

> They believe we came in here with free will. They believe we come to the earth experience because there is something we can get on planet earth that you can't get in any other school of enlightenment. This is the only planet that has bodies like this. This is the only place that we have the senses that we have here of smell, sight, tactile sensation. And that is all tied in with the nervous system that we have because this experience on this planet has to do with emotions. *We are here to feel and deal with emotion.*

> We are here spiritually to experience love— unconditional, nonjudgmental, absolutely blissful joyous love. Love has no strings attached to it whatsoever. It is total acceptance of the person. They also believe mutants don't even understand what love is.

This ancient tribe from Australia allows children to express their emotions.

> If a child is angry they are never told, "Don't be angry. Straighten up. Act some other way." They never force someone to feel other than how they feel. They allow children to express themselves the way that they are.

BECOMING THE MASTERS OF OUR EMOTIONS

As spiritual beings on planet earth we are here to learn to be the masters of our emotions. At the present time too many people are servants of their emotions. In other words, their emotions control them. When we do not learn to be the masters of our emotions we develop problems at all four levels of our being: spiritual, mental, emotional, and physical.

Being the masters of our emotions involves truly feeling the full range of our human emotions. It requires us to feel and release our painful feelings of fear, sadness, anger, and hurt. It also requires us to feel and revel in our positive feelings of hope, excitement, peace, joy, and love. Being the masters of our emotions means to live with our hearts wide open so we are radiant, passionate, and alive.

Most people do not know how to be the masters of human emotions. They have no training about emotions and they are very fearful of experiencing the painful emotions of fear, sadness, and anger. Consequently, they try to control their emotions using mechanisms like denial and repression. They close off their hearts and build an energetic wall to protect themselves from feeling their painful life experiences.

People who are masters of their emotions know that emotions are very powerful tools. The common belief is that sensitive people are weak human beings who are too vulnerable because of their emotions. Nothing could be further from the truth. The reality is opposite of what most people believe. The more sensitive we are to all our emotions the more powerful we are as human beings.

Emotions are so powerful they can kill. When people do not learn to feel and release their emotions they can actually lose their physical bodies. We have all heard the expression, "He or she died of a broken heart." It is possible for human beings to die because they do not know how to express and release their human grief or heartache.

Human beings who do learn to process and release their emotions in a healthy manner will never die of a broken heart. Instead, they will be able to feel and release their pain so their wounded heart may heal. The key to healing a wounded heart is in releasing the heartache.

POSITIVE ASPECTS OF EMOTIONS

Our emotions are the powerhouse of our human nature. They are the cornerstone of our creativity. Our emotions give us the ability to live our lives with passion. Out of this passion comes the creative genius in all areas of life: the arts, music, literature, inventions, science. Without the energy of emotions the artists would be empty shells or robots devoid of the human passion we see in their work. It is the energy of the emotions that the artist captures on canvas or the musician captures in sound. It is the energy of the emotions that is transferred from the soul of the artist to the soul of the beholder. It is the energy of the emotions that strikes a chord in our hearts and opens each of us to the soul experience of art. It is the energy of emotion—the passion for the work—that is the driving force of a scientist who must spend years researching some minute aspect of an atom before finding the key to a scientific breakthrough.

Our emotions are there to guide us in our decision making. If we are in a situation that generates positive feelings of love, joy, harmony, or peace we know this experience is good for us. If we are in a situation that generates painful feelings such as fear, anger, frustration, or sadness, we know we need to change something or remove ourselves from this situation. Our emotions become the compass for guiding our direction as we travel along the pathway of life. People who are not in touch with their emotions have no compass for their journey. They meander through life avoiding decisions or turning their decisions over to other people in their life.

They also make decisions based only on intellect, leaving out their heart. These decisions of the head, without involving the heart, can be disastrous. A typical example might be someone who marries for money or prestige without considering love. There is a high probability for a very negative outcome from such a decision-making process.

EMOTIONS ARE ENERGY

Gabrielle Roth, a New York psychotherapist, works with feeling energy using movement and dance. In her book, *Maps to Ecstasy*, she describes feelings as energy:

> Feelings are real. They are not ideas that can be turned off. They are not abstractions. They are physical manifestations of energy, uniting body and mind and bringing them to the moment.

Feelings are energy. Feelings which are repressed are stored as energy in the cells of our physical body and in our human energy field. The energy of feelings holds the information of our feelings at specific electromagnetic frequencies. We can sense the various vibrations of our emotional energy. We know the vibrations of joy, of happiness, of excitement as they resonate within us. We also know the vibrations of fear, sadness, and anger as they resonate within us.

Human beings have the natural ability to pick up the information in feeling energy vibrations. We can intuitively sense the emotional state of other people. These feeling energy vibrations extend beyond our physical bodies as a part of our human energy fields or aura. Others can sense these vibrations when they come within contact of our extended energy fields. In this way, they can pick up an awareness of our feelings.

Have you ever met a stranger and liked him or her instantly? Have you also met a stranger you disliked intensely? Your reactions result from sensing the vibratory frequency in their energy field. People who are peaceful, kind, and loving give off a soft vibration with a higher frequency that attracts others. People who are filled with anger give off a harsh vibration at a lower frequency that repels others.

Love is energy. Love has the highest vibratory frequency of all the emotions. The energy of love is a healing vibration that is very powerful. Menninger Clinic researchers, who originated biofeedback, reported that healers whose energy output is motivated by love emit a life energy that is one million times stronger than the voltage of the human heart. This energy of love is responsible for millions of healing miracles around the world. These healing miracles include healings on all four levels of being.

I often ask clairvoyants to observe while I do emotional release work with my clients. The clairvoyants report seeing clouds of gray, black, or dark brown energy leaving the body, moving through the aura and drifting out into the room as repressed emotions are released. Often these dark clouds of energy hang in the air of the treatment room for five or ten minutes before they dissipate.

I do not have the gift of seeing the human energy field, so I have not seen these energy field changes. However, as I move my hands through the client's energy field I can feel the energy leaving the client's body. It feels like a stream of hot or cold air blowing and pushing against my hand. This movement and force of energy are very subtle but definitely there.

BENEFITS OF RELEASING EMOTIONS

Releasing the lower frequency emotions alleviates depression and invites people to be radiantly alive with a full flow of human feelings.

Releasing emotions also opens the door to the unconscious mind and allows people to make major shifts in consciousness at two levels, the conscious mind and the unconscious mind. When we clear our bodies of repressed emotional energy we clear the energy blocks that cause physical illnesses. Clearing the energy blocks allows the natural healing forces to flow through the body and bring healing to any imbalance.

Ideally, people need to release the lower frequency feelings in the very moment of the emotional trauma. If they have not done this the energy is stored in the cells of the body. Then the energy of these repressed emotions needs to be released in the process of psychotherapy.

RELEASING EMOTIONS ALLEVIATES DEPRESSION

Depression is not a feeling. It is actually the absence of feelings. We close off our hearts and block the normal flow of emotions when our feelings become overwhelming. We numb ourselves saying, "This pain is too much for me to feel." We mentally deny the pain and repress the energy of the emotions in the cells of our body. This common human process is one of the causes of depression. Dr. Arthur Janov, in his book *The New Primal Scream*, describes a safety valve that limits the maximum level of pain we can experience:

> One can experience only so much pain at one time, and beyond that there is a fail-safe mechanism which sets an upper limit to our ability to respond to pain. Such a mechanism determines the outer boundary of feeling. When we are driven beyond that boundary we are beyond full reactivity. We stop crying and are therefore beyond healing.

RELEASING EMOTIONS INVITES SHIFTS IN CONSCIOUSNESS

Consciousness refers to our beliefs about ourselves, other human beings, and life in general. These beliefs are often erroneous, but they become a self-fulfilling prophecy simply because we believe them. For example, children who have decided, "I'm unlovable," close off their heart chakras and will not allow anyone to love them. Their belief makes it impossible for them to receive the energy of love.

Often these beliefs are held in the unconscious mind and people do not even know they hold such beliefs. Parents unconsciously program their children with these mistaken beliefs through their own behaviors and the things they say to their children. These mistaken beliefs are usually passed from generation to generation until someone breaks the chain. Releasing emotions invites people to open their unconscious mind and achieve important shifts in consciousness.

RELEASING EMOTIONS PROMOTES HEALING OF PHYSICAL DISEASE

Many holistic medical practitioners have explored the relationship between repressed emotions and physical disease. In *Maps to Ecstasy*, Gabrielle Roth writes about the toxic effects and medical consequences of repressed emotions:

> Unexpressed, repressed, or suppressed, this energy becomes toxic. Without release, it surfaces in lumps, clots, tumors, spasms, migraine headaches, and other symptoms of physical distress. It is now clear that the repression of feelings has medical consequences. A wide variety of recent research has shown that repressing emotions takes its toll on our health—'repressor' personalities are shown to be much more prone to disease. The only real option, the only healthy alternative, is to embrace our emotions, to befriend them, to make them our own, and to learn to experience and express them appropriately in the moment.

TEARS, ONE OF THE MOST POWERFUL FORCES ON EARTH

Dr. William Frey, of St. Paul Ramsey Medical Center in Minnesota, is probably the most knowledgeable researcher on the biochemical effects of crying. He reports that tears release ACTH, a stress hormone triggered by the pituitary gland in the brain. Frey's research also makes these claims about tears:

> Tears also release endorphins. Tears wash away pain. They help remove the biochemical aspect of stress and are therefore a biological necessity.

Dr. Janov supports the premise that crying is healing. He writes:

> Tears are uniquely human. We differ from animals in our
> ability to cry and tear. Crying is a curative process. I do
> not believe that one can cure either mental illness or a
> host of serious physical ailments without it.

Research done by Dr. Janov shows there is a biological difference
when people release tears about a real event in their own life verses
releasing tears about something in a movie. When people are crying
about events in their own lives there is a change in hormones, brain
function, and personality. However, when people have a catharsis
about a disconnected emotional event in a movie these changes do not
take place.

Dr. Janov also makes a case for the relationship between repression
of emotions and physical illness. He states:

> Tears have the power to transform our physiology,
> change our personality, and refire the evolutionary
> engine. What has seemed like a weakness to so many of
> us turns out to be one of the most powerful forces on
> earth.

> The number one killer in the world today is neither cancer
> nor heart disease. It is repression. Unconsciousness is
> the real danger, and neurosis the hidden killer. . . .
> Repression—a stealthy, hidden, intangible force—
> strikes many of us down. It does so in so many disguised
> forms—cancer, diabetes, colitis—that we never see it
> naked for what it is. That is its nature—diabolic,
> complex, recondite. It is all pervasive, yet everywhere
> denied because its mechanism is to hide the truth.
> Denial is the inevitable consequence of its structure.

> There is almost no disease, mental or physical, without
> repression.

RELEASING OR RECYCLING FEELINGS

To be beneficial, crying must include a process of release. It is a
release of the repressed lower frequency energy of the painful feelings
of sadness, hurt, or despair. When people truly experience a feeling
and release it they are finished with it. They don't have to keep

recycling it. I call this powerful crying. When people learn how to release they feel lighter after crying. They will spontaneously announce, "I feel lighter," or "I feel like a load has been lifted." People who are listening to this powerful crying respond easily with a compassionate heart.

Since most people have no information about releasing painful feelings they usually try to be strong and repress them. This process forms energetic blocks in the body and the aura. These blocks can be released in psychotherapy by imagining the scene of the original emotional trauma and releasing the repressed energy through visualizations or through crying.

Not all crying is beneficial. Sometimes when people cry they hold onto the feeling instead of releasing it. They seem to get stuck in the feeling and grind with it rather than moving through it to the end goal of release. When this is happening the tone of the cry has a whining quality to it. Listeners sense the crying coming from the throat rather than the heart. The person seems to be sending out the message "poor me," or "feel sorry for me." The person who is not releasing usually does not feel any relief from this "poor me crying." In fact, he or she often feels worse both during and after this kind of crying, often developing a headache from the internal pressure of the energy that is not being released. Also, people listening to this kind of crying have difficulty being compassionate.

All mothers know the difference when their baby is crying in need and crying to manipulate. There is a difference in the tone of the cry. Manipulative crying has a whining quality to it. Manipulative crying is unhealthy and does not end with a release. This kind of crying is usually intended to control others. It is a very destructive process because feelings are not meant to be used to control others.

POWERFUL CRYING AND POOR ME CRYING

April and her sister Debbie had very different feeling responses to their father's announcement of his second divorce. April knew how to release her feelings through powerful crying. She reports:

> When my dad told me he was getting another divorce I cried really hard. I could feel energy moving through my body as I released the sadness. I also got really mad about it. I yelled real loud just a couple of times and released the anger. Afterwards I felt so much better. I was peaceful, calm, and able to think clearly.

Debbie had a very different experience:

> I cried for over an hour when I heard the news of my
> dad's divorce. Afterwards I felt like total shit. I had a
> migraine headache and a stomachache. I went to bed
> feeling miserable both physically and emotionally. I felt
> totally wiped out from the process. Believe me, it
> doesn't do any good to cry. Crying makes me feel
> worse.

OWN IT - FEEL IT - RELEASE IT

"On a long journey even a straw weighs heavy."
— Spanish Proverb

A healthy process for experiencing any lower frequency feeling is
to own it, feel it, and release it. Most people have no knowledge or
training about how to do this. A major portion of my time as a
psychotherapist is spent teaching my clients how to feel and release
their lower frequency feelings in a healthy way. The purpose of this is
to facilitate people in raising their level of energy vibrations to a
higher frequency in the emotional part of their being.

OWN IT

Owning the feeling involves identifying a particular feeling and
admitting that you are actually experiencing it. To own it, people must
break through denial about their own feelings and experience both the
agony and the ecstasy of life's experiences. People who own their
feelings express them clearly in the first person, using the pronoun "I."

I am angry and I know it.
I feel scared right now.
I am excited about life.
I love you.
I love life.
I feel such joy watching a sunrise.

People who own their feelings live life with a passion. They cry
easily and enjoy the experience of being a feeling person. They feel no
need to apologize for crying in public. They cry when hearing *The Star
Spangled Banner* or while watching a touching scene in a movie. They cry
when they feel love or compassion towards another human being.
They cry when their heart is touched by a loving experience. They get
misty-eyed holding a baby.

FEEL IT

"What you feel you can heal."
— John Gray

Feeling a feeling means to experience it and allow the energy of it to flow through the body. This is a very natural process that can be completed in a few seconds or minutes. Rarely do feelings last for hours if the person is flowing with the process in a healthy way. Even deep grief has an ebb and flow to it. Grief often moves in waves with relief, laughter, or joy spaced between the waves.

Sensitive people can perceive energy moving through their own bodies when experiencing their emotional feelings. The higher frequency feelings of love, compassion, pride and joy are all felt in the heart chakra. So are the lower frequency feelings of sadness, grief, heartache, and hurt. Fear creates energy sensations in the solar plexus and abdominal area. Anger is usually felt as energetic sensations in the shoulders, arms, neck, jaw, and eyes. Anger is also felt as a movement of energy in the abdomen.

The English language demonstrates that people unconsciously know about this movement of energy associated with feelings. Consider these common expressions:

My heart burst with joy.
He was so proud he was popping his buttons.
Fear gripped my stomach.
He vented his spleen.
A shudder of fear passed through my body.
The grief was so intense it tore my heart out.
I am sick with grief.
Anger makes my blood boil.

Feelings are also reflected in the aura. As the emotional state of the person changes, the vibrations in the aura change. Changes in vibration make the colors in the aura change. For centuries, many people blessed with the gift of seeing energy fields have reported color changes in the human aura. Love is usually reflected as a rose-pink around the human body at the heart level. Anger shows as spikes of red color shooting out into the aura. Depression makes the aura gray.

CHILDREN EXPRESS FEELINGS NATURALLY

Babies and little children usually express feelings very naturally. Their energy flows easily through open channels, often releasing as quickly as it started. They scream in fear, they yell out in anger, and they shriek with joy. As the tone of their cry changes, the sound vibration also changes and parents are able to intuitively know the meaning of the cry. Babies and little children have not yet learned to suppress, repress, or inhibit their feelings.

As children get older, parents or other adults send out many messages that inhibit the natural flow of feelings. The child usually complies and makes script decisions that inhibit the ability to feel. These mental decisions also block the normal flow of energy through the body. As the energy stops moving, the vibratory rate slows down and the person appears deadened or flat. Parental messages that inhibit the natural flow of feelings are:

Don't be so noisy.
Stop crying.
Big boys don't cry.
Quit being a sissy.
Shut up.
If you don't stop crying, I'll give you something to cry about.
I'll love you if you don't upset me by showing your feelings.

Some children decide to shut off their feelings completely, ending up as depressed adults. They experience life mentally and physically, but without the emotional aspect of their being. They actually close off the heart chakra energetically and feel very little vibration in their chest. Thus they avoid pain, hurt, and heartache; but they also close down the feelings of love, compassion, and joy. Most people in this state only intend to shut off the lower frequency feelings. They do not realize that closing the heart chakra to avoid pain will also result in the loss of their ability to experience the higher frequency feelings. These people give off a sense of being distant, closed, even robotic.

Most people have a strong "Don't Feel" message imbedded in their unconscious mind. Consequently, they become extremely cut off from the emotional part of their being. In psychotherapy, I work diligently to help my clients overcome this deep-seated resistance to experiencing natural feelings. A great deal of my time and energy is spent teaching my clients to open to their feelings so they can release them.

RELEASE IT

All lower frequency feelings need to be felt and released from all four levels of being. At the physical level, release the energy stored in the cells of the body at the time of the event. At the mental level, release the negative thoughts associated with the event. At the heart level, release the emotion through crying or sounds of some kind. At the spirit level, release the energy from the energy field.

There is no need to recycle lower frequency feelings. We need to release them and be finished with them so we are free to express higher frequency feelings. People who recycle painful feelings develop a pattern of emotional suffering. They become the martyrs of this world. Their life motto becomes: "Life's a bitch and then you die."

A most important step for my clients is identifying repressed painful feelings and releasing them. Eventually they learn to do this without my assistance. I also teach my clients ways to create positive feelings, so they can take charge of their vibratory frequency.

Feeling release work takes courage. Most people begin with the idea that crying is weak and resist the process of moving into and through the painful feelings. The truth is that feeling release work requires a deep level of trust in the therapist and a great deal of courage to move into and through the pain. It takes courage to become vulnerable and let our defenses down. However, for the courageous there are great benefits.

Often in feeling release work there is a movement through layers of feelings. The person may begin with anger, move into sadness, and then into fear. After the release of the pain, there is a spontaneous shift into laughter, joy, peace, or love. For me as a therapist, this is the real essence of the emotional release work. I love being with the person in this moment. There is nothing quite like sharing the vibrations of pure joy or pure love.

SENSING AND WORKING WITH EMOTIONAL ENERGY RELEASE

Emotional trauma from the past is held in the very cells of the body in the form of energy. As people do their feeling release work, this energy is released from the cells and can be seen or felt by people who are sensitive to perceiving energy.

People who have developed the capacity for intuitive sight "see" it as waves of energy coming off the body. It looks just like the heat waves rising from a hot pavement on a hot summer day. The waves of energy are easiest to see with peripheral vision. The observers need to sit quietly and focus their gaze beyond the person releasing feelings. There will be a shimmer of clear energy coming off the body in waves as the feelings are released. Some gifted observers also see colors coming off the body during feeling release work.

Others have the gift of sensing energy kinesthetically—through experiencing sensations in their physical body. In doing work of this kind, the therapist can tune in to the client's vibrations on such a deep level that his or her body becomes a reflection of the vibrations happening in the client's body. The same physical pains, the same energy blocks, and the same energy releases felt by the client can be experienced by the therapist at the same time. In that way, the therapist can use his or her own body as a biofeedback machine for sensing and diagnosing the movement of energy occurring in the client's body.

Another way to sense energy kinesthetically is to use one's hands like a detector device. As the therapist moves his or her hands through the energy field of a person, he or she can sense cold spots or hot spots in the energy field. As the client releases emotional feelings through crying, moaning, or yelling there is usually a stream of energy coming off the body at various places. Some therapists have reported that it is often so strong that it feels as though a blow dryer is inside the body blowing out a stream of hot or cold air. By passing his or her hands over the client's body, the therapist can find the stream.

After completing feeling release work, the client usually reports feeling physically lighter. People spontaneously describe it in many different ways:

I feel lighter.
I don't feel so weighted down.
I feel like I took a load off my shoulders.
It's easier to walk.
I can move more easily.

After feeling release work, people have a different look to their faces. The muscles are relaxed because the muscle tension used to restrict the feelings is now released. People usually look five to ten years younger and the energy about the face is alive and moving. There is a radiance about their smile and a sparkle in their eyes. The whole being seems to be shining from within, and appears to glow or light up.

People have the ability to experience the lightness and freedom that come from doing feeling release work with a therapist, regardless of the nature of the blocked or repressed feelings. Whether they are the feelings of sadness, fear, anger, or rage, people can choose to allow their expression, and thus free themselves to become emotionally and physically healthy.

SADNESS

Sadness is a normal, healthy feeling in response to loss and change. People experience sadness as a heaviness in their heart, or sometimes even as a weight pressing down on their chest, or a heaviness throughout their body and their energy field. The body of a sad person appears to sag under the weight of the sadness: the eyes look heavy, the face droops, the mouth curves down, the shoulders sag, and the feet drag.

Denying and suppressing the sadness allows it to build and grow bigger until it becomes a pervasive feeling. Suppressing sadness also leads to depression. To heal the sadness people need to own it, feel it, and release it. Releasing sadness means moving through it rather than becoming mired down in it. Releasing it allows for the feelings of joy, laughter, and peace to surface. Releasing the pent-up sadness and blocked tears through crying releases more energy which the person can use for healing themselves. The natural healing mechanism for sadness is tears.

As I assist my clients with releasing the sadness, I can feel repressed energy leaving the area of the heart chakra. It comes out of the body in different ways. Sometimes it's a gentle all-over release through the entire aura. Sometimes it comes out of the heart chakra in a gush. Other times it releases in waves that seem to come from the very core of the person's being. As the energy of the sadness leaves the body, the level of the energy field changes to a higher vibration.

FEAR

Fear is a normal, healthy response to danger. Fear is our friend because it mobilizes us to take action to protect ourselves from danger. Fear is usually felt in the body in the abdominal area or the solar plexus. Many people describe fear as a sinking feeling in their stomachs, as if they are going down a roller coaster. Fear also shows in the eyes and the face of a scared person. Fear often is reflected in the body by stomach problems, ulcers, and gastrointestinal problems, such as diarrhea and colitis.

Again, expressing the emotion of fear is the key to releasing it and moving through it to a place of peace. Each time I facilitate feeling release work about fear I must trust that the fear will release and stop. I must also trust that underneath the fear there is a place of calmness. Finding this calm, quiet place in the center of the fear is like finding ourselves in the eye of a hurricane. The storm is still raging all around, but in the center we remain safe and untouched.

As I facilitate the feeling release work I provide lots of protection for my clients. I tell them things like:

I know you're scared.
It's OK to be scared.
Of course you're scared.
You can feel the fear.
Feel it and release it.
Go into the fear.

I interact with them as a sensitive but strong, protective parent dealing with a terrified five-year old. As the parent I am both powerful and nurturing at the same time. My calm power gives the client permission to "fall apart" and know I can handle whatever feelings come up. My sensitive nurturing part gives the client the message that I will accept his or her feelings with nonjudgmental love.

The fear release work is probably the hardest for clients. They have such resistance to feeling the fear. I find they have various conscious or unconscious beliefs about moving into the fear that inhibit the release. They believe ideas like:

I might go crazy.
I'll fall apart.
I'm weak if I feel.
I'll never come out of it.

Group work facilitates releasing fear and other emotions. Clients see others bravely overcoming their resistances, going through intense releases of long-repressed feelings, and joyfully coming out of the release—often markedly transformed. As the person releases the fear there is a corresponding release of energy from the cells of the body. The energy usually is coming from the solar plexus area and moves out of the body in various patterns.

Since I tune in kinesthetically, I can feel the same movement in my body as the energy moves through the client's body. I can detect when it gets blocked in the client's body and facilitate removing the block. Sometimes the energy flows out the solar plexus like a geyser of water. Other times the fear energy leaves the abdomen in a rush through the legs and out the feet, or moves from the gut up through the torso and out the mouth.

As I feel these energy releases with my clients I know they are healing the fear at a cellular level. I know they are doing the transformational work to become whole again. Each time I must trust in the process of feeling release work. Time and time again, I see my clients rewarded with feelings of love and joy as they continue their healing journey.

ANGER

Anger is a normal, healthy feeling that is a response to the invasion of one's personal boundaries. Gabrielle Roth defines the benefits of healthy anger:

> There's nothing cleaner, more effective than appropriate anger. Authentic anger is specific and justified, and its direct expression exposes impropriety and defends integrity in a way that benefits everyone.

Most people have been taught that expressing anger is mean, unkind, unloving, unchristian, non-spiritual, and even against God. Anger is probably the most disapproved feeling in our culture, and therefore the most repressed.

People have gross and subtle body signs of repressed anger, such as tight jaws, TMJ problems, muscle tension, tension headaches, clenched fists, stiff shoulders and neck, lower back problems, and more. Repressed anger also shows in behaviors such as sarcasm, avoidance, and passive-aggressive actions such as back-biting and gossiping. Many people use "nice" words for "I'm angry." They say, "I'm frustrated," or "I'm slightly irritated." These euphemisms are a sign that people do not have permission to be angry in a straightforward way.

Anger is probably the easiest feeling for people to learn to feel, express, and release in the process of psychotherapy. I first have the person recreate the experience that generated the anger. This can be done by role playing the scene, or using imagery to recreate the feeling, or acting out a Gestalt exercise of being the person you're angry with. It cannot be accomplished effectively by talking about the incident. Therefore I discourage clients from "talking about" the experience in an intellectual way.

I facilitate anger release by helping people move into their inner child and express feelings as children do naturally. I have people do physical activities like kicking a pillow, hitting a pillow with a tennis racket, hitting a punching bag, or pushing against another person in a safe way. I also have them use their voices in various ways (yelling, growling, or toning) to move the feelings through sound. I direct them to imagine there's a ball of angry energy in their abdomen that needs to be moved up through the torso and released out the mouth. Making loud sounds helps move and release the energy.

Many people I have worked with are angry about some tragedy in their lives. As they release the anger they express deep feelings of rage at fate and even at God for allowing this tragedy to occur. They are often angry with God for not having prevented it or for not working a miracle and taking away the pain and its consequences. They are angry with God because they feel abandoned by God. I encourage this expression of anger by having them talk to God on the empty pillow. I believe God to be a loving Mother/Father who is willing to listen to this anger in a compassionate way just as earthly parents are willing to listen to a hurt angry child.

After releasing this anger, people usually move closer to God and become more open to the unconditional love available to them. Repressing the anger blocks taking in the spiritual love. Releasing the anger opens the heart chakra to receiving the love.

This anger release work is done with the specific purpose of healing their relationship with God. At some point I redirect the clients' thinking towards self-responsibility for creating their lives and their health and not holding God responsible. After releasing the anger people are more able to change their thinking on this issue.

CLIENT STORIES DEMONSTRATING EMOTIONAL RELEASE WORK

"Though you can barely remember your experiences from childhood, the imprint of hurtful words and negative experiences has made an indelible mark upon your wounded spirit."

— Susan Dexter, *Angel Cards*

The following client stories are examples of emotional release work using Radiant Heart Therapy in group treatment. They show how emotional release work alleviates depression, facilitates the shifts in consciousness, and clears the blocks causing physical illnesses.

TRANSFORMATION OF THE "GLOOMY CHILD"

Diane first came in for psychotherapy at age eighteen when she graduated from high school. As Diane began her therapy she was incredibly resistant. She came at her mother's insistence and she definitely did not want to be there. It took all my clinical skills to just keep her in treatment. She hated her sessions because I expected her to open her heart and deal with her feelings which she most certainly did not want to do. She had closed off her heart to avoid feeling her pain and she wanted to keep it closed. Actually Diane was quite depressed and had been depressed since early childhood when her parents divorced. At age four her mother nicknamed her the "gloomy child" because she looked so sad most of the time.

At the personality level Diane had numerous problems. She had closed off her heart to deny her painful feelings. This created a block in her normal flow of vital life force energy causing both psychological and physical problems. Diane had both depression and anxiety which she covered over with a workaholic lifestyle. She was also in a very destructive relationship with a boy who was emotionally abusive to her. Physically she suffered from asthma, insomnia, migraines, and tension headaches. She had severe tension headaches every other day and debilitating migraine headaches about once a week. She had no idea that the root cause of all her problems was that she was denying her feelings.

In her intitial sessions, Diane was extremely resistant to working through her pain. Eventually, she opened her heart and flowed with the process of releasing. She opened her heart to all the anger, sadness, and fear she had stored there since childhood. She reported these changes from doing the feeling release work each week in group:

> Each week I felt lighter and lighter as I was letting go of all the pain of my parents' divorce. I pounded a huge pillow with a tennis racket and felt the hot energy of my anger move from my abdomen up through my torso and out my mouth. I felt the energy of my deep sadness coming out of the center of my chest as I went back into those scenes of my dad moving out of the house. And I felt this hot energy leave my solar plexus as I released all the fear I stored there. I felt and released all the feelings I should have felt back then.

> Releasing all this anger, sadness, and fear had the biggest effect on me. I had held all this inside me for fifteen years. I pretended it had no effect and I really believed myself. After the release work I cleared my tension headaches, my migraines, and my insomnia. They all just went away.

> Clearing the insomnia surprised me the most. All through high school I would lie awake till three in the morning. I just couldn't turn my brain off. I thought it was hereditary since my dad and his mother suffered from the same thing. Probably they have blocked off their feelings, too.

> I know the feeling release work allowed me to open my heart. Each time I released more feelings about the divorce another layer came off the wall around my heart.

NO MORE ABUSE

Anne came into treatment to deal with her heartache about her marriage. At age sixty-six, she was a retired nurse and a very spiritual person. However, she felt unable to cope with her emotionally abusive husband.

Anne called me in crisis one day. She was crying so hard on the phone that I could hardly understand what she was saying. She had just discovered that her husband was having numerous affairs through placing ads in the singles magazines. She came to group the next day and did the most powerful anger release work since she had begun her therapy. She took a tennis racket and hit a large pillow and yelled at her husband, releasing her anger at this insult to her.

Her feelings were so intense she was able to stop denying her anger. As she hit with the tennis racket, she yelled at him, bringing hot energy from a ball of anger deep in her abdomen. Kneeling next to her with my hand pressing on her abdomen, I could feel the energy release like an explosion. It came off her entire body and even her face and head. She released her present anger, as well as years of repressed anger about his verbal and emotional abuse. She yelled at him on the empty pillow:

> I'm so angry at you. I don't deserve this abuse. I'm furious with you and I won't take it anymore. Do you hear me? No more abuse.

The whole group started cheering as she finished this work. She surprised herself, feeling powerful and jubilant when she finished.

This event and her response to it was a turning point in Anne's therapy. She made her life script redecisions and dramatic behavioral changes. For the first time in her sixty-six years she claimed her right to express her feelings. She went home and expressed her anger to her husband and asked him to move out of the house. She told him very clearly :

> You have been abusing me for forty years. I'm angry with you for doing it and I'm angry with myself for allowing it. I've made my decision. No more abuse. I won't take it another minute. Get out, now!

Anne maintained this powerful position and her husband actually moved out of the house to an apartment. She was uneasy living alone for a few months, but then she came to love the peace and quiet. She felt peaceful for the first time in her own home after years of abuse and quarreling. Every day she congratulates herself for having the courage to stay in therapy and make her redecisions.

Anne had been miserable because of her inability to deal with her emotions and her emotional needs—her needs of the heart. Like most people in her generation she had no education about her feelings or how to deal with them in a healthy way. She had used all her spiritual teachings to support her early childhood script decision, "I won't feel my feelings." She was doing spiritual bypassing: "I'll bypass my feelings and rise above them in order to become a more spiritual person."

Anne had been trying to deny her human feelings. She focused on being spiritual and tried to rise above being human. She did not want to admit to having emotional pain nor did she want to express the pain. Therefore, she was all bottled up with this repressed pain. She had been storing her painful feelings for over sixty years so it was obvious to me that every cell of her body must be filled with the negative energy of her denied pain.

After two years of releasing repressed emotions Anne cleared several physical symptoms. Her elevated blood pressure returned to normal and she was able to give up her blood pressure medication. Also, her eyes had been constantly watering for about ten years. After releasing her repressed emotions her eyes stopped tearing and returned to normal. She was delighted with both of these physical changes.

I WAS ROBBED OF MY INNOCENCE

Elizabeth began treatment at age twenty to heal her depression. After several months she revealed conscious memories of sexual abuse and we uncovered a script decision of "I deserve abuse." She had experienced ongoing verbal abuse from her mother, years of physical abuse from her older brother, and five years of sexual abuse from her uncle. Her parents had no conscious awareness of her emotional state from all of this. She didn't even know it herself. Underneath her depression she was filled with rage at the ridicule, the put downs, the unfair treatment, and the sexual abuse.

She remembers being a bright five year old who was at the top of her class in kindergarten. Suddenly, in first grade she began failing in school. Her parents and teachers could not understand why she began doing so poorly. Elizabeth herself decided she was stupid. What she did not realize was that her mind could no longer function because she was so overwhelmed with emotions about the sexual abuse that began soon after starting first grade. As a child she could not comprehend any cause-and-effect relationship between receiving sexual attention from her uncle and getting poor grades at school. Since she kept the sexual abuse a secret the adults in her world did not have a clue about the root cause of the change in this little girl.

Elizabeth was willing to go back into those early scenes of sexual abuse and release the many emotions she repressed and buried at the time. She had numerous sessions in group where she released the fear, the humiliation, the hurt, the heartache, and the rage she held for her uncle. She opened her heart and cried for the lost innocence of her childhood. I remember her saying:

> I was robbed of my innocence. I always felt dirty after he touched me. I had this sad look in all my pictures and I felt so different from my friends. I wish I could have told somebody why I was so sad, but my uncle threatened to kill me if I told.

As we did the release work, I knew we could not give back her innocence to Elizabeth but we could release the buried emotions that were causing blocks to the natural flow of her vital life force energy. Each time she did the feeling release work she released hot energy from various areas of her physical body—her heart, her face, her solar plexus, and her abdomen. Those in the group with the ability to see the higher vibrations could see waves of energy coming out into her aura. At times, some group members could see blobs of color coming off her body.

In the final session about the abuse she released a huge cloud of very dark energy from her abdomen. This dark energy came out with a rush when she was toning and moving a loud sound from her abdomen up through her torso, her heart chakra, and out her mouth. In the next second, her heart chakra opened with a rush and was flooded with this hot energy. It was the suppressed energy of her life force. I felt it rush from her root chakra, through her heart chakra and out her crown chakra. She spontaneously began laughing and announced, "I feel so loved!" I will never forget this wonderful healing moment.

As Elizabeth healed from the emotional damage caused by the sexual abuse, she seemed to walk a little taller, her eyes began to sparkle, and her face brightened. I knew these were signs that her aura was getting bigger and brighter. We were removing the energy blocks caused by the emotional pain in her childhood. As these blocks melted away, the natural flow of life force energy moved through her system and brightened her eyes and face. Each week she seemed to come more alive as she released the hurt and pain of the past.

I WANT TO BE LOVED FOR JUST BEING ME

Marilyn, age fifty-three, entered therapy for assistance with her fears about her diagnosis of cancer, a third-stage lymphoma. After clearing her body of cancer using chemotherapy, she stayed in treatment to transform herself at the other three levels of being: spiritual, mental, and emotional. Each week in her Thursday morning group she worked on various aspects of her life script. She came to understand that she was doing a lot of unhealthy emotional caretaking with her friends and family members. One morning I asked her to complete this sentence with as many ideas as she could bring to consciousness:

If I don't take care of others, then . . .

She pondered this question for a few moments and then plunged into expressing the thoughts that were surfacing in her consciousness. She looked each group member in the eye, one by one, as she repeated the sentence and her various responses. She surprised herself with her answers that surfaced from the dark places of her unconscious mind. She spoke from her inner child saying:

If I don't take care of others . . .
  I feel like I'm not doing my job.
  I have no value.
  Nobody will notice me.
  Nobody will love me.
  Then I'm nothing.

As she proceeded around the group expressing her inner thoughts about her caretaking, I could feel the emotions beginning to build in her abdomen and her heart chakra. I knew because I was tuned into her energy field and my body was resonating with her energy vibrations. I could feel this tension building in my own abdomen and a feeling of pressure in my chest. I knew Marilyn was opening to the childhood pain about these beliefs she held in her unconscious.

As she said the words, "I'm nothing," the buried feelings gushed from her abdomen, moving up through her torso as she broke into sobs and released the deep pain of feeling so worthless. She cried and cried as if her heart would break. And as she released these tears she also released a cloud of hot energy from her abdomen and a stream of hot energy from the front of her heart chakra. I sat next to her, providing support by putting my arm tightly around her shoulders. As the stored energy released from the cells of her body I felt the same releases in my own body.

As the storm of feelings subsided Marilyn sat very quietly with her eyes closed for a long time. She seemed to go deep within. Intuitively,

I knew she was listening to her inner voice, the whispering voice of her soul. I sat with her holding my breath as I watched the energy shift in her face. Her eyes brightened, she started smiling, and she seemed to light up. She suddenly opened her eyes and announced:

I want to be loved for just being me!

I knew this was a profound moment. She had just achieved the shift in consciousness that I patiently wait for with each of my clients. I had just witnessed the light bulb go on in the darkness of her unconscious mind. In this magical moment after the release of the repressed energy of deep pain, she allowed the voice of her soul to be heard. She let go of the old thought patterns regarding her unworthiness and reprogrammed her unconscious with this redecision. Now she could more easily change her behavior and stop taking care of others to get love.

Marilyn had her old programming for almost fifty years. I knew she would need to reinforce this redecision for months so she didn't revert back to her old programming. For weeks after this redecision work she programmed these new thought patterns into her consciousness:

I am lovable.
I deserve love just because I was born.
I have value because I exist.
I am worthy of love.
I deserve to get my needs met.

As Marilyn cemented these changes into both her conscious and unconscious mind, she could look back at her old behaviors and her old personality as if it belonged to somebody else. She says of her former self:

I feel like a different person. I look back at the old me and I wonder how I could possibly have believed such crazy ideas. They no longer make sense to me.

INTENSE AGONY AND INTENSE JOY

I work with many cancer clients and I have observed that the diagnosis and treatment invites cancer clients to feel angry. When surgery, chemotherapy, and radiation are used to eradicate the cancer, there is a deep violation to the entire body of the cancer client. This violation produces a sense of rage that moves through all parts of the body and permeates every cell. The grown up part of the person can understand the necessity for the treatment, but the inner child still needs to express the rage at the violation. The negative energy of this rage needs to be released from the cells of the body.

Rusty's case is a good illustration of the rage that needs to be released after surgery and radiation. Rusty was diagnosed with breast cancer at age fifty-six. Since the cancer had progressed to include eight lymph nodes she was given chemotherapy, radiation treatments, and a mastectomy of the left breast. Rusty began psychotherapy with me several months after her mastectomy. She was still in the process of finishing her radiation treatments, which she hated with a passion.

Rusty was extremely hostile as she began her therapy. She was angry about having cancer, angry about the side effects of the radiation, angry about losing her breast, angry about being in pain, and angry at her doctors. Each week I feared she might get angry with me and stop treatment. Somehow she bonded with me and we proceeded to work together for several years. After her body was clear of cancer she stayed in psychotherapy doing the work to heal herself spiritually, mentally, and emotionally.

After six months of individual therapy Rusty reluctantly joined an ongoing weekly psychotherapy group which was designed to facilitate feeling release work. She was fearful of talking in front of a "group of strangers" and she much preferred to continue with me in individual sessions. But once she bonded with the group and trusted them, she began to release feelings of anger, sadness, and fear about her cancer experience.

Two years after her mastectomy Rusty came to group one night with a vague sense of uneasiness. Her feelings were triggered by a visit to a friend in the hospital. She left the hospital feeling extremely disturbed but unclear as to the root of her internal discomfort.

As we explored her feelings she felt her anger about her own hospital and surgery experience. She got in touch with her rage at being violated and disfigured. In the process she released agonizing screams that pierced the heart of each group member. She must have screamed for ten minutes or more.

The whole group felt her pain and was deeply touched. In that moment there was an emotional bonding among members of the group that is difficult to describe. The group then bonded with Rusty, forming a supportive healing cocoon and surrounded her with love and compassion. They held her and rocked her wounded inner child. Within minutes after the release Rusty was taking in the love and began laughing with relief, excitement, and even joy. Her joy was as intense as her agony. She was very alive in the expressions of all her emotions. Her face looked radiant and she exclaimed to the group:

> Wow! That was something! My whole body feels lighter. I feel great!

Indeed, I believe she was lighter. I was physically close to Rusty as she lay on the mat doing the release work. I could feel waves of energy coming off her entire body. It felt like heat off a stove. As I felt it, I knew Rusty was releasing the repressed energy stored in her cells two years earlier when her body was traumatized by the surgery.

After the release of this repressed energy her energy system was open to receiving the healing energy of love and compassion. Her heart chakra was open and she bonded energetically with the open hearts of her group members. I felt such joy as I watched Rusty healing her anger and her disconnectedness. This was a joyful healing moment for Rusty, for all her group members, and for me.

Over a period of three years Rusty did the work to transform herself on all four levels of her being. Spiritually, Rusty opened to the experience of giving and receiving love. Mentally, she changed from thinking mostly negative thoughts to positive thoughts. Emotionally, Rusty moved from the lower vibrations of fear, anger, and depression to experiencing the higher vibrations of peace, joy, and love. Physically she implemented diet changes, vitamins/minerals, and exercise to attain a very healthy body. She looked ten years younger than when she began treatment and her personality was so different that she seemed like a different person.

Rusty's thirty-three year old daughter entered treatment four years after Rusty began. I casually asked her if she had noticed much change in her mother. Her response was rather surprising:

> My mother is like a different person. You know those stories of aliens coming in and taking over somebody's body? Well I think there must be an alien in my mother's body. She's not the mother I knew as a kid. She's become so loving. It's rather amazing.

Rusty's daughter gave me further evidence that releasing the rage facilitates opening to the natural feelings of love.

THERE'S MOTION GOING THROUGH ME

Mandy, age twenty-two, entered therapy to heal her depression and lack of self-confidence. Mandy attributes much of her personal empowerment to learning about identifying feelings and being able to move the energy of her feelings through her body as she releases them. She says:

> Before therapy I spent my life holding onto things and being stuck. I'd be angry and I'd get stuck in it. Now there's motion going through me rather than something sitting inside me. I can sense the energy of my feelings moving inside me. Now I feel more alive because I move through feelings and I let them go.
>
> Before our family went to therapy, feelings were discouraged in my family. My parents wanted me to be positive so I wasn't allowed to be angry, sad, or scared. I wouldn't tell my parents my feelings because they would say, "You shouldn't feel that way." I knew I didn't want to share with them but I didn't realize it was because I felt criticized for feeling whatever I was feeling.
>
> The biggest change in our family is that we have learned to listen to each other's feelings with open hearts. I used to hide a lot from my parents because I didn't want to deal with their criticism. Now I'm open with them and they are open with me and we love spending time together.
>
> Our whole family now has a heart connection. I feel an energy connection between our hearts when we hug. Because of this I feel more like we are a family. I want to be there. Before, my goal was to get away but now I want to spend time with my parents sharing and being close emotionally.

I HAVE A VERY TENDER HEART

Joseph, Mandy's father, entered therapy to heal his marital relationship and his problems with addictions. He also transformed the way he handled feelings. After three years of therapy he said of himself:

I've become a very sensitive man. I'm not the old callused individual that can survive anything. I have opened to my feelings and I know when my heart hurts. I didn't used to know. I am a very feeling person. I used to only feel about other people. Now I have feelings about myself.

When my wife criticizes me I can tell her, "That hurts me." I used to just get angry to cover the hurt. I have discovered I have a very tender heart. I can share that tenderness with my wife and my daughters.

Last week I lost control of the car on the ice. I felt this rush of fear in my body. It is so strange to be feeling my feelings. Before I would have stayed in my head and had no feelings about it. I would be thinking, "Whatever happens happens." It was easy to keep a fatalistic attitude when I had my deathwish and a closed heart. I have lost my fatalistic attitude about life now.

Now that I have feelings I care about what happens to me and my family. Two years ago I lost a lot of money gambling. My wife was all upset, but it meant nothing to me. Nothing meant nothing to me. I just didn't care about anything.

LOVE IS NO LONGER A MYSTERY

Jake, Mandy's boyfriend, also came into therapy. He joined the same therapy group and together they learned the Radiant Heart exercises and the Radiant Heart process. Jake made his redecisions about love so that he could open his heart and connect in a healthy, loving relationship with Mandy.

Jake learned to open his heart chakra and feel the sensations of energy moving through his chest. He describes the difference between having a closed heart and an open heart:

When I started therapy I didn't know my heart was closed. I had never even thought about it. I just knew I didn't feel happy with myself, my life, or my relationships. I had no idea what the problem might be nor did I have a clue how to fix it.

When my heart opens, the inside of my chest feels warm. I get this weird feeling like something is shifting in my physical body. It's like a big weight is being lifted off my chest. I start feeling calm and peaceful.

Before I opened my heart I didn't know how to love. I didn't know what love was and I didn't know how to feel it. I could think about it but I couldn't feel it.

Now I know love is the feeling of energy moving in my chest. I can feel the warmth when my heart is open and I can feel the coldness when my heart is closed. These sensations of energy tell me whether I'm feeling love or not. It's no longer some nebulous, intangible thing. *Love is no longer a mystery.*

I never used to be sure about my relationship with Mandy. Now I realize I often had my heart closed and I couldn't really feel a connection with her. I would open it for a time and feel "in love" and then I would lose the feeling. Then I would start doubting whether she was right for me. I didn't realize I was closing off my heart. Instead, I blamed her and started thinking we were wrong for each other.

Now when I look at her my heart opens and I feel this rush of hot energy in my chest. I know I'm in love and I have no doubts. I sit and watch her and think, "She's smart and she's pretty, and most important, she has an open loving heart. And I'm the luckiest guy in the world to be able to feel our heart connection."

"It is in the acknowledgment of the deathwish that the real self is born. One must come to grips with this shadow side of one's being."

– Rita Benor, Devon, England

CHAPTER 6

THE DEATHWISH: THE DESIRE TO RETURN TO DIVINE LOVE

his chapter is intended to define the deathwish, explain its nature, and provide case histories of transforming the deathwish using Radiant Heart Therapy.

At the soul level there is no death because the soul by definition is eternal. There is death at the human level. However, it is only a death of the physical body. We know from fifteen years of research on the near death experience (NDE) that consciousness goes on after the death of the physical body. Dr. Elizabeth Kübler-Ross and Dr. Raymond Moody pioneered the early research on NDE. George Meek continued their research and published his findings in *After We Die, What Then?*. He traveled to twenty different countries and spent sixteen years investigating NDE and life after death. He states:

> There is now a sufficient accumulation of research data to show that the energies that make up an individual person's thoughts, emotions, personality, memory banks, and soul continue in existence after death and decay of the human body.

Others have written about the soul being eternal. In her book *Heart Thoughts*, Louise Hay states her views about death:

> There is no loss. There is no death. There is only cycling and recycling of energies—a changing of form.
>
> We are on an endless journey through eternity.
>
> Our spirit, our soul, the very essence of who we are is always safe, always secure, and always alive.

ALIGNING THE WISHES OF THE PERSONALITY WITH THE WISHES OF THE SOUL

As spiritual beings incarnate on the earth plane we have consciousness at two levels. At the soul level our consciousness forms a plan for coming to earth and learning certain lessons through emotional experiences. This soul plan is commonly called *fate* or *destiny*. Most human beings are not conscious of either their soul or their soul plan. However, one of the goals of spiritual awakening is to become conscious of the existence of the soul as well as the existence the soul plan.

There is a dynamic interaction between destiny at the soul level and free will at the human level. The ideal scenario is that the soul and the personality are constantly communicating and negotiating about major life decisions as the human being journeys along the path of life. The plan at the soul level is created with numerous options. The human being has free will and makes choices about these options all along the path.

Just as everyone has a soul, they also have spirit guides, although not everyone is aware of them. Human beings who are spiritually evolved have a conscious connection to soul and to their spirit guides. These are the multisensory human beings who can tune in to their intuition and receive guidance from the spiritual realms. Gary Zukav even defines intuition as the "whispering voice of the soul." In this case the wishes of the personality are most likely to be aligned with the wishes of the soul. The free will choices made at the personality level will ensure that each person uses his or her natural talents and gifts to achieve the highest potential as a human being.

One of my clients gave a wonderful description of discovering his soul plan:

> I was meditating and I got this wonderful vision of my life unfolding. I saw myself as a spiritual healer working with human beings in pain. I was a radiant being and I had this wonderful energy coming out of my hands. It was such a beautiful vision. I'll never forget it. When my doctoral program gets overwhelming and I feel like giving up, I remember the vision and it keeps me going.

Another client described his soul plan as he said:

> Since I was a little kid I always wanted to work on cars.

> I have this dream to have my own business and rebuild cars. I feel happy whenever I think about it and I seem to have this natural ability to do mechanical work. I seem to just "know" what to do without any training.

Less spiritually evolved human beings have no conscious connection to their soul and spirit guidance. These are the five-sensory human beings who have closed hearts and are unable to hear the internal whispering voice of the soul. In this case the wishes of the personality are more likely not to be aligned with the wishes of the soul. These people often say things like, "I don't know where I'm going. Why am I here? I don't know what I'm supposed to do here." These people are also less likely to achieve their true potential as human beings because they are probably not using their natural talents and gifts.

According to Dannion Brinkley, author of the best-selling book, *Saved By The Light*, only the most courageous souls choose to come to earth because they already know life can be extremely difficult here on this planet. He calls all of these souls "great spiritual warriors" because they had the courage to dare to come.

The soul leaving home in the spiritual realms to come to the earth plane might be likened to a human being who leaves home to go off to a trade school or college. The human being is often homesick and longs for the comforts of familiar surroundings and family love. However, the inner drive to learn new knowledge and create a better life helps the person maintain the motivation to stay in school and overcome whatever obstacles are in the path of learning.

Sometimes human beings decide these school courses are too hard and return home without learning the lessons. Other times people complete all the courses and learn the lessons. Graduation ceremonies are the ritual which celebrates the successful completion of learning the lessons after a long course of study.

At the soul level, birth into a human body is the result of choosing to enroll in a school called the earth plane. Just as humans can decide to leave trade school or college without learning their lessons, they can decide to leave the earth plane school without learning their spiritual lessons. Human beings can also decide to stay in the earth school and overcome the obstacles and challenges to learning their spiritual lessons they came here to learn. When they leave the earth plane at this more appropriate time there is cause for celebration of their graduation.

Choosing to return home to the spiritual realms means the death of the physical body. This choice needs to be negotiated between the personality and the soul. When the personality has a desire to give up the physical body and return to the spiritual realms the human being makes a mental decision called the *deathwish*. This deathwish at the personality level might be as simple as, "My life is too much of a struggle and I don't want to go on."

We all know we must leave the earth plane at some time, so the choice to leave is neither right or wrong. However, we need to look a this deathwish in relationship to the soul plan. This deathwish at the personality level may or may not be synchronized with the soul plan at the spiritual level.

THE PREMATURE DEATHWISH

Many times people form a deathwish at the personality level when the soul plan still contains many more lessons for the human being to learn. In this case the deathwish is a premature decision to leave the soul path and return to the spiritual realms of divine love. Most people make this premature decision when they experience a lack of radiance and have no faith or hope of reclaiming it. They believe there is no hope of attaining peace, joy, or love on their journey through the earth plane. When the deathwish is premature the wishes of the personality are not aligned with the wishes of the soul.

The near death experience literature is filled with hundreds of case histories in which people return to their human bodies with the message from a spiritual being on the other side of the veil, "Your work is not completed yet. You must return to earth."

THE MATURE DEATHWISH

"No one dies unless the life force agrees to leave the planet."
　　　　　　　　– Elizabeth A. Johnson, *As Someone Dies*

Many times people form a deathwish at the personality level when the soul plan is complete. This completion has nothing to do with the chronological age of the human being. The soul plan can be complete for an infant or a teenager as well as an elderly person. The mature deathwish signifies that the human being has successfully completed all the lessons in the soul plan.The person knows intuitively that the lessons are complete. There is no further need to remain on the earth because the journey is finished and it is graduation time from the earth school. In this case, the wishes of the personality are very much aligned with the wishes of the soul.

In *Mutant Message Down Under*, Marlo Morgan describes the customs of an aborigine tribe in Australia. These people are very spiritually evolved even though they live in primitive conditions as nomads in the bush country. They are in constant communication with their souls through a process of mental telepathy. They never make a decision without consulting their Soul Self. They know how to use spiritual healing energies to heal their own physical bodies. Consequently, they live very long lives with very little physical disease.

When a member of the tribe believes it is time to leave the earth plane he or she first asks permission from his or her soul. If the answer is yes, the person announces this to the tribe and sits down in the center of a tribal gathering. The person goes into a meditative state and closes off the chakras using a process that is taught within the tribe. The energy of the soul leaves the human body peacefully within several minutes. The last words this person hears is the whole tribe saying in unison, "We love you and we support you on your journey." These words have a familiar ring because the first words spoken to every new baby born into the tribe are, "We love you and we support you on your journey." These primitive nomads already understand that the time spent in a physical body on the earth plane is only a very tiny part of the soul's longer journey of evolution through eternity.

Indeed, the idea of death becomes much less frightening when we view life on earth as only a tiny portion of the soul's journey through eternity. *The Urantia Book* substantiates this viewpoint with this interesting definition of death:

> Love of adventure, curiosity, and dread of monotony—these traits inherent in evolving human nature—were not put there just to aggravate and annoy you during your short sojourn on earth, but rather to suggest to you that death is only the beginning of an endless career of adventure, an everlasting life of anticipation, an eternal voyage of discovery.

> Curiosity—the spirit of investigation, the urge of discovery, the drive of exploration—is a part of the inborn and divine endowment of evolutionary space creatures. These natural impulses were not given you merely to be frustrated and repressed. True, these ambitious urges must frequently be restrained during your short life on earth, disappointment must be often experienced, but they are to be fully realized and gloriously gratified during the long ages to come.

PREMATURE DEATHWISH DUE TO LOSS OF RADIANCE

When people develop a premature deathwish something happens at the personality level and they become disconnected from the inborn drive to evolve to a higher level of consciousness. At the personality level people become discouraged, depressed, and filled with self-doubt and emotional pain. They believe they are incapable of experiencing and transcending the painful emotions of their life lessons. They develop fears, feelings of inadequacy, and negative thought patterns that diminish their sense of personal power. They lose their sense of curiosity, their spirit of adventure, and the natural urge to learn. They lose their sense of connection to soul. It is a crisis of existence at both the human level and the soul level. They lose their connection to divine love and, therefore, lose their radiance.

The premature deathwish can be overcome if people are willing to open their hearts, release their current emotional pains and repressed emotional pains, and learn to receive unconditional love. Then they can reconnect with their soul and reclaim their radiance. The soul then reclaims its basic curiosity and sense of adventure about completing its life plan.

When people develop a premature deathwish they are trying to solve their life problems and complete their mission from the personality level. They have a disconnection from soul and consequently a sense of "doing it all alone," so of course the task seems overwhelming. Opening to a reconnection to soul and the spiritual forces increases the sense of personal power in the world. Following intuition and inspiration from the spirit world makes learning the lessons and completing the mission so much easier.

LIFEWISH: A REASON FOR BEING

The *lifewish* is a wish at the personality level to stay in the human body on the earth plane and complete the lessons planned at the soul level. The lifewish is often called the will to live. It is a desire to complete the mission and achieve the ultimate goal of expanded consciousness while still a human being.

The process of transforming the deathwish to a lifewish requires people to find meaning and purpose to their lives here on earth. I help my clients understand that the very reason for being here on earth is the learning of the spiritual lessons—lessons about love and universal truths about our existence in the universe.

Survivors of the near death experience report unanimously that there are only two important goals to be accomplished in life before crossing over to the other side. The most important goal is developing the *capacity to experience love*. The second important goal is to *accumulate knowledge*—knowledge about what is true about our existence in the universe.

Money, prestige, success, power, and the accumulation of material things are of no consequence in the afterlife. The only things we can take with us to the other side are our capacity to experience love and the knowledge we learned through completing our mission on the earth plane. Those who cross over and return to their physical bodies drastically change their priorities in life. They become more loving and devote more time to relationships and less time to achievement oriented activities.

PSYCHOTHERAPY AND THE DEATHWISH

The concepts of a premature deathwish and a mature deathwish have important implications for the process of psychotherapy. First, the deathwish is unconscious for most people. It takes a highly skilled therapist to facilitate bringing the deathwish to consciousness. Once this has been accomplished it takes even more skill to facilitate the client in defining his or her purpose in life and evaluating whether or not it has been completed.

If the person has a mature deathwish, the task of the therapist is to facilitate a conscious dying process that enables the person to cross over with much less fear. In fact, it is possible for the person to cross over with much peace and joy, knowing death is only another transition and a graduation process after successfully completing his or her course of study here on the earth plane.

If the person has a premature deathwish, the task of the therapist is to facilitate the client in transforming the deathwish to a vibrant lifewish so that the mission for this life in a physical body might yet be accomplished.

And who is to decide whether the deathwish is premature or mature? And what criteria do we use for making this decision? These are extremely important questions that are not easy to answer. Certainly the therapist is not the one to decide such an important question for the client. I believe the answer can only be found in the client's soul. Usually people with a deathwish do not have a conscious connection to soul, so they cannot answer the question from the soul level. Therefore, it becomes the task of the therapist to facilitate the reconnection between the personality and the soul so the person can find the answer from within. This can be accomplished through various techniques such as guided imagery, meditation, hypnosis, dream analysis, and working with the chakras and the energy field.

TRANSFORMING THE DEATHWISH TO A LIFEWISH

Transforming the deathwish to a lifewish is only appropriate when the deathwish is premature. I am using the term *deathwish* to indicate premature deathwish throughout the rest of this chapter.

DEFINING THE DEATHWISH

The deathwish is a mental decision at the human level of existence. This decision has repercussions physically, emotionally, and spiritually. Physically, the body becomes weakened and more susceptible to illness. Emotionally, the person is likely to experience mostly negative feelings and depression. Spiritually, such a person experiences a disconnection from soul and disconnection from God, and consequently a loss of vital life force. It is a decision to choose death over life, to leave the physical body at a particular time in the journey of the soul. The deathwish can be conscious or unconscious, subtle or pronounced, fleeting or pervasive, dormant or active.

I believe the deathwish is a universal phenomenon. I believe this because I have experienced it myself, and for twenty years my psychotherapy clients have been spontaneously describing it to me using various words, phrases, metaphors and dreams. It can be as simple as any of these thought patterns:

I want to give up the struggle.
Life is too hard.
Life sucks.
I don't want to go on.
When will it be over?
Anything has to be better than this.
I can't go through this anymore.
There's really no way out of this.
I don't want to spend one more day here.
My family would be better off without me.

I have an outpatient psychotherapy practice consisting of middle-class Americans who would be considered rather high functioning adults. My clients represent a broad spectrum of occupations including students, housewives, parents, farmers, salespersons, industrial workers, secretaries, managers, nurses, teachers, lawyers, entrepreneurs, and others. They range in age from teenagers to adults in their sixties, with the majority between thirty and fifty. They are just ordinary people at various stages in life who choose to use psychotherapy as a tool to improve themselves and improve their ability to cope with their life problems.

These ordinary people all experience normal life problems such as relationship conflicts, difficulties in achieving career goals, financial problems, anxiety, depression, marital difficulties, and psychological issues centering around low self-esteem and lack of love. Most of these ordinary people also report thoughts and feelings that indicate the existence of a deathwish.

The deathwish exists on a continuum from a fleeting thought to an all-consuming preoccupation with wanting to die. Almost everyone at some point in life has at least a fleeting thought, "I want to give up" or, "Life is too hard." These destructive thoughts usually come with life experiences of failure and loss during adult life, but may be initiated at any stage of life, from conception to adulthood. They can be prompted at any time by an awareness of emotional emptiness or lack of love. Only a very small percentage of people with a deathwish actively plan to commit suicide and take action to carry out such a plan.

UNCONSCIOUS DESIRE TO RETURN TO RADIANCE

Our lives on earth are chosen by our souls as lessons in emotional experiences. The deathwish is so pervasive because as spiritual beings we carry with us an unconscious memory of living in the spiritual realms surrounded with the vibrations of unconditional love. With the decision to incarnate and live on the planet earth, we left that spiritual world and are now living in this human world which, by comparison, seems cold and unloving. We naturally have a desire to return home to this blissful world filled with spiritual love. We want to return to the world of radiance.

As we incarnate, we select a life purpose and a pathway designed to learn certain lessons so that our soul might evolve. This is done at the soul level, and at the human level this life plan resides in our unconscious mind. For most people the life purpose remains hidden from our conscious mind. People develop a deathwish when they cannot accept the reality of what is occurring in their human experience.

Usually they feel incapable of dealing with the emotional pain or terror of their human existence and so they make the choice to self-destruct. They want to leave their soul path prematurely because they believe they cannot find love, peace, or joy on their journey. The formation of the deathwish is actually an attempt to ferret out and destroy the very part of them that is human—their emotional self. People develop a deathwish when they want to turn from the very purpose of incarnating, which is to learn about emotions while dwelling on the planet earth.

The deathwish is evidence that this soul is having difficulties in merging with its human nature—its emotional nature. When people learn to master their emotions they can feel and release the emotions of pain, fear, sadness, and anger and then open their hearts to the energy of love. When their hearts are filled with this spiritual love it is like being back home in the spiritual realms. Then life as a human being on the planet earth becomes worth living and they can replace the deathwish with a lifewish. This is the ultimate purpose of life here on this earth: to remain as human beings with physical bodies and feel the spiritual love that we once knew on the other side of the veil.

It takes a skilled, caring practitioner to deal with the deathwish. When the deathwish is unconscious, people will deny that they even have one. These clients vehemently deny this possibility and often get very angry with me for suggesting it might be true.

If people are in denial, they cannot see reality. They really are not in touch with something that is very obvious to a skilled observer looking in from the outside. Often, it takes six months to a year of psychotherapy for my clients to break through their denial and begin to deal with this demon that is hidden deeply in their unconscious.

SECRETS FROM THE SELF
THE STOREHOUSE OF INNER VIDEOS

The unconscious mind might be described as a vast storehouse filled with secrets. These secrets are hidden from the conscious mind; therefore, I call them secrets from the self. These secrets are powerful in terms of influencing one's thoughts, feelings, behaviors and decisions in everyday life. They are also powerful in terms of influencing a person's physical body and ability to defend against illnesses.

The secrets from the self include anything that has ever happened to a person which the person cannot consciously remember. These secrets might include consciousness as a fetus in the womb, memories of the birth trauma, early childhood experiences, early childhood script decisions, repressed painful feelings, or all forgotten events.

The secrets are stored by the unconscious memory in a way that is complete and perfectly detailed, as if on an enormous mental "video tape." This internal video camera has been recording every moment of the person's existence. Thus, the camera has captured every scene, every thought, every feeling, and every vibration experienced in the person's life. When existence is defined in terms of consciousness at the soul level, the video must also include past life experiences. Therefore, I envision the unconscious mind as a vast storehouse of video tapes filmed from the moment the soul came into existence.

Often the conscious mind of the person repressed an event or feeling because it was too painful to experience. The unconscious mind keeps the videos locked away in the storehouse to protect the person. The unconscious holds the key to the lock. The unconscious will not allow repressed material to become conscious until the person is emotionally strong enough to handle the information at the conscious level.

BIRTHSTORY

For many years psychologists, psychiatrists, psychics, and hypnotherapists have been exploring the psyche of the unborn child. Much research is currently being done in this emerging field called prenatal psychology. The International Association of Prenatal Psychology was founded in 1988 to promote research in this field and provide an international forum for exchanging research results. Their yearly conferences are attended by health professionals and educators from around the world. One of their goals is to educate the public about the psychological aspects of the fetus in the womb.

Much research has established that the fetus in the womb has consciousness. In other words the fetus has intelligence, memory, feelings, and the ability to make decisions about the self and others in the family. Research has proven the newborn infant remembers and recognizes music played while still inside the mother's womb. Babies also have a recognition response to the unique vibration of their mother's voice. Hypnotherapists all over the world have thousands of case histories where their clients have remembered sensations, memories, emotions, thoughts, and experiences while they were still a fetus in the womb.

The origin of the deathwish is most often found in the psyche of the unborn child. This information is often revealed to the client by their parents in the form of their birthstory. I always ask my clients these questions:

What stories were you told about your birth?
Was the pregnancy a planned pregnancy?
How did each parent feel about the pregnancy?
Were there any complications during pregnancy or delivery?
Did you bond energetically to form a heart connection with your mother?
Did you bond energetically to form a heart connection with your father?
Were you loved or rejected from the moment of conception?

The birthstory sets the stage for the psychological development of the inner child. A child conceived in love and blessed with the energy of love will make very different decisions than a child who is rejected from the moment the mother knows she is pregnant.

THE AWARENESS OF THE UNBORN CHILD

Canadian psychiatrist, Dr. Thomas Verny, spent six years gathering research information about the psyche of the unborn child. He interviewed professionals around the world, including psychiatrists, psychologists, physiologists, fetalogists, obstetricians, and pediatricians. His book, *The Secret Life of The Unborn Child*, is a phenomenal text on this subject.

Dr. Verny believes the unborn child has an active mind. Research information in the scientific literature by Dr. Lester Sontag (1930s and 1940s) substantiated this belief. Sontag demonstrated that maternal attitudes and feelings could leave a permanent mark on the personality of an unborn child.

Verny also found exciting research in the fields of neurology and physiology. Investigators in the 1960s and 1970s were able to use new medical technology to study the fetus undisturbed in its natural habitat. Dr. Verny summarizes his work in the forward of his book:

> Thanks, in part to all of them [world researchers], I have been able to present here a fundamentally new portrait of the unborn child, one that is very different from the passive mindless creature of the traditional pediatrics texts.

> We now know that the unborn child is an aware, reacting human being who from the sixth month on (and perhaps even earlier) leads an active emotional life. Along with this startling finding, we have made these discoveries:

> The fetus can see, hear, experience, taste and, on a primitive level, even learn in utero (that is, in the uterus –before birth). Most importantly, he can feel—not with an adult sophistication—but feel nonetheless.

A corollary to this discovery is that whatever the fetus feels and perceives begins shaping its attitudes and expectations about itself. Whether it ultimately sees itself as a secure or anxiety-ridden person depends, in part, on the messages it receives while in the womb.

The child's mother is the chief source of these modulating messages. However, it should be recognized that each and every fleeting worry, doubt, or anxiety a woman has does not rebound on her child. What does matter are deep persistent patterns of feelings, chronic anxiety, or wrenching ambivalence about motherhood. These can leave a deep scar on the personality of the unborn child. On the other hand, life-enhancing emotions such as joy, elation, and anticipation can contribute significantly to the positive and beneficial emotional development of a healthy child.

New research is just beginning to focus much more on the father's feelings. Until recently his emotions have been disregarded.

FAILURE TO THRIVE IN INFANTS

Infants, like adults, will present physical manifestations of their mental decisions. Many infants who have "a failure to thrive syndrome" are examples of this phenomenon. The infant with failure to thrive may already have a deathwish. The infant who refuses to eat may be saying, "I do not want to nourish myself. I do not want to keep my body alive." These babies who survive usually have a life filled with both psychological and physical illnesses.

I have worked with numerous adult clients who report they had failure to thrive syndrome as infants. A young man named Darrell is a vivid example of this condition. Darrell entered psychotherapy with me at age thirty-two to alleviate depression. His mother had been in treatment with me four years previously. She also came in for depression. The mother gave the following family history:

> Darrell has been sickly since he was born. His dad rejected him from the moment I told him I was pregnant. It was a miserable pregnancy and I almost lost him several times.
>
> I couldn't get this baby to eat. The doctors finally diagnosed him as failure to thrive. I didn't really understand the root of it. My doctors kept saying, "There's no known cause."

Darrell had no conscious memory of any of these details about his birth. He did rather well in life in spite of his poor beginning. He looked fairly normal on the surface, but a closer look revealed severe psychological damage that he expressed in this way:

> I have been depressed all my life—ever since I can remember. I did not know how to feel good emotionally. I have had a few happy moments, but they do not last.
>
> Also, I cannot seem to connect with people. My wife and I are having serious marriage difficulties. Sometimes I think things like, "What am I doing here?"or, "Maybe I will just end it." I do not act on these thoughts but I think about it often.

Darrell obviously has a deathwish. He carried this out behaviorally even as an adult by not eating. He was extremely thin and eventually came out of denial about his eating disorder. As an infant, he had the failure to thrive syndrome and, as an adult, his diagnosis was depression and anorexia nervosa.

THE PSYCHIC CONNECTIONS OF THE UNBORN CHILD

From the moment of conception, the fetus has its own human energy field. The fetus is also affected by the energy field of each parent. The vibrations emanating from each parent impact on the fetus in a profound way. The energy field of the fetus also impacts on the energy field of each parent. The interaction of these energy fields provides the possibility for a psychic connection between the baby and the parents.

Dr. Verny reported on some research that demonstrates the existence of a psychic connection between a mother and her fetus. Pregnant women and their babies were monitored with very sophisticated equipment that could measure the baby's heart rate and other vital information. Dr. Michael Lieberman showed that an unborn child grows agitated physically each time his mother smokes a cigarette. The agitation was measured by the quickening of the heartbeat. The more interesting finding was that the research team could produce the exact same response from the baby by having the mother *think about* having a cigarette.

I believe this type of psychic connection between mother and baby is responsible for the transmission of psychological messages from mother to baby. The unborn child knows, "I am wanted and loved in this family" or the opposite, "I am not wanted and there is no love available to me." The unborn child who knows, "I am not loved" is the child who decides, "Life is too hard and I do not want to live." This is the infant with a deathwish.

This information has enormous implications regarding both the psychological and physical health of all human beings. *The programming for psychological immunity against life-threatening illnesses must start at conception.* The healthy messages given to the fetus can establish a psychologically healthy baby with host resistance to physical illnesses. Unhealthy messages given to the fetus initiate a deathwish that may lead eventually to life-threatening illness, depression, or self-destructive behaviors.

EARLY CHILDHOOD TRAUMA

The origin of the deathwish can often be traced to an emotional trauma in early childhood. A cancer client named Lucy reported making her deathwish decision after an emotional trauma involving the death of her brother. In this family the brother was the favored child.

Lucy was rejected and left in the background. At age seven, Lucy came home from school one day to find her mother crying hysterically. The mother's words of explanation were embedded forever in Lucy's memory.

> Your brother was killed by a car today. He's gone. I am
> so heartbroken. Why couldn't it have been you?

Needless to say, Lucy became severely depressed and suicidal from that moment in time. Her mother may not even remember saying these words, but they left an indelible mark on Lucy's psyche.

THE LOSS OF A LOVED ONE

People often make a deathwish decision when the death of a loved one causes such emotional pain that life seems unbearable. This reaction is common when a person believes, "I lost my only source of love" or, "I lost my most important source of love." The reactive depression following the death of a loved one is one sign that the survivor has shut off his or her own vital life force energy and indicates that the survivor has a deathwish. The deathwish decision may be conscious or unconscious.

People with a conscious deathwish are usually aware of their thoughts and fantasies about dying to achieve their goal of uniting again with their loved one. Their fantasies are focused on joining their loved one in the after-life rather than that person coming back to earth.

Many people are unconscious about their deathwish decision at the loss of a loved one. However, they will think or say things that indicate the formulation of a deathwish decision. The following statements are examples of these:

I just do not care anymore.
I hate my life without my husband.
I do not want to go on without my mother.
My life is so empty now.

RECLAIMING RADIANCE BY RELEASING GRIEF

The ability of the survivor to process his or her grief will determine the effect these thoughts have on the survivor's physical health. Those who grieve and release their pain about their loss will be able to release the deathwish and revitalize their own life force. Thus, the will to live will be regenerated. Those who deny or repress their grief are the ones who are most susceptible to manifesting their own life-threatening illness to carry out their deathwish.

Wilma's experience demonstrates the deathwish decision in response to the death of her husband from a heart attack. She reacted to his death by stopping her own life. She stayed home, pulled down the blinds, became severely depressed, and essentially gave up on life. Wilma described herself as being obsessed with this thought, "I do not want to go on without him." Two years after her husband's death, Wilma developed colon cancer at the age of fifty-six. I believe her body created her cancer in response to her depression and her conscious deathwish.

Psychotherapy for Wilma was focused on healing her grief. When her husband died she had never really grieved, believing that crying would not bring him back. I helped her release the repressed emotions of anger, deep sadness, and fear of going on alone. The emotional release work facilitated the lifting of her depression. At some point, she made a redecision to create a life worth living even without her husband. She established her own identity, probably for the first time in her life. Her relatives were amazed at the transformation in her personality.

She not only healed her cancer but she also healed her personality and her life. She opened her heart, released her repressed pain, and reclaimed her radiance. At the end of working together for two years she actually said:

> This cancer was a blessing. I have changed so much and I have learned so much. I would never have done therapy without getting cancer. I like myself so much more than before my illness. In fact, I have learned to love myself.

HEALING UNRESOLVED GRIEF

Shirley, forty-eight, came to me for psychotherapy after having a lumpectomy to treat her breast cancer. The doctors had assured her that they had discovered the lump very early and she would be fine. She was not at all interested in exploring the psychological causes for her cancer. She was also in great denial about her deathwish.

Shirley did not seem to fit the emotional pattern of unresolved grief before her diagnosis of cancer. Her father had died five years earlier, but she had worked through her grief well. Neither did she fit the common pattern of the empty nest syndrome. Her two sons had recently married, but her sixteen-year-old daughter was still at home. We only uncovered what was happening when Shirley witnessed another group member expressing grief about her daughter leaving home. Shirley began crying rather deeply at that moment and said:

> I felt that kind of pain when my second son got engaged [one year before her diagnosis]. I could hardly bear the thought of him leaving home. I am not at all connected to my husband and this son was my strongest emotional bond within the family. Now, I have no one to talk to. The house seems terribly empty without him. In fact, I feel terribly empty without him.

As she said this she began to sob, releasing the repressed emotional pain from her heart chakra.

Gradually, Shirley came to terms with her deathwish and understood that she had unconsciously given up on life when she knew her son was leaving. She processed her unresolved grief about the loss of her son. She released great pain that she had suppressed because her rational mind kept saying, "Nobody died, you know."

Unresolved grief over other losses may produce similar reactions. People may make a deathwish decision when they lose a job or a dream or their purpose in life. In many instances we find that the deathwish was probably present but dormant from childhood or in the womb. The loss of purpose later in life then re-activates the deathwish.

FACILITATING REDECISIONS TO LIVE

Marilyn, a cancer client introduced in Chapter 5, identified her deathwish in the first few weeks of therapy. She came to group therapy week after week and proceeded to work with releasing her repressed feelings and transforming her personality. She had not yet dealt with her deathwish and I wondered when she would open to working with this core issue. I couldn't force her readiness so I waited, knowing that it would surface when the time was right.

One Thursday morning another group member did some powerful grief work about the death of her mother. Marilyn witnessed this release work and began to release her buried feelings about the death of her own mother. As these feelings began to bubble up from deep within her body she tried to repress them saying:

THE DEATHWISH ■ 129

> I don't know why I'm crying. I shouldn't be feeling this.
> My mother died twelve years ago. It's been over for
> such a long time.

I directed Marilyn to stop judging her feelings and allow her inner child to express whatever was coming to the surface. She opened her heart chakra and poured forth this agonizing grief. As the energy of the repressed grief began to emerge from the cells of her body, Marilyn flowed with it and started releasing these deep, heart wrenching sobs. As she released she closed her eyes and went back in time to the moment of her mother's death. At that time she had appeared stoic. Actually she was in shock. She went through the whole funeral process denying her grief with the rationalization, "Crying won't bring her back."

Now, as she released the pain of her loss, she cried as if her heart would break. Her pain was so immediate and real it touched the hearts of all the group members. There was not a dry eye in the room as they opened their own hearts and connected with her in loving compassion. As she released her pain she also released her deathwish from its hiding place in the dark recesses of her unconscious. Her inner child cried out:

> Mother, come back. Come back and be with me here. I
> don't want to go on without you.

With these words, I felt the hot energy of Marilyn's pain sear through my own heart chakra. I recalled my own pain of losing my father twenty years earlier. I remembered saying those exact words from my own wounded child. Marilyn's release work touched that part of my heart that still yearns to be with my father in the physical world and walk together once more on the earth plane. I truly knew the depths of her grief.

At the same time, I felt this intense joy, for I knew Marilyn had just uncovered the very root of her deathwish. Staying in her logical mind she never would have been able to remember saying those words, for she had repressed them in the secret vaults of her unconscious. She had to go beyond the mind and open her heart to her feelings. Then she could retrieve the memory of her decision. In her conscious mind she didn't remember making such a monumental decision. However, the very cells of her body remembered and they responded to her wish, creating a life-threatening illness. I also believe that her soul remembered that moment in time when she cut off the flow of vital life force energy. By closing off her heart chakra to deaden the pain of her loss, she blocked the natural grieving process.

All the repressed grief flowed out of the cells of Marilyn's body, through her energy field, and out into the universe. Hot energy came off her face as she released the need to hold her face in a mask so no one would suspect she was grieving. A rush of heat poured out of her abdomen as she cried for her mother. The heat poured out of her chest as her heart chakra opened to allow the stored energy of grief to come to the surface. Marilyn held onto me like a terrified child as she released her pain. After about ten minutes of releasing, the storm of feelings gradually subsided and she spontaneously announced:

> Mom, I need to go on without you. I want to live! I have
> my own life to live. I really do have my own life to live!

Marilyn said this last sentence as if it were a revelation to her. She had such a stunned look on her face. She had just experienced a major shift in consciousness. She had just made a decision to stay on her own soul path and continue her life journey on the earth plane. For the first time she realized she could carry on without her mother. Her shocked look was a reflection of this major shift in perception. The whole world looked different to her in this moment. My heart felt such great joy to be part of her transformation. I knew she would be different from this moment forward.

Over the next weeks Marilyn processed her feelings about her relationship with her mother as she worked to understand her unconscious urge to self-destruct. Marilyn had been born into a very loving family. She was the oldest of two girls and she had a very strong heart connection with her mother. She described her mother as kind, loving, and full of unconditional love. However, Marilyn believed no one else could love her like her mother. All her life she held the thought pattern, "My life would not be worth living without my mother." She kept this thought hidden from her friends and family members. She really didn't think about it very much herself. And she certainly had no awareness of the problems this attitude could create in her life.

Marilyn received her diagnosis of cancer ten years after her mother's death. The research shows that the diagnosis of cancer usually comes eighteen months to two years after the loss of a loved one. I believe there was a significant reason for the delayed onset of her cancer. Marilyn's life purpose was to be a wife and mother. She was very comfortable in this role and was fulfilling her life's purpose. Marilyn's diagnosis of cancer came two years after her youngest son graduated from high school. Unconsciously Marilyn saw her son's graduation as the end of her purpose in life. In a later piece of work she discovered her unconscious belief, "I'm nothing without my role as a mother." It's my belief she had held her deathwish at bay until she finished raising her last son. Then the loss of her purpose in life allowed her immune system to stop functioning. This in turn allowed the cancer cells to spread in her lymphatic system.

SPONTANEOUS REDECISION TO LIVE

Spontaneous redecisions to live often occur without therapy or outside the therapy room. Sometimes the shock of the diagnosis of cancer awakens the person's desire to live. Dr. Bernie Siegel, author of *Love, Medicine & Miracles*, calls cancer "God's reset button." Indeed, the diagnosis of cancer can sometimes reset the deathwish.

Other events can lead to a redecision to live. Bertha came for psychotherapy to change her lifelong suicidal thoughts. For eighteen months she made little progress in redeciding that life was worth living. Then, one day she had a terrible car accident. As her car slid under the back of a semi-truck, she threw herself prone on the front seat screaming, "God, help me. I don't want to die!"

She survived with only minor scratches from the accident. She never had another suicidal thought again. In that terrifying moment, facing death, she spontaneously redecided to live.

TRANSFORMING THE DEATHWISH PROMOTES GROUNDING

Julie began therapy with me because she suffered from Crohn's disease, a severe disorder with chronic, uncontrollable diarrhea and painful intestinal inflammation. Medical science has not yet identified the cause of Crohn's disease. It strikes mostly among young adults and may be connected to a deficiency in the immune system.

The intestinal tract is very sensitive to emotional states. Julie's internist referred her for therapy to reduce her emotional stress. She was so seriously ill she had been hospitalized four times in five years and almost died twice.

Julie was in her mid-forties, divorced, with two children ages twenty-one and sixteen. She had a very stressful job as a real estate salesperson. She grew up in a dysfunctional, alcoholic family where she learned the patterns of chaos. Consequently, she kept herself constantly stressed to the maximum both personally and professionally. She was in total denial of her stress levels. She also did not understand that her severe emotional stress contributed to her Crohn's flare-ups.

Julie was not energetically grounded. Since I don't "see" energy fields, I have to use other clues. My first impression was that Julie appeared extremely off balance when we exchanged hugs. She would often fall forward or backward during our hug. Sometimes she would pull me off balance. I also noticed that she felt "spineless." Her back felt too mushy, as though she had no backbone and no strength in her back muscles. I often wondered how she could hold herself up.

Mentally, Julie presented more clues that she was ungrounded. She had great difficulty making decisions. She often used the phrase, "I'm up in the air about this." She did not realize this phrase about her indecision described her problem of being energetically ungrounded. She also had great difficulty with logical sequential thinking. Often she would jump to illogical conclusions or skip from topic to topic in her conversations.

Julie was a menopause baby and knew she had been unwanted from the moment of conception. The pain of being unloved was so great that she closed off her heart in the womb. She often had thoughts like:

> Life is too much of a struggle. I want out of here.

It was no accident that Julie developed a life-threatening illness. One day I hugged Julie and exclaimed:

> My God, you have a spine! You're grounded! What
> happened? How did this transformation take place?

I had been gone for a week's vacation and Julie had literally transformed her energy field during this time. Hugging her was like hugging a totally new and different person. She was now grounded to the earth and no longer pulled me off balance during our hug. Her back felt normal instead of mushy. For the first time, she felt like she had a backbone.

Interestingly, Julie was unaware that her energy field was so strikingly different. She had been in therapy eighteen months and knew she was making gradual changes, but she was surprised at my exclamations about her energy field transformation. We traced the transformation to a particular piece of therapy in our last session and some imagery work Julie did alone in the privacy of her home.

The shift in consciousness emerged while Julie was struggling to release repressed feelings of being unwanted and unloved as a child. We were imagining her mother in front of her in an empty chair. This process from Gestalt therapy is designed to bring old buried emotions to the surface. Julie was resisting the process, so I gently pressed her to move into her feelings so she could release them. She responded saying:

> I'd rather die than face the fact that my mother didn't
> want me.

She surprised herself with this statement. It "popped out" of her inner child without thinking. Suddenly, she grasped the profound meaning of her statement. Indeed, she had been near death several times in the past five years with her Crohn's disease. Bringing this to consciousness triggered the shift in consciousness. Julie returned her attention to the empty chair and said to her mother:

> I'm not going to die over this. I can face this. I'm
> furious you couldn't love me. I deserved better. I
> deserved for you to love me!

She exploded with years of repressed rage, hurt, and deep resentment over being ignored, pushed aside, and rejected. The energy rushed from her abdomen as she released the buried emotions. No wonder her body developed a disease in the abdominal area.

The next week Julie sat quietly at home creating mental movies with her imagination. She saw herself walking up to a huge white door, putting her hand on the doorknob, and standing there filled with indecision. After a long debate she turned and walked away, leaving the door closed. As she pondered the meaning of her spontaneous imagery, she heard this conversation between two parts of herself:

> Where is this door leading?
> It is the door to the "other side."
> Why didn't I open it?
> I guess I'm NOT ready to die. I'm staying right here on earth.

She reported this experience with a rather nonchalant attitude. She seemed unaware that she had quietly achieved a major shift in consciousness. Her next words confirmed she had indeed made the shift:

> I guess I'm ready to get well. Now that I'm going to
> stay here I need to figure out how I can make things
> easier. I'm ready to give up my struggle script.

Julie had achieved her redecision to live! Eighteen months into her healing journey, the emotional release work and the mental imagery both facilitated the shift in consciousness which allowed her to become grounded for the first time in her forty-five years.

Julie's behavior changed almost effortlessly after her energetic shift. She gave up her hostility towards her mother and forgave her for being unloving. They formed a heart connection and developed a friendship. Julie made numerous decisions that alleviated her long-standing financial worries and made her work life much easier. For the first time in her life she was "able to get a handle on things and do what she needed to do to clear the chaos from her day-to-day living." These changes had important effects on Julie's health. Since starting psychotherapy, Julie has not had even one flare-up of Crohn's.

GETTING GROUNDED TO MOTHER EARTH

The most important component of getting grounded is the mental decision to stay in the physical body and remain on the earth plane. It's a decision to remain fully human and enjoy the benefits of life with a physical body. It's a decision to find purpose in the day-to-day existence of human life.

People who are grounded have a sense of personal identity. They send out vibrations that carry the message, "I know who I am and I know where I'm going." People who are grounded have a sense of personal power and have given up victim consciousness. They are truly inner-directed people who have learned to listen to the inner voice in the stillness of their heart. It's the voice of their soul guiding them to find their purpose in this lifetime. It takes great courage to listen and follow our hearts. Interestingly, courage comes from the French word for heart—*coeur*.

Often the choice to follow our own path does not please other people in our lives. I tell all my clients, "You are here to follow your heart and your soul. You are not here to please your parents, spouses, children, teachers, or your therapist. You cannot find your dream while listening to what others say you *should* do. Look inside your heart for your own answers. Let your feelings be your guide. Only you and your soul can find your path."

CLUES THAT INDICATE YOU HAVE
A DEATHWISH

Throughout this chapter, I have mentioned factors that indicate the presence of a deathwish. Here are fourteen clues that indicate the deathwish is present:

1. A fascination with music, poems, or books about death; reading such material often; writing poems or other material about death; collecting favorite songs about death.

2. Creating fantasies about your own death or funeral; daydreams about how you might die; imagining how others would feel if you died; visualizing your own funeral.

3. Having a longing to "go home and be with God;" praying for God to take you home.

4. Thoughts of not wanting to go on because life is too painful, too hard, or too much of a struggle; thoughts such as "I would rather die than go through a divorce," "I hate my life," "I cannot face this problem so I want out."

5. Inability to plan for your future; nothing to look forward to; no interest in creating a future.

6. Longing to be with a loved one who is dead; wanting to join the dead person in the after-life rather than bringing that person back to earth.

7. Being accident-prone, with the accidents being serious or nearly fatal.

8. Exhibiting self-destructive behaviors such as alcoholism, smoking, obsessive eating, and workaholism.

9. Suicidal thoughts, plans or attempts; often thinking about dying; understanding why people commit suicide; planning how you might carry out a suicide.

10. Thoughts of not wanting to have a physical body such as "I have always wanted to be a spirit," "I have never felt comfortable in this body," "I have always wanted to be free of my body," "I want out of this body to avoid physical pain," "I hate this body."

11. Thoughts of dying before or at a certain age such as "I will die at fifty like my father," "I could never see myself living past twenty-five."

12. Thoughts like "What is the use?," "What is the use of going on?," "Nobody would care if I died," "Nobody would miss me if I were gone."

13. Believing your purpose in life is completed; "I have raised my children so I am of no use now," "I have completed my career goal and I have nothing useful to do now."

14. Feeling helpless and hopeless to create a life worth living.

CONCLUSIONS

Acknowledging the existence of the deathwish is the first and essential step in affirming life. Denying the existence of the deathwish leaves it lurking in the unexplored regions of the unconscious mind. Left there, it suppresses the vital life force, causing first depression and then physical illnesses.

To truly affirm life and live it to the fullest, a person needs to deal with this demon called the deathwish. Each person needs to clear it from both the conscious and unconscious mind so the life force is free to be used in the creative process of life in the physical.

Dealing with the deathwish means moving into and through the pain of it to a place of joy about life. To heal a deathwish, the person has to break through denial of its existence, own it, feel it, and then release it. The very expression of the deathwish allows it to dissolve and dissipate, making space for a redecision to live.

After identifying the existence of the deathwish, I usually work with clients to identify the root cause of the deathwish. In this process I look for the earliest experience when the person decided, "I want to die" or, "I do not deserve to exist." That experience then becomes the main focus for the redecision therapy.

Denying and repressing the thoughts and feelings surrounding the deathwish serve to keep it buried in the unconscious. People think they are making it go away by pushing it down and out of their consciousness. Actually they are reinforcing it and keeping it longer. Expressing it allows for movement and for its release. Only after the release of the deathwish can the redecision to live be made. The redecision to live allows the phoenix of one's life path to rise up out of the ashes of the deathwish.

A visual representation of this phenomenon was demonstrated in one of my ongoing psychotherapy groups. I was working with a very depressed client who was releasing the pain of her deathwish. As she finished the release, there was a surge of her vital life force that appeared to come from the her root chakra. I felt the force of it in my body and immediately got the mental image of a geyser of water spouting high into the sky with the power of Old Faithful.

After this process, the deathwish is truly cleared from the person's energy field. Releasing the deathwish frees the vital life force energy and allows emergence of the will to live. The person is then free to make a commitment to life. The individual is free to focus energy on affirming life and creating a life that is worth living.

THE DEATHWISH ■ 137

THE REDECISION TO LIVE: RECLAIMING RADIANCE

The emergence of the life force spontaneously facilitates the redecision to live. This redecision comes from the inner child, and the therapist cannot predict or force this to happen. I can only "be with" the client to facilitate the feeling release work and trust the process. Each time I guide a client to work through the deathwish, I must trust that the spark of life still exists underneath and that it can be gently coaxed and fanned into a flame with the energy of love.

POWERFUL SPIRITUAL RESULTS

The redecision process with the deathwish is a powerful, transformative experience. I am awed by the depth of this work. After each piece of release work, a quiet peacefulness descends over me, the client, and the whole group. Eyes meet in the silence and people seem reluctant to break the connectedness. In the quiet I sense that this work is profound and life changing for myself and every group member.

Each time I participate as a facilitator in the healing of a deathwish I experience my own heart opening. The energy of divine love flows through my open heart and into the client's heart. Facilitating the emergence of the vital life force is like being a witness to the birth of a baby. I have this awesome feeling and great wonder at the creation of new life.

I feel an inner awareness that something very spiritual is happening. I believe this process reconnects the soul energy with the physical body. Indeed, during this process, I feel very close to God. Often there is a feeling of God's presence in the room and I know I am merely an instrument for God's work. It is truly an exhilarating experience for everyone in the room and feelings of peace, joy, and love descend upon the whole group. I have great joy in knowing I am doing my life's work. I feel my own radiance as I facilitate these clients in reclaiming their radiance.

"The mind thinks
The body acts
The soul imagines."

— Thomas Moore,
Care of the Soul

CHAPTER 7

HONOR YOUR SOUL

he soul essence—the radiating light—is present in all human beings. It cannot be absent. To honor your soul means to become conscious of this spiritual energy so that you can feel it, experience it, and believe in its existence. Our life force is an energy and the physical manifestation of our soul. It is the tangible evidence that our soul is present in our physical body. The energy of the soul vibrates at such a high frequency that most people cannot perceive it because they are still operating in a five-sense reality. However, as we learn to tune in to the higher frequencies of our soul we are more able to connect with our Higher Self or the God-consciousness within. To sense the presence of the energy field is to sense the presence of the divine.

As a soul we are on an endless journey of evolution through eternity. At birth we lost our conscious connection to our soul. The ultimate purpose of our journey here on earth is to remain in our human bodies and reconnect with our soul energy. As conscious human beings we can learn to use our higher mind to bring the light of our soul down into our physical body. Then we will become the radiant beings we were meant to be.

SPIRITUAL AWAKENINGS

"Our problems cannot be resolved at the same level of consciousness from which they originate; we must move to a higher level of energy."
— Richard Moss, M.D., *The Black Butterfly*

When people are unconscious about their spiritual nature they are often guided by the spiritual forces to find the experiences that will bring about a spiritual awakening. Many clients come to me in total denial of their spiritual nature. They come for help with their heartaches, health problems, and life problems and discover that they must evolve to higher levels of consciousness to heal themselves. I become their guide on their spiritual healing journey as they transform themselves. Most of my clients transform from ordinary five-sensory human beings who relate only to the physical reality, to multisensory beings who begin to have experiences in the fourth dimension.

I am able to lead my clients on their journey of spiritual transformation only because I have traveled the same path. Indeed, at times I feel like I am only one step ahead of them as we journey along on our individual pathways of self-discovery and spiritual awakening.

As I traveled on my transformational journey I also continued to search and explore the spiritual dimension. I had this inner yearning to reconnect with the spirit of my father. After my experience of seeing my mother-in-law as a radiant being I wondered if he were alive and radiant somewhere in the universe. I truly believed he was alive and well in another dimension and I had a secret hope of seeing him just as I had seen my dear Golda. Year after year I searched for teachers who could help me learn more about the spiritual dimension.

HEAVEN IS ALL AROUND US

Dr. Marilyn Rossner of Montreal, Canada became one of my teachers on my journey to the invisible world of energy. She is a wonderful teacher because she can actually see into that world. She had a spiritual experience at age four and from that time forward had the ability to perceive the invisible energies. She could actually see energy chakras in the body and the aura all around the body. She could also see and hear spirit beings. In 1986 I began attending spiritual conferences in Minneapolis and Montreal, sponsored by her organization, International Institute of Integral Human Studies.

These conferences were the real impetus for changing my mind about the validity of psychic readings and receiving messages from spirit beings on the other side. Marilyn herself was a psychic and I sat through many sessions where she contacted people from the other side. One most dramatic case involved a therapist friend of mine whose daughter had been murdered just six weeks before the conference. It was an unsolved murder with no apparent motive. She had been brutally stabbed while taking a nap in her own bed in a townhouse in Chicago.

In a group of thirty people this mother asked Marilyn to contact her daughter. As the daughter "came through" she told her mother that her grandmother had prepared a bed of pink rosebuds for her to sleep on. She awoke on the other side lying on this beautiful bed with her grandmother right beside her. The mother broke into sobs saying, "Pink roses were always her favorite flower." Believe me, there was not a dry eye in the room. My own heart opened with a rush and I burst into tears hearing of this scene of such tender love.

The daughter proceeded to tell her mother through Marilyn that the man who had killed her was a drug dealer. He thought she was an informant to the police. It was a simple case of mistaken identity. The message came through, "I want you to forgive him, Mother. I already have. I wasn't supposed to have a long life. I'd always known that. I'm here now with Grandmother. Everything is as it is supposed to be." With that the mother broke into deep sobs and released her grief from the depths of her very being. It was both heartbreaking and heartwarming at the same time.

This process lasted about thirty minutes, with the daughter communicating information to her earth mother. Numerous times the mother would confirm how the bits of information fit her knowledge about her daughter. I will never forget that scene, the feelings of the mother, or my own feelings as I watched this healing process. It took place on a spiritual level that was most profound.

MY FIRST SPIRITUAL READING

After witnessing this reading for my friend, I wanted to have my own experience. I decided to book a reading with one of the spiritual mediums at the conference. I looked over the list of mediums in the conference brochure and intuitively chose Roy Waite from Montreal, Canada. I was so excited it didn't occur to me to be scared.

I had no idea what would happen but I secretly wished to communicate with my father. He had crossed over twelve years ago. Now I just wanted to know how he was. I decided not to tell Roy about my father's death or my secret wish to speak with him. I didn't want to spoil the believability.

I sat opposite Roy with a great deal of excitement trying to look calm. The first ten minutes were fairly interesting but nothing profound happened. Suddenly, he asked, "Did anyone you know cross over with a great deal of chest pain? I ask because I'm getting these pains in my chest." I knew immediately that my father's spirit was present. I burst into tears of joy and I thought, "He really still exists!! He is here even though I can't see him with my own eyes." Then Roy said, "He's standing behind you with his hand on your shoulder. He wants to know if the song *You Are My Sunshine* means anything to you." I had been singing that song over and over with a group of people at a weekend retreat just two weeks earlier. I immediately knew he had been there observing. I was deeply moved.

The next words are embedded in my memory. I know I shall never forget them, though I have a tape recording if I ever need it. Roy said:

> He wants you to know he has so much love for you. When he was here on earth with you he didn't know how to tell you. So he bought you presents, like the blue bike for your seventh birthday.

By this time I was in a state of shock and the tears were streaming down my face. My parents had indeed given me a blue two-wheeler for my seventh birthday. I held my breath hoping he would continue. I was afraid to talk for fear I might frighten him away. The connection seemed so tenuous. Roy continued with the following message:

> He says to tell you that he is sorry for the way he raised you. There wasn't enough touching. There wasn't enough feeling. There wasn't enough loving. He wants to know if you will forgive him?

I felt this rush of energy in my chest. My heart opened even more and the tears flowed even more. Without having to think about it I responded, "Of course; there's nothing to forgive."

I spent months savoring this contact with my father. I played the tape over and over to be sure it's what I really heard. In many ways it was so unbelievable and in many ways it was absolutely believable. There was no way this medium from Canada could have known of my father's heart attack. I was also absolutely sure he had no knowledge about my blue bike or this silly children's song about sunshine. Thank goodness for these little details. They convinced my doubting, logical mind that this reading was valid. My father actually talked to me from the other side, remembering details from my childhood as well as from a time just two weeks previous to the reading. He was not asleep somewhere. He was very much awake and aware of events in my current life. I was impressed.

ASKING SUCH A FOOLISH QUESTION

The next summer I returned to Minneapolis for the same spiritual conference sponsored by Dr. Rossner's organization. I went with great anticipation of contacting my father again. As I sat with Roy he surprised me by saying:

> There's somebody here who loved you a lot in the
> physical. It feels like a mother vibration. Is your mother
> on the other side, please?

I felt very confused as I answered no. I wondered who might be
coming through.

Next Roy said, "She is showing me some tools for gardening and
she is planting flowers. This person loved to work with flowers when
she was here on earth." Then I knew it was my mother-in-law because
every spring she took great pleasure in planting her flower gardens. I
remember thinking she was very clever to give me such an easy way of
identifying her. My heart opened and I felt the tears start flowing
gently down my cheeks. I was so thrilled to hear from her. I
immediately thought of her visitation just two days after her funeral. I
wanted to know if I had really seen her. So I said to Roy, "Ask her if
that was really her in my living room two days after her funeral." The
answer came back, "Of course. You already know that. Why are you
asking such a foolish question?"

I laughed out loud realizing she hadn't changed a bit. It sounded
just like her when she was here with me in the physical. And I suddenly
realized I was laughing and crying at the same time. My tears were
tears of joy that she was present and with me again. It had been eight
years since I saw her in my living room. Many times I had sensed her
presence but I had not had another vision. Often I would get a sense
of someone watching me and I would turn and look only to find no one
there. And I would think of her and wonder. Roy continued:

> She's sending you a bouquet of roses. She wants you to
> know how much she loves you. She is so happy that you
> know when she is around. She says she tries to contact
> other people in the family but no one else is aware of
> her. She wants them to wake up and know she still
> exists.

I was so joyous to have my vision confirmed in this way. It was an
important step in my process of learning to trust my own intuitive
knowings. As she left I found myself thinking, "Someday I won't have
to ask such foolish questions. Someday I will be able to trust my own
perceptions of the higher frequencies."

Then I was pulled out of my thoughts as Roy announced that my
father was coming through again. He had another important message
for me. Roy said:

> He says to tell you that he sits on a big rock and watches you as you walk by the lake. That's why you often think of him as you pass that spot. He knows you are happy when you are by the water. He's laughing as he says, "You always were such a water fairy."

Again his message was one only he and I would have known. I did have a special rock that I passed on my daily walk down the beach. It was quite unusual in shape and much bigger than any others along the lakeshore. Indeed, I did often think of him at that very spot. I was happy to get yet another confirmation of my intuitive abilities. I cried knowing it was really him and he was watching over me as I went about my daily life. I remember thinking that I'm really never alone as I journey along my path in my every day life. That thought was such a comfort. It soothed the longing I had to be with my father again in the physical.

A LOVE SONG FROM THE OTHER SIDE

It was my third year to attend the spiritual conference in Minnesota. I was looking forward to more communication from my father during my appointment with the medium Roy Waite. I felt sure he would "come through" again as he had in the past two years.

The morning of my appointment I went for a walk by the river. It was early—just past dawn—and I was alone as I walked along this meandering river. It was turbulent with rapids and water spraying up on the banks. I was lost in the sounds of the rushing water when I was suddenly startled by a song playing in my head. It was an old familiar song: *I Love You Truly*. All the words to all the verses were running through my head. I was hearing it in my own voice but it seemed very strange because I didn't consciously know all the verses.

Suddenly, I felt this welling up in my chest and I began to cry as it dawned on me that this might be my father singing to me. I remembered it was one of his favorite songs when he was here on earth. And I remembered Dr. Marilyn Rossner saying that our loved ones on the other side often communicate with us by putting a song in our head. I came to the conclusion that it was really him and I let myself enjoy this moment of receiving this message of love from the other side. Indeed, my heart swelled and my chest was filled with the energy of love. I felt so loved. I silently thanked him for coming and communicating with me. It was such a magical moment. I didn't want it to end.

However, it did end and I went on to my classes at the conference, wondering if it was really him. I couldn't wait for my appointment with Roy to get some kind of confirmation for my intuitive knowing. My father appeared in the first few minutes of the reading. I asked him, "Was that you singing to me this morning down by the river?" His response through Roy was a surprise:

> Yes, that was me. And I also had my brother Bill and my sister Agnes singing with me. You were able to hear us because we had the strength of all three of us. That helped the vibrations travel into your consciousness. I was so happy knowing you could feel the love as we sang to you.

I was so thrilled with this confirmation from Roy. I knew my Uncle Bill who had crossed over just a few years before this experience. I never knew my Aunt Agnes who had died as a young child, but I did know that my dad had a younger sister who died when he was a teenager. I was thrilled to know I could feel my dad's presence and hear an accurate message with my spiritual ears. My hope was that someday I could communicate easily with spirits on the other side and not have to use a medium to get my messages or for confirmation of my messages.

A CLAIRAUDIANT EXPERIENCE

Not long after hearing my father sing to me I had another clairaudiant experience as I was working with clients. I was leading a retreat weekend for thirty clients in St. Louis. The purpose of the retreat was to do redecision work healing the inner child. The process consisted of a mixture of group exercises and individual pieces of work.

I had a unique experience with a woman at this retreat. I asked the woman my standard questions to begin the work, "What do you want to work on? What's your goal for today?"

She could not answer these questions. We spent the next fifteen minutes getting nowhere because she could not define her goals for the session. As we talked, I began hearing a silly children's song playing in my head. It was playing over and over like a broken record. I kept trying to ignore it because I truly did not know what to do with it.

The song was *I'm a Lonely Little Petunia in an Onion Patch*. I could clearly hear the words in my own voice inside my head as I sang along to the catchy tune I remembered from childhood.

I'm a lonely little petunia
In an onion patch
An onion patch
An onion patch.

I'm a lonely little petunia
In an onion patch
And all I do
Is cry all day.

The whole time this tune was playing in my head, I was talking to the client and also hearing this left-brain chatter in my own voice saying:

> Singing this song to her is a big risk. It's a big retreat week-end. I'm working in front of thirty clients. There are three other therapists in the room and six of my trainees are present and watching. I have a doctorate in clinical psychology. I can't make a total fool of myself. I never learned this kind of an intervention in graduate school or in any other training, for that matter.

I kept listening to my left-brain chatter and tried to tune out the singing.

Finally, after three full times through the song, I decided to risk it—mainly because nothing else was working. I kept talking to her and I was getting nowhere. She was totally blocked! As I thought about telling her about the song my heart was pounding in my chest and my left brain was saying, "What if you're wrong?" Finally, I put my hand on her knee and said, "I'm hearing this song in my head. I don't know what to make of it. I'm going to tell you what I'm hearing so you can tell me if it means anything to you."

I stopped talking and there was this long pause. The room was dead quiet. You could hear a pin drop. It was like everyone was holding their breath. The long pause was because I was too scared to say out loud what I was getting psychically. Still the song played on and on. It just wouldn't stop. Finally I actually said it, "Do you know the song: *I'm a Lonely Little Petunia in an Onion Patch?*"

The client burst into tears, and covered her face with her hands. When she could stop crying she said, "I sang that song in a third grade play. It's become the theme song for my life. And I am so lonely."

This response gave me the key for the focus of her therapy. The direction for the work became obvious. I used Radiant Heart Therapy to facilitate opening her heart and releasing the pain of her loneliness. Then I helped her establish a connection to love. She needed to love herself, receive love from others and connect with a spiritual love. She was able to actually open her heart and take in the energy of love during the retreat.

Afterwards I thought, "If I'm going to get psychic communication could it at least be a little more profound? Then maybe I'll believe it sooner." Hearing a silly children's song in my own voice inside my head was not my idea of important messages from the spirit world.

However, I learned from this experience that the spirit beings are very wise. My guides gave me the perfect song to describe her current behavior. We discovered that she was spending a great deal of time being lonely and crying. However, her crying was not productive because she was crying from a victim position rather than releasing her feelings in a powerful way. She needed to stop this nonproductive crying and connect heart-to-heart with people. This heart connection then allowed her to solve her loneliness by filling up with love.

A HAND ON MY SHOULDER

I was going through another emotional time one spring. My twin sister was hospitalized with a seizure and had a near death experience. At the same time my son was in the same hospital having his own crisis. I was extremely stressed dealing with the emotional aspects of both these events at the same time.

I decided to have a healing session for myself with two women healers. We were holding the session in my group room at my clinic. I lay on my back on a massage table while they worked to rebalance my chakras and my energy field. I was in a deep state of relaxation when I felt a hand press gently but firmly on my right shoulder. I opened my eyes to see which one of the healers was touching my shoulder. To my surprise they were both working near my feet. Neither of them could have possibly reached my shoulder from where they were standing.

I was puzzled for a moment wondering about my senses. I started to doubt my own reality and thought I must be imagining things. Then I immediately started thinking about my father. I wondered if he was sending me a message of support. I decided to believe that he was present and I carried on this mental conversation with him. I thanked him for being present and supporting me during this time of family crisis. I felt this overwhelming sense of gratitude that he was here in whatever way he could be. And I heard this little voice in my head saying, "You are not alone." Again, my heart opened and I began to cry as I felt his presence and heard this message.

A month later I sat with Roy for a spiritual reading. I had not thought to tell Roy about my experience during the healing session. Roy said to me, "Your dad is here. He says to tell you that you were right. That was him who touched your shoulder during a healing session. Do you understand this, please? I'm not quite sure what he is talking about." Of course, I understood exactly what he was talking about. I was so pleased to have this confirmation. And still I look forward to the day when I can trust my own senses for perceiving spirit communication.

CLIENT STORIES OF SPIRITUAL AWAKENING

"Stories do not 'cure' problems, but they open the heart and the mind to new possibilities; they offer new choices, new understandings, renewed hope. These are the elements that treat the soul."

— Clarissa Pinkola Estes

All these personal experiences in the fourth dimension prepared me to facilitate experiences of spiritual awakening for my clients who are ready to open to the fourth dimension. My clients report numerous experiences of psychic dreams, spirit communication, communication with angels, hearing a "little voice," which is usually the voice of their soul, getting inspiration for solving a problem, and pulling wisdom from what Jung calls the pool of knowledge in the collective unconscious. They also open to clairvoyant experiences of seeing auras, seeing energy come off the body during emotional release work, seeing flashing lights in the room, and seeing spirit beings in the treatment room and other places as they go about their daily lives.

Many of my clients open to the awareness that their coming to work with me is guided at a higher level. Usually within a month of starting therapy they will spontaneously say something like, "This feels like it was 'meant to be'," "I feel like fate brought me here," "I feel like I was guided to come here." Some even say, "I think God sent me here."

Many who come to me for help with their personal problems open to the first glimmer of a desire to become a professional in holistic medicine or transpersonal psychology. Their illness or heartache is the door opener for aligning with their soul and finding their true purpose in life. As I observe this process I marvel at the ways of the universe in guiding each of us to where we need to be to find our spiritual path.

ASSISTANCE FROM THE ANGELS

Dorothy came into therapy for depression and severe anxiety attacks. She was a bank teller and was very stressed because she had been held at gunpoint by bank robbers three different times in eighteen months. Dorothy had had several mystical experiences of seeing into the spirit world before she started therapy with me. Her parents were on the other side and had both come to visit her in her own bedroom. They stayed about ten minutes without talking. They just sat on the bed and smiled at Dorothy. She was not scared by their visit. In fact, she felt very comforted. She hesitated to tell me about this incident, thinking I might define her as "crazy."

When Dorothy joined a weekly therapy group she could see energy leaving the body as we were doing the energy work and the emotional release work. Each week the other group members were anxious to hear her descriptions of what was happening in this other reality. One particular night stands out because several people were in crisis. Don was in crisis because his wife Susie had just been diagnosed with a relapse of leukemia. Another woman named Nancy was attending the group because she had advanced breast cancer metastasized to the bone. As each of these people did their emotional work love poured out to them from the hearts of the other group members.

Dorothy reported that love was also pouring out to Don and Nancy from the spiritual realms. She said at the end of the group session:

> As soon as Don started talking, this beautiful angel appeared over his head. She had a flowing, long, white gown and was holding a large ball of brilliant white light in her hands. She hovered over Don for about fifteen minutes and left only when we focused on another client. Another angel appeared over Nancy as Sher and the group worked with her in a healing circle. This angel held an open book in her hands. She stayed over Nancy's head for about ten minutes. She held the book out toward Nancy as if there was something she needed to read. There was also a huge square of brilliant white light that stayed above and behind Sher's head the whole time she worked with Don and Nancy. It had large rays of energy going off in all directions.

I believed Dorothy's perception of the angels in the fourth dimension even though I didn't perceive them myself. It was not the first time that a group member or a visiting clairvoyant had seen angels appear in the treatment room. I thought it was interesting that they appeared above the two group members in crisis and not above any other group members. When I have had my own angel experiences it has always been when I was in an emotional crisis. They seem to appear when human beings are most in need.

Many of my clients have also reported having angel experiences outside the treatment room. Patricia, one of my cancer clients who was hovering near death, saw an angel standing guard by her bedside for two full weeks. She described the angel as golden and huge, reaching from floor to ceiling. The angelic being didn't speak, but Patricia felt extremely comforted by his presence.

Patricia found it fascinating that the doctors and nurses seemed to walk right through the angel with no recognition of his presence. She told me six months later that I also walked through him many times as I visited her for energy treatments. At the time she was fascinated with viewing the two realities at the same time. She could see all of us going about our work in the physical reality while the angel went about his work in the spiritual reality. She decided not to share this secret with anyone because she didn't want to dilute the experience or have anyone criticize her for "making it up."

A VISITOR FROM THE OTHER SIDE

One night in group therapy I was doing some feeling release work with a woman who had lost her father to cancer five years earlier. She needed to release her sadness and grief because she had not let herself cry at the time of his death. Rita Benor, a visiting therapist with clairvoyant abilities, observed the therapy group that night. As we finished, Rita said to the client:

> A man appeared behind you in the spiritual dimension soon after you started talking about your father. He was about six feet tall, balding, with a rather large paunch. He stood right behind the couch for about twenty minutes. He says to tell you that he loves you and he is okay. Do you know who that might be?

The client touched her heart chakra and burst into tears saying, "You have just described my father. I'm so happy he is here. My God! What a blessing to know he is okay."

CREATIVITY: CONSCIOUS CONNECTION TO SOUL

Dara began treatment with me as a high school senior. She came into treatment with the goal of healing her depression and improving her performance at school. Dara was a very talented actress and excelled at drama and theater in high school. However, she had trouble focusing her mind and was usually disorganized about her studies and responsibilities. She learned in treatment that these difficulties were due to an Attention Deficit Disorder (ADD). She also suffered from severe anxiety and depression.

At the personality level she learned to cope with her ADD and alleviated much of her anxiety and depression. She stayed in treatment during her college years and opened to her most important work which involved her spiritual transformation. She found she was very sensitive to energy and very adept at perceiving energy patterns in the spiritual dimension.

Dara joined a weekly group where we focused on integrating the Radiant Heart energy work into the process of psychotherapy. As she did more and more energy work she became very adept at tuning in to the higher energy frequencies. She became conscious of seeing energy in the environment around her. She describes this experience:

> I was sitting in Thursday morning group after we finished the Radiant Heart energy exercises. Suddenly I saw something like light shining off the surface of everything in the room. It was a bit shocking to tune into this other reality.

> The group room at the Center always has more light than other places. I sit there and see sparks of light all around the room. Sometimes I see large blobs of light just hanging in midair. Often there's this subtle light flashing around the room. It's almost like watching a light show.

> It is a very active process to be able to see energy. The more I am at peace with myself the more I can see the glow around people, energy, and sparks of light in the room, and even energy coming off trees.

Dara also awakened more and more to an ability to see human auras as she went about her daily life. She was having a private lesson in music theory with one of her favorite music teachers when she first became aware that she could see colors in the human energy field. She describes this experience:

> I was sitting there relaxed and just enjoying being with my teacher. I liked her and she liked me, so I never felt uptight in her presence. We had a real heart connection from the first day we met. She was an intense and passionate teacher and I started focusing my vision on her eyes. Suddenly out of the corner of my eye I saw this hot pink color coming off her body. It was like hot pink cotton candy coming off her shoulders and her upper torso.

There were certain interesting variables that allowed Dara to perceive her teacher's aura at that moment. This college professor was very passionate about what she was teaching. Therefore her heart was more open and the energy of her soul was flowing more intensely into her heart chakra and out into the space around her human body.

Dara's teacher was standing against a blackboard, a perfect background color to provide Dara a visual screen of contrast for the light of the teacher's aura. Dara accidentally focused on her teacher's eyes allowing her to defocus on the body. Dara didn't consciously know it at the time but this defocusing is an important part in the process of learning to see auras.

Dara also became adept at seeing her own energy body and the energy body of other people. She really has as much ability as most professional healers who have had years of training. Dara seemed to be able to do it naturally. She could close her physical eyes and focus her inner eyes on her inner screen of vision. She would get a picture of the person's energy body and see a different color wherever they had a block in the flow of energy. She could also see when the blocked energy began to clear and the vital life force began to flow smoothly.

Dara became a valuable resource for me and the other clients in her group. I learned to use her feedback to validate my own perceptions as we did the healing work of removing blocks in each client's energy field. Each week in group she would also report her perceptions of spiritual beings who were present in the fourth dimension. She reported seeing departed loved ones, angels, and "energy beings" as we proceeded with the group process. All these benevolent spiritual beings seemed to come closer as people opened their hearts to release their repressed emotional pain.

As Dara awakened more and more spiritually, she also opened to some hidden memories of seeing energy as a child which she used to call "things in the air." She did not talk about these experiences at the time nor did she really think anything about what she was seeing. She remembered seeing a glow of some kind around one particular grade school teacher. It happened fairly frequently and she decided it was a reflection of the fluorescent lights. She did not think to question why she didn't see it around other people who were also under the fluorescent lights. As she evolved in consciousness and learned to trust her perceptions she would ask her fellow group members, "Do you see the glow?"

Dara also remembered being scared in the night as a small child. Her parents kept a night light on in the adjoining bathroom. As she looked through the doorway she could see "blobs of something" hanging in midair. They had various shapes and colors. Dara says of those childhood visions:

> I didn't know what to make of these forms I was seeing. I didn't know if they were real and they scared me.
>
> They are hard to describe. Sometimes I just saw fuzz in the air—like a fuzzy TV screen. Other times I saw globs of grayish looking material. They were like the balls of gray lint that you get out of the clothes dryer. Occasionally, I saw globs of color in the doorway as I looked toward the light coming from the bathroom. I didn't tell my parents about these experiences. I never gave anything I was seeing any value.

Dara also opened to her ability to perceive messages or information from her Soul Self. Actually she had always tapped in to the wisdom of her soul. She describes doing this in her teenage years:

> At age fifteen I loved to just sit and write. I'd start writing and put down whatever ideas came into my head. Often I would be very surprised at what I put on that paper. Through this process I would come to a great realization. Usually these were ideas that were beyond my understanding.

Dara is using her own words to describe moving from the human mind to the soul mind. These realizations were the wisdom of her soul. Her soul is connected energetically to the energy fields of all other souls. By tapping into the wisdom of her soul she could tap into the universal pool of knowledge and write ideas that were coming from beyond her own personality level. Carl Jung called this pool of knowledge the collective unconscious. This is the process that allows numerous inventors to get the same creative ideas at the same time in different parts of the world.

Dara joined a spiritual organization because she wanted a place where she could talk about her energy experiences and feel accepted. At their weekly meetings she connected with many other like-minded people who were also learning about the sensing of vibrations at the higher frequencies of the spiritual dimension. Through this organization she attended various workshops on developing her psychic abilities. As she went through the classes on channeling she realized she had been channeling ever since she could remember. She just didn't call it that.

Dara spent much time alone as a child and a teenager. In her aloneness she daydreamed a great deal and developed a very creative imagination. She wrote plays and stories just for the pleasure of writing them. She had not realized it at the time but her creative ideas were coming from her soul. She had a natural ability to tune in and receive inspiration from her soul. This is the process for all creative genius in the world. Inspiration is the energy of the soul coming into the human mind and generating new ideas at the personality level.

As a sophomore in college Dara wrote and produced her own play. She also gave acting lessons and trained the cast for the production. Dara implemented the Radiant Heart energy exercises into her daily practices with the cast over a period of two months. She taught them to open their hearts and make heart connections with each other. Consequently, the cast members bonded at the level of heart and soul. These cast members experienced an emotional bonding and a subtle spiritual awakening that made a significant impact on each of them. They came alive on stage and were able to perform at a much higher level.

When people do their creative work with passion they open their hearts and the soul energy flows through every cell of their body. This soul energy brings excitement for the work and a level of excellence that is not possible when people work at the personality level. Dara always wrote with her heart wide open. She loved doing it. In fact, she got high doing it. When she talked in group about her theatre work she lit up and looked radiant. This radiance was the light of her soul shining through her eyes and her face as she talked with passion about her love—acting and producing plays.

SPIRITUAL AWAKENING:
"I AM THAT SPARK OF GOD"

Shoshanna came into treatment in her late forties to deal with her severe depression and suicidal thoughts. She was a very competent critical care nurse and felt very good about her professional life. However, she felt terrible about her personal life and felt incapable of changing it. She had been married for twenty-six years to a man she described as a stone, and she felt totally frustrated because her emotional needs were not being met in the relationship. She was severely codependent with her husband and four children, who all had serious emotional problems, including drug and alcohol addictions. At the personality level Shoshanna healed her depression and her codependency. At the soul level she experienced a major transformation, including opening to spiritual vision and a conscious connection to her soul.

Many of my clients first open to the experience of seeing energy beyond the body during a treatment group that involves emotional release work. I think this happens because the process of releasing emotions causes the field to brighten and become more intense. Also, we begin each group with a half-hour of Radiant Heart energy exercises. These visualizations invite the clients to be in an altered state that allows for these perceptions of the higher frequencies. Shoshanna describes her first experience of seeing the energies beyond the body:

> I was in group therapy watching Marilyn do emotional release work about having cancer. She started talking and moved rather quickly into her deeper feelings. As she released the words, she also released tears and cries of fear, pain, and rage. I'm not a therapist, but I could hear a distinctly different tone to each feeling.

> As I watched this emotional release work, I was suddenly aware of something rising out of her body into the air above her. There were columns of dark gray energy spewing gently out of her abdomen. They looked exactly like the clouds of smoke coming out of smoke stacks at the steel mills. The grayness formed a cloud that hung in the air above Marilyn and Sher.

> I was shocked beyond belief. I had no previous

experiences with visual perceptions beyond the five senses. I trusted my experience because Marilyn was such a down-to-earth person. She seemed to feel wonderful after the release so I trusted the process was helpful for her.

Shoshanna was able to see the gray energy of Marilyn's repressed negative emotions as it came out of the cells of the body. She saw the gray energy leave the body, move out into the aura and form clouds that hovered near the ceiling in the treatment room for several minutes. Shoshanna reported her perceptions to the whole group with a sense of awe at what she was seeing. She knew the theory of repressed negative emotions forming blocks in the energy field, but this was the first time she was actually able to see a block being removed during emotional release work.

This experience became a case of 'seeing is believing' for Shoshanna. She had a major shift in consciousness about the truth of these theories. She continued to be able to see the energy being released in other pieces of emotional release work. It was usually gray or black. Shoshanna reported her perceptions to the rest of the group. This helped the other clients to begin to believe, even if they couldn't perceive the energy with their own eyes. Shoshanna was also able to see other colors in the auras of the group members:

> Gradually, I began to see other energy patterns around the various group members. Sometimes it would be a faint white light around the head and shoulders of a person. Other times I'd see a blob of green or yellow in a person's aura. Sher's aura was usually very bright with lots of green energy coming off her arms and hands.

Shoshanna stayed in group therapy about two years. During this time she transformed herself at both the personality level and the soul level. To accomplish this she had to achieve numerous shifts in consciousness. Some of these included opening her heart to receive love and loving herself for the first time in her life. She also opened to an awareness of being a spiritual person. She says of this shift in consciousness:

> The most important shift in consciousness is to realize that I am a spiritual person. It's not the most important thing in my life—It *is* my life!! When I came into this group I was unaware of the spiritual aspect of my being.

After about three months of doing the Radiant Heart energy exercises, I began to experience my connection back to soul. I connected with a part that is truth for me. I can feel the energy of it flow into me and through me. I truly know the feel of my soul from experience—not from some theory.

I believe this soul connection occurred because I opened my heart chakra and released the stored energy of old emotional traumas. This removed the energy blocks and opened the energy pathways. Then my soul energy could flow into my body and enhance my own vital life force. When this happens I get very hot and I radiate energy all around me. I feel so alive—so radiant. It's almost unbelievable that I could feel so good.

The energy exercises at the beginning of each weekly group paved the way, but at first I thought they were dumb and did them reluctantly. When I finally realized the benefits, I gave up all my doubts and critical thoughts.

Gradually, I realized these simple visualizations were having a profound effect. Doing the energy exercises of grounding to the earth and opening my crown chakra to the radiant universal energy taught me to be sensitive to the existence of my own life force and the subtle energy flowing around me. Without this sensitivity, I could never have perceived the energy of my soul.

My connection to soul is my true strength. I now know I'm connected to divine love at all times. My whole being is filled with the energy of love since I opened to my soul connection. I no longer experience depression, loneliness, or anxiety because I feel secure in this love vibration.

I now know what people mean when they talk about a spark of God. The spark is the energy—the light that is invisible to people who are limited to a five-sense reality. I know from experience *I am that spark of God.* In this group I have nurtured that spark of God so it has grown to be the true me. I now think of me as my energy, my vital life force, my aura, my spirit or soul.

Shoshanna accomplished this transformation at the personality level by awakening to her spiritual nature and integrating her intuitive knowings of the heart with her logical knowings of the mind. Like Dara, she also accomplished the true purpose in life, the integration of the human and the divine.

CANCER CRISIS: DOORWAY TO THE SOUL

"Following your feelings will lead you to their source. Only through emotions can you encounter the force field of your own soul."
— Gary Zukav, *The Seat of the Soul*

Jennifer came into treatment just one week after receiving a diagnosis of Hodgkin's disease. She was a freshman in college and still in a state of shock from hearing this devastating diagnosis. I worked with her individually for two months while she went through her radiation treatments. She rarely cried, even while talking about important emotional issues like exploratory surgery and the possibility of not being able to bear children. The first two months in treatment Jennifer learned about her feelings and how to use visualizations to strengthen her immune system.

Finally I felt Jennifer was strong enough physically and emotionally to attend group therapy. After two weeks of doing the Radiant Heart energy exercises she opened to an awareness of energy moving through her body. She had never felt anything like this before. She also opened to a rush of anger moving through her body while sitting in a college class listening to one of her professors talk about cancer. She felt this ball of hot energy in her abdomen. She also felt it begin to move up through her torso as she was sitting in class. She stopped it for the moment and came to my office terrified that she was going crazy. I explained to her that she was just feeling the energy of anger in her body. For the first time she was conscious of her anger about having cancer. I facilitated a ten-minute anger release and this hot energy spewed out of her abdomen in a forceful stream. Within a few minutes she returned to a peaceful and calm emotional state. We both considered this a real breakthrough in Jennifer's therapy.

The very next week Jennifer had another breakthrough. She came into my office looking absolutely radiant. She had so much energy she seemed to bounce from the waiting room to my office. She sat down and proceeded to tell me about opening to the spiritual dimension and seeing a spirit guide. She was talking really fast and her eyes were as big as saucers:

I saw my spirit guide! Nothing like this has ever happened to me before. I wasn't even scared—just excited. I was working at the cash register at Arbys at noon. First I thought I saw a flash out of the corner of my eye on my right side. I looked again and nothing was there. Then I looked up and standing right in front of me was a spirit. It had a body and a head but no face. It was as tall as a person and it was radiating this beautiful white light. And I could feel all this love coming from it to me. This being was just so loving. I didn't get any message, just its presence.

I opened Barbara Brennan's book *Hands of Light* and showed her some pictures of spirit beings. She was delighted to discover these pictures looked just like her vision of a spirit. I reassured Jennifer that she wasn't going crazy. She was just opening to an awareness of another dimension. Then she proceeded to tell me some other interesting information that she had not shared with me in our four months of treatment:

I feel like someone is guiding me. I get these messages coming into my mind. I hear them in my own voice talking inside my head but they are things that I would never think or say. So I know they are not coming from me.

These messages are always positive, never negative. My dad gave me your card and I let it lay there for two days. One day I heard a voice in my head say, "Call the Wellness Center. You have to call now, Jennifer." So I picked up the phone and called for my initial interview with you. I know I didn't think that command. I trusted the voice and I just knew it was right for me to come. I just knew that you would help me.

As I listened to Jennifer I marveled at her simplistic trust in listening to her inner guidance. She described exactly the process of getting intuitive messages from spirit guides. I found it fascinating that she was able to do this without any training.

Jennifer began to have many experiences of communicating with her spirit guides and angels as she went about her daily life. She learned to ask them for help in solving her life problems as well as her emotional problems. She decided she wanted some help with releasing her tendency to be angry most of the time. Actually Jennifer was using anger as her favorite bad feeling. She did not allow herself to feel fear, hurt, or sadness. One afternoon she lay down on her bed in her room and asked her angels to take away her anger. She described the following scene to me:

> I was lying on my bed and these two angels flew towards me. They were wearing bluish-purple long flowing gowns and they had huge wings. I know I left with them but I am not aware of where we went. It is blocked from my consciousness.
>
> I know I went somewhere because as I came back I found myself up by the ceiling in the corner of my bedroom. I was looking down at this body asleep on my bed. I thought it was my sister who had come in to take a nap in my room. Then I woke up and sat up on the bed as my sister walked into the room from the hallway. So I said to her, "I thought I saw you asleep on my bed." She answered, "No, you couldn't have. I've been out working all afternoon."

Then Jennifer realized that she had been above her bed looking down at her own body. She thought it was her sister because she could not comprehend looking down at herself.

This is very typical of people who have an out-of-body experience (OBE). Jennifer estimates that she was out of her body approximately fifteen minutes. She has no memory of the angels working with her but she changed dramatically after this incident. She stopped escalating anger and began to experience her other, more vulnerable feelings of sadness, fear, and hurt. For a few weeks she felt overwhelmed with fear. She soon realized that she felt defenseless without her usual fits of anger. She could no longer manipulate and distance people with her tantrums and explosive fits of anger. Gradually she learned how to identify, experience, and release her more vulnerable feelings of fear, hurt and sadness. She thanked her angels for helping her achieve this transformation.

On the human level Jennifer came to me for cancer counseling while she also did the traditional medical treatments. This was an important part of our process together and I did indeed assist her in dealing with her feelings about cancer and in learning numerous holistic techniques that would facilitate her overcoming her cancer.

However, I believe the real reason Jennifer came to work with me was for her spiritual awakening. At the soul level she was guided to me because she was ready to awaken to who she really is. She was ready for opening her heart and she had the courage to go on an inward healing journey to find her soul.

SPONTANEOUS OPENING TO SOUL CONNECTION

Diane, whom you met in Chapter 5, began treatment in her senior year at high school through her mother's insistence. Like most teenagers she was focused on the material world rather than the spiritual world. She was very concerned about getting good grades and making money to pay for her own car.

At the spiritual level Diane was completely disconnected from her soul. She had no conscious connection to her soul energy. She did not trust her intuition nor did she have any desire to become intuitive. Spiritually she was in the dark.

During the first year of treatment Diane mostly resisted. She would come for three months, then drop out for three months. She would return for another three months, only to resist again. She resisted joining a group that I believed would help her open both her mind and her heart. All this resistance was most frustrating for me because I could see so much potential in Diane at both the human and the soul level.

Diane left treatment for a whole year. I was very sad and felt I had failed in some way. My own heart felt heavy because I had not been able to help her break through the thick wall she built around her heart. Then, one day, out of the blue she called to tell me that she wanted to come back into treatment and was ready to do group therapy. She gave this fascinating explanation of her decision-making process:

> My mom and I were taking our dog for a walk in the woods. As I was telling her about my unhappiness with my boyfriend and trying to figure out what to do, I suddenly got this rush of energy. It came into the top of my head and went through my whole body in a flash. It was a jolt going all through me. I still remember the feeling like it was yesterday.

I suddenly felt inspired to make three major changes. I decided to break up with my boyfriend, call my father to reconcile our relationship, and return to therapy with you. I knew in my heart all three decisions were absolutely right for me. I didn't really even think about them. I couldn't wait to get back to the house and make all three phone calls.

At the time I didn't know what happened to me. Now I know I experienced a conscious connection with my soul. The flood of energy was my soul energy. I felt as if my energy body jumped up and stood at attention. The message I received was much stronger than inspiration. It was like a direct order from my soul that said, "You need to do this to survive. You need to do this to save yourself."

As Diane described her experience in the woods, I understood that she had allowed this opening to her soul energy because she felt relaxed and safe. She was grounded to the earth because she was walking on it. She was enjoying the sun as it shone down on her. I suspect that the sun helped open her crown chakra. She was walking amongst trees, which have healing energies. She was talking with her mother about an emotional issue, so she probably had her heart open. All four of these factors were important in setting the stage for such a spontaneous spiritual awakening.

This jolt of soul energy caused a major shift in consciousness for Diane, and it was effortless. She suddenly perceived possible solutions to her life problems that she could not see before. Her perception of herself and her problems changed in just one instant. As I listened to her I silently thanked the unseen forces for giving her this gift. She experienced a major shift in consciousness and I knew she would never be the same old Diane.

A GENTLE SPIRITUAL AWAKENING

Jill originally came into therapy as a sophomore in high school to deal with her heartache about her parents' divorce. At that time she was only interested in healing her heartache, anxiety, and depression. She accomplished those goals at the personality level during her high school years. Because of her successful therapy experience Jill decided to become a therapist. She enrolled in a college program and returned home each summer to continue her process of personal growth at my center. During this time she experienced a very gentle spiritual awakening.

When Jill first joined a weekly group she had a great deal of doubt about the validity of doing the energy exercises of grounding, opening the crown, and bringing the earth energies and the radiant universal energy into her heart chakra. She was typical of most of my other clients who have not had any experiences of sensing the higher frequency energies. She describes those early experiences with the exercises:

> In the beginning I did it because I trusted Sher. I didn't necessarily believe it would work. At some point along the way I realized I'm really sensing something new and different in my body. I could actually feel subtle sensations that moved through my physical body in response to what I was creating in my mental imagery. I felt rushes of very subtle electrical energy moving through me.

> It was always different. Sometimes I felt rushes of heat. Other times I felt cool energy moving through some part of my body. I learned not to have expectations but to just tune in and allow the awareness of sensations.

> At some point I stopped questioning why it works. I started simply trusting that it does work. I trusted it because I felt it myself. I trusted it because of my own experience. I had to learn to trust my own perceptions of these experiences. It is an inner experience, so I could not look to anyone outside myself for confirmation.

> As I pull in the energy with my mind I feel it moving in my body. It's there. I know it because I feel it. It doesn't make sense to question it. I get it and I use it.

Jill learned to let go of her analytical, linear thinking and allow herself to perceive the energy sensations. She learned to trust her perceptions of subtle energy moving through her body. She stopped criticizing her experience with thoughts like, "This isn't real. It is just your imagination. You are just making this up."

She learned to defocus on the physical world around her and focus her consciousness on her inner world. She learned to get images on her screen of inner vision as she had her physical eyes closed. She started getting ideas that seemed to come from someone smarter than herself. Most importantly, she learned to trust her intuitive knowings—the knowings of her heart rather than her mind. Jill described her energetic experience of getting grounded:

> When I'm not grounded I feel like I'm in chaos. My mind is racing and yet I'm going in circles because I'm not thinking clearly. I can't seem to quiet my racing thoughts.
>
> When I do the grounding exercises I experience this real shift from chaos to letting go into peace. I feel very much here in my body on the earth. I feel a peace and a solidness all at the same time.

Jill describes some of the energy sensations as she opens her crown and visualizes bringing in the radiant universal energy:

> I visualize opening a spot in the top of my head and bringing in the radiant energy. I sense my scalp relaxing and a subtle warmth fills my head. Sometimes I feel heat around my head—like I'm sensing a subtle warmth out in my own aura. The tightness in my face muscles disappears. Sometimes I feel hot or cool energy coming out of the pores of my skin on my face.
>
> Last week I spontaneously changed the visualization. I visualized opening the whole top of my head instead of just a spot. The experience was totally different. I got this rush of energy coming into my head. It was such a rush that I got a bit dizzy. I felt the energy move into and through my head, my heart, my arms, and my torso down to my waist. I had never felt anything so strong. I had the sensation of being filled with warm, pulsing energy through my whole torso.

Jill is describing this energy experience in terms of the sensations in her body. If a clairvoyant was watching her, he or she would probably see light moving into and through all the areas where she felt the heat and movement of energy. In this experience Jill used her mind to form a conscious connection to her soul and bring the light of her soul down into her physical body. This light was already present but the imagery enhanced it or increased it so that it was possible for Jill to perceive it in her consciousness.

Jill reports some of the changes she experiences after doing the Radiant Heart visualizations:

> I usually come in with all this stuff bubbling inside of me. After I do the energy work I can let it all go. The stuff that was keeping me up at night just doesn't matter. I stop worrying. I am able to rise above my daily problems and get a spiritual perspective about them. I can go away in my imagination and come back feeling peaceful instead of scared about my life. It could be just an escape but I don't think it is because I come back with solutions.
>
> I don't hear a voice telling me what to do. I just start looking at the problem differently in a way I hadn't looked before. While doing the energy exercises I often get this flood of spontaneous ideas. I call it *spiritual brainstorming*. Usually all the old ideas didn't work but these new ideas usually solve the problem.

Jill is describing the process of being able to tune in to her Higher Self or her Soul Self for answers to her everyday problems. She is learning to think independently to solve her life problems. She is also learning to think more creatively through receiving inspiration from her Soul Self. The human mind thinks logically and the soul mind thinks creatively. What she calls *spiritual brainstorming* is a flood of creative ideas coming from the wisdom of her soul. This process of opening to the soul level is the true genius of all great artistic people. Jill is integrating the wisdom of her soul with the intelligence of her human mind. She is truly accomplishing the real purpose of life, the integration of the human and the divine.

Over the past five years Jill has had numerous experiences of awakening to her conscious connection to soul. Some of these she experienced in group sessions with me leading guided visualizations and some she experienced by herself as she practiced the Radiant Heart visualizations alone in the quiet of her own home.

Whenever I lead this visualization for contacting the Higher Self, I give the following instructions to the group:

> Ask your Higher Self, which is also called your Soul Self, to present itself to you in whatever form it would like to appear. Tune your senses to the higher vibrations

and allow yourself to see an image with your spiritual vision, or hear a message with your spiritual ears, or feel sensations in your energy body. You may even notice a taste or smell in your spiritual senses. Trust the intuitive impressions that you receive.

During a group therapy session Jill came out of such a visualization bursting with excitement. She described her experience to the whole group:

As the process started I thought I wouldn't be able to do it. But I followed the instructions and the most amazing thing happened. When Sher said, "Allow your Soul Self to appear," I suddenly saw this light being appear in front of me. It was a mirror image of myself sitting knee-to-knee with me in a lotus position.

To do this exercise I had to defocus on the human level of the physical body and focus my consciousness in the energy dimension—the soul dimension.

The most surprising thing was that I had no preconceived notion of what my Soul Self might look like. I certainly didn't decide about this image with my conscious mind. I'm not sure where the image came from. It just appeared without me consciously creating it. That was the best part for me—it just appeared.

My Soul Self was made of brilliant white light and it was radiating hot energy all around its form. It was really something!!

I asked my Soul Self for help about finding a job and I heard this calming message, "Trust yourself. You are on your path. The job will unfold as it is meant to be. All is as it should be."

Whenever I tune into my Soul Self I hear messages that are very different than what I'm thinking with my conscious mind at the human level. It is not the usual mental banter I hear when I'm stuck in my human struggling. I always learn that none of that dialogue is necessary if I trust myself to turn the problem over to my Higher Self.

At the end I asked my Higher Self to send love into my heart chakra. I consciously opened my own heart and I felt the sensations of hot energy flowing into my chest. It filled my whole chest cavity till I thought it might burst. It was a wonderful sensation. That's when I started crying. I wasn't sad or hurting. I was crying because I knew I was feeling the love from my very own soul.

A major part of Jill's spiritual awakening involved opening to spirit communication from her grandfather who died in a car accident when she was twelve years old. Since Jill did not have a heart connection with her father, she had bonded heart-to-heart with her grandfather. His death was her first experience in losing a loved one. She reacted by closing off her heart to deny her feelings, which were too painful. This emotional crisis became a major component of the depression which was present when she first entered treatment. She describes her reactions to her grandfather's death:

His death really shook me. I looked to God for help. I started praying a lot—actually it was more like begging. I pleaded with God for help with my heartache but I didn't feel like I got anything back. I couldn't feel any connection with God.

As I prayed I began to feel a connection with my grandfather in the spirit world. I could sense his presence—I just sort of knew his spirit was around me and taking care of me. It was very comforting.

I would go to the farm and sit under the apple tree where we spent time together. One day I couldn't sense his presence anymore. I thought he may have gone and I cried hysterically. Suddenly, I felt these two hands placed gently on my shoulders. And I wondered if I was making it up or if it was really him. I wanted to believe it was him but I was afraid to trust my perceptions.

In her therapy process Jill dealt with her repressed grief about her grandfather's death five years earlier. As she opened her heart and released her pain she became less and less depressed. However, she had this burning question about her grandfather in the spirit world so I recommended that she have a session with a spiritual medium. She had great apprehension and great doubts but she decided to try it. The medium surprised her by saying without any prompting:

> Your grandfather is with you a lot. He tries to communicate with you to let you know he is there protecting you. I see him putting his hands very softly on your shoulders. This is his way of showing you how much he loves you. He knew you felt it in the moment.

As she heard these words Jill felt her heart open and she could not deny the rush of feelings in her chest. She went into the experience of the reading doubting that any other human being could really contact her grandfather She had not told the medium that she wanted to communicate with him, nor had she told the medium about her experience of feeling her grandfather's hands on her shoulders. This one, tiny detail made the reading seem very believable to her. It also gave her permission to trust her intuitive knowings. She went into the reading filled with anxiety and doubt. She came out of the session filled with excitement, enthusiasm, and a feeling of being very loved from the other side.

Jill had a goal to learn to communicate with her grandfather in the spirit world and trust the intuitive messages that she received from him. For months she went back and forth between believing in her ability to accurately receive messages from him and returning to a place of disbelief. She always trusted that he existed in the spiritual dimension and that he could hear her thoughts. She did not trust her own ability to perceive the messages he might be sending her.

Six months after her first session with the spiritual medium Jill decided to have another reading with a different medium that I recommended. While driving home from college she mentally prepared for the session. She had already asked her grandfather to be present at the reading and she talked out loud to him as she drove. She remembers saying to him:

> I'm sorry I have to go through a medium to be able to communicate with you. I hope this is not too uncomfortable for you. I feel like I need the go-between. I don't seem to be able to do it any other way.

Suddenly her consciousness was flooded with a video that showed little clips of her childhood times spent with her grandfather. The video seemed to be playing by itself.

Jill was overcome with emotion. She kept driving and crying deeply as the video played out in her inner mind. She described this experience:

> I've never had anything like this happen before or since. I got this flood of obscure memories of times with my grandfather. I have a standard set of memories that I can recall at anytime and tell the stories. These scenes were all different. As I saw them I knew they had really happened and I wept with the joy of seeing them again.
>
> The video played on for about ten minutes. It was almost like watching a life review with only scenes of our special moments together. I had no conscious control over what scenes were being shown to me. That's why it seemed so incredible.
>
> It was a very emotionally charged moment. Luckily I was alone on the expressway with hardly any traffic. I was afraid to pull over for fear of messing up the moment and somehow interrupting the flow.

Jill believes that this experience was her grandfather showing her that she definitely could receive communications from him. It was such a strong, vivid experience that there was no way she could deny the reality of seeing the video. She believes she was given this experience so she could learn to trust her own ability to receive accurate messages from her grandfather:

> I was just saying to my grandfather, "I can't do this." And he seemed to be saying to me, "You talk to me all the time. Now here comes something back." This experience was like an earthquake in my consciousness.
>
> I needed the earthquake so I could trust myself. Now I have a much deeper trust in the subtle messages that I get. I trust the impressions I get when I ask my grandfather to communicate with me. I no longer feel the need to ask a medium if my impressions from the spiritual dimension are true.

Jill has not been able to tap into the obscure memories shown to her on the video that day. Try as she might they are lost in her consciousness. I explained to her that in that moment she was in an altered state of consciousness. The childhood memories hidden in the secret vaults of her unconscious mind were made known to her in that altered state. Now that she has returned to a normal state of consciousness the vaults are locked up once again.

Jill has since had many experiences of communicating with her grandfather as she goes about her daily life. On her grandmother's eightieth birthday, as Jill sat in church with the family, she started thinking about her grandfather. She had a deep desire to really see him again. So she started looking about the church to see where he might be. She looked up at the front of the church where the family had placed a cross in memory of him. She didn't see anything but she reports getting this message:

I'm not up there. I'm over here next to Grandma.

Jill's grandmother always leaves an empty seat next to her when she sits in church. Jill did not see her grandfather in the physical sense but she had the distinct impression that he was sitting right next to her grandmother in the empty space.

After church the whole family attended a brunch for the birthday celebration. Jill sat next to her grandmother at the head table. Grandma leaned over and said to her, "This is really wonderful but I wish your grandfather could be here with us today." Jill responded quite confidently:

Well, I asked him to come to church with us. And he was there sitting next to you in the empty seat. I also asked him to come to the party, so I'm sure he is here now with us.

Jill was surprised with herself for talking like this to her grandmother. She was even more surprised with her grandmother's reaction. She smiled and nodded her head, accepting Jill's explanation as fact. She didn't seem to think it was an unusual thing for her granddaughter to be talking about him as if he were conscious and present at the party. They had never discussed spiritual communication before nor the possibility that Grandpa could be conscious somewhere in another dimension.

Jill has awakened to her ability to receive spirit communication from more than just her grandfather. She believes she has spirit guides and guardian angels who guide her as she travels down her path. Often she hears unusual messages from them when she is having a hard time in life. Recently she was looking for a counseling job and getting very discouraged. As she lay in bed one morning half-awake, she heard a song playing in her mind. It was a familiar tune from her childhood, although she could not consciously remember the words. She says of this experience:

> I heard this music playing and this phrase kept repeating over and over in my head, "Give me hope. Help me cope with this heavy load." I think it was a spirit guide singing to me. It was a message and it did indeed give me hope. It was almost like a prayer but I didn't think of it myself.

Jill has learned to pay attention when she hears a song or a phrase inside her head. Like most people she used to think, "I'm just making this up" or, "It is just my own thought processes." Now she asks questions like, "Who is singing this to me?" or, "Why is this message coming through now?" She tries to connect it with a spirit guide who is sending her some inspiration so that her life might become easier.

THOUGHTS ON MY WORK WITH JILL

It does my heart good to think about how Jill has evolved and transformed using Radiant Heart Therapy. It has been a seven-year process of both personality transformation and spiritual transformation. She started with me as a high school sophomore who was in severe emotional pain about her parents' divorce. She worked with me during her last three years of high school and returned each summer for more personal growth work when she was home from college. During this time she opened her own heart and connected with her soul path, which was to become a therapist. After her college graduation she also came into my professional training group to learn these techniques as a therapist. It was no accident that our paths crossed.

When Jill began her therapy she had no expectations about awakening to her conscious connection to soul and becoming a spiritually-evolved person. She only wanted me to take away her heartache. Gradually she learned she had to take away her own heartache herself. To do this she had to learn new knowledge—knowledge of the heart rather than the mind. She had to transform herself in order to accomplish her goal of mending her broken heart.

The joy of it was that she was willing to risk evolving to higher levels of consciousness. She was willing to risk the process of transformation—giving up her old ways of being and moving into new perspectives about life. She accomplished much more than she ever dreamed when she began her therapy process.

I also feel great joy because she is planning to become a therapist. She has already finished her bachelor's degree in psychology and plans to enroll in a doctoral program. Working with Jill was like planting little seeds for the future. I believe she will take the heartwork and teach it to hundreds of other people in her future years as a therapist. She will be one of many who will carry the light on the planet. She will help with the spiritual awakening of others who come to her in pain. Her goal is to work with children—especially children of divorce. I can imagine that she will work with these children with her heart wide open sending them the healing energy of divine love. I can imagine that she will teach these children how to heal their hearts just as I taught her to heal her own heart. And I can imagine her using her own radiant heart to help these new little ones to reclaim their radiance.

"The true purpose in life is the integration of the human and the divine."

– Valerie Hunt, Ph.D.
International Healing Conference,
London, England

CHAPTER 8

HONOR YOUR HEART

INTEGRATING THE HUMAN AND THE DIVINE

s spiritual beings incarnate in human bodies, we all exist in two states of consciousness—the physical and the spiritual. For most people, daily life on earth is confined to an awareness of only the physical reality. Yet there is another level of experience happening simultaneously at the spiritual level. My goal is to help people make the necessary links to become conscious of this spiritual level of reality. As each human being becomes conscious of this other reality he or she takes a giant step along the pathway of spiritual evolution. As more and more people evolve to this state of expanded consciousness, we as a race will attain a new level of evolution. When this reaches critical mass it will transform the consciousness of the planet.

Energy is the link between the physical dimension and the spiritual dimension. Tuning in to the spiritual energies requires the same process as tuning in to a particular radio station. Sound is transmitted through space via waves of energy that have various frequencies. For sending and receiving to occur by radio, the frequencies have to match. The dial on the radio has to be tuned to the same frequency emitted by the radio station. Likewise, for awareness and communications to occur between the two worlds, the vibrational frequencies have to match. The reason most human beings cannot tune in to an awareness of the spiritual realm is that they have not yet opened to their ability to tune in to the higher frequencies.

At this time on the planet, these two worlds are coming closer, and the veil between them is becoming thinner. For the link to occur, the beings in the spirit world have to lower their vibrational frequency and the beings in the human world have to raise their vibrational frequency. Then the psychic connections can be made and communication can occur between the two worlds. Developing the ability to tune in to the higher frequencies of the spiritual realms is a necessary prerequisite for achieving the integration of the human and the divine.

MERGING THE ENERGIES OF
THE TWO WORLDS

Radiant Heart Therapy facilitates the integration of the human and the divine using imagery as the tool to create this integration in the human energy field. The basic Radiant Heart visualization (Chapter 3, page 54) creates the energetic pathways for the earth energy and the spiritual energy to merge in the heart chakra. The heart chakra is the bridge between the lower three chakras that relate to the physical aspects of the person and the upper three chakras that relate to the spiritual aspects of the person. Another way of saying this is that the heart chakra is the bridge between the body and the soul. Therefore, it is the perfect place to merge the earth energies and the spiritual energies. The Radiant Heart process facilitates this merging of energies through the following steps:

1. Opening the root chakra and bringing the earth energy into the body—the human element.
2. Opening the crown chakra and bringing the spiritual energy into the head—the spiritual element.
3. Opening the heart chakra and merging these two energies in the heart—the integration of the human and the divine.

THE ROOT CHAKRA

Each chakra vibrates in harmony to a particular color when it is in balance. The root chakra vibrates in harmony with the color red. It is the seat of our very life force and the energetic opening for connecting with the energies of the earth. The earth energy vibrates at 7.83 cycles per second. This is the exact frequency of our healthy cells in the human body. Visualizing sending roots from the feet down into the earth and pulling up the earth energy into the body gives our cells the message to attune to the healthy vibration of the earth energies.

The energy patterns in the root chakra reflect the person's consciousness about survival issues. People who have a deathwish also have a block in their root chakra which stops the natural flow of the life force. People who have a strong lifewish have no blocks in their root chakra. As people make a shift in consciousness their energy patterns change. As people release the repressed pain from a scene which is the root cause of their deathwish, their root chakra opens and the life energy rushes up through the body.

THE CROWN CHAKRA

When the crown chakra is in balance it vibrates in harmony with the color violet. This chakra is the opening for the spiritual energies to flow into the human body. The crown chakra is also linked to the pineal gland. The Radiant Heart visualization opens the crown chakra and establishes an energetic pathway for people to form a conscious connection to the energy of their soul.

THE HEART CHAKRA

The heart chakra vibrates in harmony with the color green when it is in balance. This is the chakra that processes emotions in general, and in particular, the emotion of love. In *Vibrational Medicine*, Dr. Gerber states, "The capacity to love and be loved is related to the heart chakra."

When people make a shift in consciousness regarding receiving love themselves, the heart chakra opens to receiving. The heart chakra also opens to sending out loving energy when people develop a mature consciousness about loving other human beings.

In *Subtle Body*, David Tansley describes how human beings radiate love through the heart chakra, "Through this centre man learns to radiate the energies of love flowing from the soul, out into the world he inhabits." The Radiant Heart visualization enhances our ability to connect with the energy of our soul and radiate divine love to our own inner child and other human beings.

LOSS OF RADIANCE

As children most of us closed off our heart chakras to avoid the pain of feeling unloved, unwanted, not good enough, criticized, and rejected. Consequently, as adults we feel disconnected from our spiritual nature, unable to love our own inner child, and unable to form healthy love relationships. The vital life force energy no longer flows through the heart chakra, which causes a spiritual disconnection, emotional problems of anxiety and depression, addictions, and numerous physical illnesses related to the heart chakra.

Most human beings have closed heart chakras and exist in a state of disconnection. This disconnection needs to be healed on three different levels. First, within each individual we need to heal the disconnection between the personality level and the soul level. Second, we need to heal the disconnection between human beings.

Third, we need to heal the internal disconnection involving our own inner child. When these disconnections are healed we will be able to experience divine love from the spiritual realms, share human love through our heart connections with other human beings, and experience self-love through loving our own inner child. Learning to open our closed heart chakras and experience the energy of divine love is the key to healing all three disconnections.

INTEGRATION OF THE HUMAN AND THE DIVINE

The need for integration is due to a false sense of separation of the human and the divine. The truth is that as human beings we are and always were both human and divine at the same time. The goal of the evolutionary process is to awaken to our spiritual nature and recognize the divine aspect of ourselves as human beings.

This divinity is given various names: God-consciousness, the God within, the Soul Self, the Higher Self, the Divine Spark, the Light, and more. This recognition of our natural divinity occurs as people attain higher and higher levels of consciousness. The problem is that we live in a time on the planet when most societies do not teach people about their divine nature. In fact, most religions of the world teach people that they are sinners and as such are very separate from the divine.

In reality, there can never be a true disconnection from our soul energy. It is only our *awareness* of the connection that is damaged and needs to be healed. However, since consciousness (awareness) affects our energy field, we create important transformations in the human energy field by forming a conscious connection back to soul.

BECOMING RADIANT

Radiance is the beauty of the soul energy shining forth from the very core of our being. This spiritual energy lights an oval around the body which is called the aura. The soul energy infuses the entire aura making it bigger, brighter, and full of vibrant colors. It particularly shines through the eyes, the face, and the heart of those persons who have connected with their spiritual nature.

Radiance is available to all human beings. Those who achieve a state of radiance have experienced a shift in consciousness—a knowningness about their spiritual nature. It is an awakening to spiritual consciousness that transforms every aspect of our lives.

In March of 1994, Stuart Geltner, a trance channel from Santa Fe, New Mexico, channeled this information about radiance:

> Radiance is a natural thing and radiance is everything. Becoming radiant is the very purpose of living life as a spiritual being in a human body. Becoming radiant is the very purpose of incarnating on the planet earth. It is not a question of how do we become radiant. It is a question of how do we let go of what is preventing our radiance.
>
> In the natural way of things everything has energy and is constantly emitting light or being radiant. The reason people are not in this natural state of radiance is because of the stuck emotions and the negative thought forms. Both of these form a constrictive armoring system in the light body—not just in the physical body. In the light body you can have bands caused by repressed emotional pain. You can also have a strap across here or there caused by negative thought patterns. So the natural light is literally enshrouded in this emotional matter and this mental matter.
>
> When the person is cleared then it is very natural for the soul to enter more into the physical body and begin to radiate light. The Radiant Heart work clears the repressed negative emotions from the light body. It also invites people to clear their negative thought patterns. These are two reasons why this work is so important.

SPIRITUAL TRANSFORMATION

"The heart chakra is a primary factor in spiritual transformation."
— Dora Kunz, *The Chakras and the Human Energy Field*

The Radiant Heart process facilitates both spiritual awakening and spiritual transformation by working with the flow of spiritual energy through the heart chakra. Many people open their hearts and feel the energy of God's unconditional love for the first time while doing the basic Radiant Heart visualization (Page 54).

These structured exercises are designed to teach the clients an awareness of their own life force energy, and to show them that this energy can be purposefully manipulated to achieve a higher level of functioning in all four parts of their being: body, mind, heart, and spirit. The purpose of these exercises is to open the heart chakra and create an open, radiant heart in each client. Then they can open to the healing power of love flowing from God, self, and other human beings. They can heal the sense of disconnectedness that is the underlying cause of both psychological and physical illnesses. They can reclaim their radiance and reclaim their health.

"I FEEL SO CLOSE TO GOD"

"Men talk of 'finding God,' but no wonder it is difficult; He is hidden in the darkest hiding place, your heart. You yourself are a part of him."
– Christopher Morley

This example illustrates the profound change possible from these simple exercises. One evening a client began crying softly as she participated in the group exercises. Her face showed much emotion and tears flowed down her face throughout the visualization. She reported at the end that she felt a dramatic increase of heat in her heart chakra and actually felt a physical sensation of opening in her chest. She declared in amazement:

> I feel so loved. I've never felt like this before. I felt so close to God. I actually felt his presence right here in the room.

She was almost overcome with joy, laughter, excitement, love, and later, peace. Her whole appearance changed. Her face lit up, her eyes sparkled, and she became radiantly alive. She was able to hold the transformation so that six months later she would often recall that experience and state that she has been different ever since. The difference is that she opened to divine love and healed her spiritual disconnection. She experienced a dramatic shift in consciousness that alleviated much of her depression, her loneliness, and her inability to love herself.

PURPOSE: A REASON FOR BEING

"You can't change the music of your soul."
– Katherine Hepburn

At some point in their lives many people begin to ask questions like, "Why am I here?," "What is my purpose?," "Where am I going?,"

"What's it all about?" Dr. Valerie Hunt, professor emeritus at UCLA, defines our major purpose in life when she states, "The true purpose in life is the integration of the human and the divine."

To accomplish this we must align the wishes of the personality with the wishes of the soul. This is certainly not a simple task, and many spiritually evolved human beings dedicate their entire life to achieving this alignment.

One of my colleagues made an interesting comment about the Radiant Heart work:

> The gift of healing that you give to your clients is what
> the French call *le raison d'être*—a reason for being.

Indeed, as I facilitate my clients in opening their hearts and connecting with the energy of their souls they become more conscious of their spiritual nature. This allows them to find purpose in their lives through aligning their personality with their soul.

Life is a dynamic interaction of destiny (at the soul level) and free will (at the human level). As we make our life choices there is a constant interplay of these two forces. It was destiny that my father died at age fifty-seven. I had no control or choice over this event. However, I had free will in my choice of how to respond to this event. Because of my choice to enter psychotherapy and deal with my painful emotions and my deathwish, I started down a path that evolved into my life's work. I intuitively found part of my "reason for being."

In *Man's Search for Meaning*, Victor Frankl discusses our purpose in life. He states:

> Everyone has his own specific vocation or mission in
> life to carry out a concrete assignment which demands
> fulfillment. Therein he cannot be replaced, nor can his
> life be repeated. Thus, everyone's task is as unique as is
> his specific opportunity to implement it.

The process of Radiant Heart Therapy teaches people to open their hearts and follow their intuition to find their soul path. Most people don't know how to define their soul path. The key is in trusting and following your feelings. What gives you joy and does not harm yourself or others is your path. If your heart is closed you will be out of touch with your feelings, as well as your intuition, and you will find it difficult to find your path.

My clients often discuss the issue of purpose and how it feels to be in touch with purpose and out of touch with purpose. One young woman in her early twenties was working in a job that she hated because it did not give her a sense of purpose. She had her bachelor's degree in psychology and was interested in spiritual psychology. She worked with people who did not want to change and who had no interest in the spiritual side of life. Consequently, she felt like she was not aligned with her mission in life. She described her feelings in these words:

> I'm so out of touch with my connection to my soul purpose. I have forgotten why I'm here. I feel lost. I'm not doing anything that makes me feel good or gives me purpose.

> I'm bored with my job and bored with my life. Nobody at work acknowledges what I'm doing. I feel like a faceless, expendable unit.

Another woman came into therapy for severe depression. She was not in touch with her spiritual nature and had no sense of purpose to her life. At the personality level she was a battered wife, although she did not see herself as such. She was also not aware that she had no sense of self. Her words are a wonderful description of how people feel when they are disconnected from soul and disconnected from purpose:

> I feel like a slave and a puppet. All I do is spend my time taking care of everybody else and doing what everyone else wants me to do. I wouldn't know how to start to love me.

FINDING PURPOSE IN LOVING A CHILD

"For one human being to love another, that is the ultimate, the last test and proof, the work for which all other work is but preparation."
— Rainer Maria Rilke

Another woman in her late fifties came for counseling for depression. In her initial interview I asked if she knew why she was depressed. She gave me a most interesting answer.

> I woke up one day and realized I am getting old. I look back over my life and I see that is has been a lifetime of

unrealized dreams. I feel like I didn't become anything and my life has been a waste.

I didn't take the risks to do what my heart wanted to do. Instead I have wrapped myself in a blanket of *shoulds* and followed what everyone else wanted me to do. I had all these dreams, but now it is too late.

I assured her that it is never too late to evolve at the spiritual level. Perhaps it is too late for her to begin developing career goals. However, she could use the last phase of her life to achieve spiritual awakening and spiritual transformation. I also asked her what had given her joy during her life. Her response gave me the clues to help her define part of her purpose. She said:

My son has been my greatest joy. I couldn't have children and we adopted him as a newborn infant. I enjoyed every moment of being with him. We used to play together in the park and go for picnics in the summers. I was never bored while I had him to raise.

Obviously, raising this son was a major part of her life purpose. Even as she talked about him her whole energy field changed. She came out of her depression and seemed to emit a wonderful energy. Her face lit up and she had a sparkle in her eye. Her deep love for him was very obvious.

In this session she came to realize that her life could not have been a waste because she nurtured and loved another human being. She had been discounting this accomplishment because it didn't fit into her definition of a "career." Part of her depression stemmed from not giving herself credit for already completing part of her purpose. Also she had not yet created a new purpose since her son left for college. She felt the emptiness of her life without her son as she tried to find something meaningful to do with what she called "the endless hours of every day."

Parents need information about healthy parenting that facilitates their children in the process of finding their soul path. Most parents try to influence their children in defining their careers and their life decisions, believing somehow, "I know what is best for my children." Nothing could be further from the truth. Parents need to encourage their children to follow their own hearts and do what brings them joy. They need to say permissions like:

You can figure out what you love to do.
Follow your heart and follow your joy.
I will love you whatever choices you make.
I don't know what is best for you.
Follow your own natural talents.
Listen to the inner voice of your soul.
Do what makes you light up.

CLIENT STORIES

A HEALING DREAM—A GIFT FROM SPIRIT

Elizabeth, whom you met in Chapter 5, came into group one day absolutely exhilarated. Her depression had lifted, her life force was vibrant and flowing again, and she looked radiant. I had never seen her so animated in the two years that we had worked together. I couldn't imagine what had happened to cause such a wonderful transformation in such a short time. Elizabeth proceeded to reveal a most intense healing dream from the previous night. I value these dreams because I know they are a message from the client's soul.

> In my dream I was talking to God about my depression, hating my life, and hating my body. I told Him/Her that I understood that I was gaining weight to keep myself grounded to the earth. God affirmed this idea and seemed to be very pleased that I had figured this out.
>
> Then the most unusual thing happened. I sat up in bed and said, "I open my heart to you, God." And my heart actually opened. I saw this beautiful white flower in the center of my chest. All the petals opened very slowly and this white light came flowing out of the center of the flower. And then the light began flowing back to me from God.
>
> This magnificent white light kept flowing out to God and coming back into my heart from God. I know I actually felt God. It was so amazing. I couldn't see God but I felt this presence.

In the dream I felt and saw my life force flowing through my body and making it really hot so that I needed to remove my covers. I woke up enough to realize that I was actually hot all over. So I got up and took the quilt off my bed and opened my bedroom door. Then I lay back down and continued dreaming.

I dreamt that I was polishing my black shoes while sitting on my bed. I got some shoe polish on the covers so I took them to the laundry room where I saw this huge, orange column of light. It was immense going from floor to ceiling and throwing off an incredible stream of orange energy.

I stood gazing at the orange light absolutely transfixed. I got even warmer as I stood looking at it. I could feel my heart opening even more. This hot energy was flowing in my heart like I have never felt before. I felt so hot and so loved. It was incredible! And then I woke up.

I'm still feeling so loved. I know in my heart that God loves me. I don't have to think about it because I felt it. I felt the energy of it. I saw it, too. But the main thing was experiencing the feeling of that energy. What a rush!! I don't ever want to come down from this high I'm on.

My thoughts and feelings have changed drastically since that dream. I'm not depressed a bit and I have no more thoughts of wanting to die. I decided that I do have a purpose in this lifetime—like a special assignment. I don't know what it is yet but I trust that I have one. For the first time in my life I believe I am not meant to die young. I had this thought driving here, "I'm God's special little girl."

Several months after the dream I asked Elizabeth to describe the lasting effects of the dream. She said:

I know in my heart that my whole life is different because of that dream. I still feel connected to God each day. I feel this wonderful love for myself. Before, when you would talk about loving ourselves, I had no idea what that would feel like. Now I know. And it is so very wonderful. I don't ever want to lose this feeling.

In the future I see myself making movies that teach about spiritual growth and help people awaken to an awareness of their soul energy. I want to make movies with a message. And my message is going to be, *"You are so much more than human."*

I am so lucky. My life is so different. I don't think I could have had that dream without all the other therapy work that led up to it. I know that I am very connected to my soul. And if I hadn't done my therapy I know I wouldn't even know that I was connected. I used to be so caught up in being human—worrying about money and making my grades. Now I can let that go. It just isn't important. I'm focused on my soul connection. And there's so much more to our souls than going to Sunday mass. *My spirituality is the most important thing to me. And love is the most important thing in the universe.*

As I listened to Elizabeth my heart opened wide and tears flowed down my cheeks. She sounded wise beyond her twenty-three years. It was such a joy to witness this depressed teenager flowering into a radiant young adult. I felt honored to be a part of her healing journey. Silently, I thanked the forces in the universe that brought us together.

A FIRE IN THE CORE OF MY BEING

This client story describes a session using Radiant Heart Therapy to facilitate the integration of the human and the divine. It was conducted in England in April, 1995, in the presence of Rita Benor, the psychotherapist who is also a clairvoyant. Her descriptions of the changing patterns of the energy fields and the presence of spiritual beings are invaluable to understanding the spiritual depth of this work.

Nathan, a homeopathic physician, scheduled a healing session with the goal of opening his heart chakra to receive love. He was very intelligent, quite well educated, and very successful in his career. However, he was quite detached from his emotions and felt a deep frustration with his own inability to form healthy love relationships. He was committed to a process of transformation at both the personality level and the spiritual level and had previously completed a year of psychotherapy with Rita Benor. I knew this session was only one step in his transformational journey.

As we began the session I sat next to Nathan on a couch with my left hand on the back of his heart chakra and my right hand on the front of his heart chakra. I asked Nathan to become centered and invite his spirit guides and Soul Self to be present with all their inspiration and guidance. I did the same. Then we both did the Radiant Heart visualizations to open our energy fields and merge the earth energy and the radiant healing energy in our heart chakras. I boosted the quantity and intensity of healing energies flowing into his heart chakra by channeling energy through my hands.

We talked very little during this session because we were both focused on sensing the presence of spiritual energies and the flow of those energies through Nathan's energy field. After several minutes Nathan perceived a gray cloud of energy blocking his heart chakra. We realized that the cloud represented his lifelong heartache of feeling unlovable. I instructed him to use imagery to release the gray color from his heart chakra. After several minutes Nathan reported that the grayness cleared and the stream of energy tuned white in color. He was seeing these changes with his spiritual vision. This was our signal that the energetic block in his heart chakra had cleared.

I was very tuned in to Nathan's energy field so I was able to feel a subtle but definite sense of expansion in his chest as the block released. He reported feeling the same sense of expansion and a gentle warmth filling his chest cavity. I continued to channel radiant healing energy into his heart chakra while giving him verbal permissions to open his heart to receive the energy of unconditional love:

You are lovable.
You deserve to receive spiritual love.
You deserve to receive human love.

Nathan then reported a sensation of opening in his crown chakra. With his spiritual vision he saw a purple energy come into his crown chakra and flow down into his heart chakra. I felt guided to have this spiritual energy move through his heart chakra, flow through the very core of his being, and connect with his own life force in the root chakra. To accomplish this I placed my right hand on his abdomen and asked him to imagine a tube of purple energy moving from his heart chakra down to his root chakra. As he did this I created my own visualization of pulling radiant healing energy into my crown and sending it through my heart chakra and out both my hands. I felt a pulsing of very hot spiritual energy flow through my whole body emerging through my hands and infusing his body. It came through me in waves as I concentrated on my visualization of pulling in radiant healing energy from a ball high in the universe. It went through my left hand into the back of his heart chakra and through my right hand into his second chakra in the center of his abdomen.

We toned together to increase the flow of the purple energy. Within a few minutes we could both sense this open tube of hot energy connecting his heart chakra and his root chakra. As we continued toning the channel of energy opened wider and became much hotter. The sound vibrations seemed to facilitate the expansion and the increase in intensity. Energetically, Nathan developed a ball of fire in his belly and a column of fire along the front of his spine. We both felt the spiritual energies illuminating the very core of his being. Heat poured out of his body and his aura became very bright and expansive. He spontaneously announced, "I have a fire in the very core of my being."

Throughout the session Rita sat quietly across the room using her spiritual vision to observe our changing energy fields and the presence of spirit beings. She recorded her observations and reported them to us as the session ended. Her visual impressions of the flow of spiritual energies matched what Nathan and I were sensing energetically. However, we were mostly unaware of the presence of the spiritual beings surrounding us.

As we began the work, Rita saw a madonna-like figure enter my energy field and stay in the background. She appeared in full figure wearing a flowing blue habit. As I pulled in the radiant healing energy she moved closer and closer to me but she did not intervene in the process. My energy field merged with Nathan's energy field creating one aura for the two of us. Rita observed my chakras projecting forward from the front of my physical body and extending towards Nathan. Each of my chakras became embedded in a corresponding chakra in his energy system. I actually used my whole energetic system (my aura, my seven major chakras, and the chakras in my hands) to channel healing energy into Nathan's energy system. As Nathan and I completed the merging of our energy systems an angel appeared between us and placed an arm around each of us.

As Nathan cleared his heart chakra of the gray cloud Rita observed several of Nathan's spirit guides appearing in his energy field. To his left she saw an old Chinese man with a long beard. He looked to be from the Mandarin period and Rita had the distinct impression he had been an herbalist. A young spirit girl with dark, curly hair sat next to Nathan on the couch. These spirit beings seemed to just be there observing the process.

As I placed my hands on Nathan's abdomen and heart, Rita observed the madonna figure move from the background and merge with my physical body so that her arms and hands actually worked through mine. She sent massive amounts of healing energy through my body and my hands and into Nathan's chakras. Together we created the purple core of energy connecting his heart chakra and his root chakra. This spirit being was very instrumental in creating the "fire in the core of his being."

As Nathan and I worked with the energies, Rita observed a huge Roman centurion next to Nathan in the fourth dimension. He came in full armor and he exuded strength throughout his aura. Rita received the message that he represented courage and justice. The centurion told Rita that he was an advocate for Nathan and he appeared because Nathan's inner child was never protected or defended by his human caretakers.

At one point, as Nathan and I were merging our energies, I became aware of being extremely tired. However, I also had a sense of being very supported from the spiritual realms. As I withdrew my attention from Nathan and focused in the fourth dimension I started thinking about the madonna figure. I was aware of her presence and felt like she was assisting me. I received an image of her dressed in blue and enfolding me so that my head rested on the front of her chest. I felt incredibly comforted as I rested against her for a few moments. I suddenly heard this phrase ringing in my head, "the peace that passeth all understanding." Indeed I felt very peaceful.

As I rested for a moment in the peace I felt the presence of angels surrounding Nathan and me as we sat on the couch. I turned to Rita and asked for confirmation about resting on the madonna figure and the presence of the angels. She confirmed both. Remember, at that point in time, I had not yet heard Rita's observations.

To complete the session I instructed Nathan to use his imagination to bring radiant healing energy from the universe, through his crown chakra, his heart chakra, his root chakra and down into the ground. His heart chakra opened even more and filled with this magnificent radiance. I was deeply moved as I felt the radiance flow through Nathan. And I felt this sense of wonder as I observed this radiant light flow out through his aura and fill the whole room.

As Nathan began this visualization Rita saw a silver light flow out of his crown chakra and disappear into the universe. Next she observed a brilliant gold pillar of light descend from the universe, enter his crown chakra, go through his torso, and leave through his root chakra. The pillar of gold light went straight down into the ground. At the same time his heart chakra turned a vibrant red and gold. We sat together quietly in this column of light and healing.

As we finished the session I suggested to Nathan that he do some meditations and toning to keep his chakras open and connected with the spiritual energies. As we were talking Rita observed the following changes in the fourth dimension. Our energy fields separated and my chakras returned to their proper place within my own physical body. The madonna figure was still present but less active and staying in the back of my energy field. The old Chinese man moved to the back of Nathan's energy field and the little girl came and sat next to him on the couch. Three angels encircled us sending a brilliant light over the whole scene.

As Nathan and I finished the session, we listened to Rita's descriptions of assistance from the higher dimension. We were both very touched and filled with wonder. And I had this inner knowing that these spiritual beings are present everywhere on the planet to assist all spiritual healers as they do this type of transformational work.

My Heart Poem

I hurt
Therefore I am;
Hurting
I know I am alive;
In the hurting fields
my childhood ran joyless
before the storm.

I am hurting now,
way down
beyond the frozen river
around my heart.
I am hurt by my hurting
Want to be free of it
Want to love
and be loved.
I hurt
Therefore I must leave
the hurting
behind.

– Andrew Morrish, Exeter, England

CHAPTER 9

THE HEALING POWER OF LOVE

"The salvation of man is through love and in love."
— Victor Frankl, *Man's Search for Meaning*

ove is the greatest force in the universe. Love is the energy that causes miracles to occur in healing. Human beings who have reclaimed their radiance have the ability to experience the healing power of love. The energy of divine love from their own soul and from the universe flows through their whole being. These human beings can use this high frequency energy to heal themselves and assist others in a healing process.

Many have written about the healing power of love. One of these is Victor Frankl. In the depths of despair from the inhuman conditions of a Nazi concentration camp, Frankl had a mystical experience in which he had a vision of his beloved wife. He was transfixed and came out of the experience knowing a truth about life. He says in *Man's Search for Meaning*:

> A thought transfixed me: for the first time in my life I saw the truth as it is set into song by so many poets, proclaimed as the final wisdom by so many thinkers. The truth—that love is the ultimate and highest goal to which man can aspire. Then I grasped the meaning of the greatest secret that human poetry and human thought and belief have to impart: The salvation of man is through love and in love.

Another author who writes about love is Gary Zukav. In *The Seat of the Soul*, he gives these definitions of love:

> Love is the energy of the soul. Love is what heals the personality. There is nothing that cannot be healed by love. There is nothing but love.

> Love is not a passive state. It is an active force. It is the force of the soul.

Love is the richness of your soul flowing through you.

The highest frequency current is love.

Much scientific research has been produced on spiritual healing energy as well as the power of love. In *Healing Research, Volume II,* Dr. Daniel Benor reports over two thousand research efforts that prove the effectiveness of healing with spiritual energies. Dr. Bernie Siegel, a cancer specialist who wrote *Love, Medicine and Miracles,* helped make the concept of love energy credible and acceptable. Dr. Larry Dossey, author of *Recovery of the Soul,* is another holistic medical physician who writes about the power of love in healing.

Radiant Heart Therapy teaches people a simple method to experience the energy of love in the heart chakra. There is a big difference in "thinking about" love, "talking about" love, and "experiencing" love. We learn to experience love through opening our spiritual senses to the presence of our energy field which is our soul energy. Using specific visualizations, ordinary human beings can learn to open their heart chakras and find the link to the God-consciousness within. This heart opening is the key to connecting to the healing power of love.

LIFE EXPERIENCES CAN HEAL
A CLOSED HEART

Many women first open their hearts at the birth of a child. The experiences of being pregnant, delivering a baby, nursing, and holding an infant next to the heart chakra are all highly emotionally charged. This emotional intensity is the trigger for the heart chakra to open to the experience of motherly love. One mother told me:

> I didn't know what love was till I had my first child. I thought I loved my husband, but I didn't really feel much when I got married. I never felt for my husband what I feel for my children.

Another mother with three teenage children also reported that she first opened her heart at the birth of her oldest child:

> When I held my son for the first time I felt this swelling in my chest—like it was going to burst. He was such a miracle. I couldn't get over how beautiful he was. I'm

not one to cry, but then I couldn't stop crying. I was overwhelmed with so many emotions. I would feel the swelling in my chest every time I held him. After a while, I would feel it just thinking of him. I felt the same swelling in my chest with each baby. I loved being a mom.

Having a child is no guarantee of opening the heart chakra. I have talked to mothers who did not bond with any of their children. I have also talked to mothers who created a heart connection with one child, but not the others. When one mother talked about her second child, her whole energy changed. Her face lit up, her eyes sparkled, and her face would soften. She was quite unconscious of her selective loving and believed she was loving her three children all equally.

EMOTIONAL PAIN OPENS THE HEART

Intense emotional pain can also open a closed heart and promote healing. The death of a loved one, the loss of a career dream, a divorce, the loss of a friendship, and the breakup of a relationship are all examples of intense emotional life experiences. Some people respond by opening their heart while others respond by closing off even more.

The healthier response is to open the heart and express the grief through crying. Heartbreak comes from shutting off the feelings in an effort to stop the pain. Going with the natural flow of deep feelings opens the heart and allows it to stay open. Expressing the feelings allows the person to move through the heartache. It really is true: An open heart will never break.

Charlotte, a depressed woman in her thirties, had her heart closed most of her life, so she did not bond with her son at birth. He had numerous physical and emotional problems including being hyperactive. When he was evaluated at age four, the psychologist told Charlotte he was autistic and so emotionally disturbed that he needed to be removed from the home and placed in an institution. Her reaction to this recommendation was exactly what her son needed. She reported her response with much emotion:

I went home and picked up my son and held him against me real tight. I was crying and my chest hurt real bad. I knew I couldn't let anyone take him away from me. At that moment, I felt like my heart opened up, and I just took him right inside of me. I remember I decided to do whatever it would take to help him.

Charlotte's intense emotional pain forced her to open her heart and begin the healing process. In that moment, she bonded with her son and began to give him the love he needed. She then started on a long journey of finding professional help to heal herself and her son. She needed the passion that comes from an open heart to overcome the numerous obstacles on her healing journey.

A catastrophic illness may be the catalyst for some people to open their hearts to receive. Most of my cancer clients are shocked and amazed at the outpouring of love that happens as a response to their illness. Some are able to take the love in and thus transform their ability to receive. They say things like:

I didn't know so many people cared about me.
I've gotten so many cards and visitors.
I didn't know how to respond to all this attention.
I'm very shocked.
I feel so fortunate to have such faithful friends.
I'm so grateful to so many who have supported me.
I feel very loved.

GENTLE OPENINGS

Intense emotional experiences are not the only way to open the heart for healing. Very soft, gentle emotional experiences can also be a catalyst to opening the heart.

Babies seem to tug at peoples' heart strings. Even the most hard-hearted person will usually melt a bit in response to a baby's smile. Baby animals seem to have the same effect. Watching ducklings learn to swim, holding a kitten against the chest, or playing with a wiggly puppy are almost all guaranteed to touch the heart. I believe people open their hearts to babies and animals because both are very safe and non-threatening.

Music, poetry, and beautiful art work are also ways to open the heart gently. Movies with an emotional component often invite people to open their hearts. *E.T.* captured the hearts of many movie-goers. Many people allow themselves the luxury of crying during a movie even if they can't cry about events in their own lives.

HEALING IN THE HUMAN CONNECTEDNESS

Shoshanna, whom you met in Chapter 7, became very adept at using the Radiant Heart visualizations to send and receive love energy. She learned to feel a heart-to-heart connection with her fellow group members. She coined the term "healing in the human connectedness." Shoshanna describes her experience of the healing power of love in group therapy:

> There's a lot of power in a group of people who have their hearts open. There's a power and an energy in a group that you can't get in individual sessions. As I think about my experience in group I think of the phrase, "When one or more gather in My name." That's what group is to me. These ten women gathered together every Thursday with honest love for one another. There's a power that grows out of that. It's a power that opens your heart. It is a power that sustains you.

> I will always be thankful for my experience in the group process. I learned that the healing is in the human connectedness. The second time in group I opened to my pain as Sher gave me a hug at the end of the energy exercises. I started crying from some place deep within my being. Sher and another group member held me between them in a human sandwich. As we stood there I felt this incredible feeling of support. As I cried I felt this hot energy move up through my body and release. I had never felt anything like it before.

> I had always thought that I couldn't stand the pain of my numerous heartaches. So I kept my feelings shut down. I learned if we are that protected and that loved we can stand the pain. I had always been afraid to let the feelings come up because I was trying to stand the pain all alone. Not being able to stand the pain is from trying to stand the pain alone.

> I have always had a spiritual connection to God. My mind says that should be enough. However, being human we can't really experience that love of God without that human touch and the human affirmation. Maybe one of the ways He/She makes the connection is through other people.

CREATING A LOVING FIELD

I believe Shoshanna was able to experience the healing power of love in her weekly group because the group members and I create a "loving field" as we do the Radiant Heart visualizations for thirty minutes at the beginning of each group session. Many sensitive people have commented that the energy in my group room feels like the same high vibration one feels when entering a place of worship. Dr. Leonard Laskow is a gynecologist who has integrated spiritual healing into his medical practice. In his book *Healing with Love*, Dr. Laskow discusses the existence of a loving field:

> In my practice I have seen again and again how the energy of love and the creation of a loving field can profoundly enhance healing, not only physically but mentally, emotionally, and spiritually. Love is not only the stuff of poets and mystics but a tangible, transmittable energy that can produce healing. . . . When you create a coherent, loving field everything within that field begins to vibrate as one, to dance to the same rhythm.

Doing the Radiant Heart visualizations in a group setting creates a loving field. In 1992 I presented my Radiant Heart Therapy in a workshop in London, England at a vibrational medicine conference sponsored by Dr. Daniel Benor. Several clairvoyants were participants in my workshop. We spent three hours doing the Radiant Heart visualizations of grounding to the earth, pulling in the radiant healing energy, and blending the two in the heart chakra. We also did numerous exercises to transfer loving energy from one person to another as well as energy exercises to bond the whole group together. At the end of the workshop one clairvoyant described the dynamic changes in the participants' energy fields:

> At the beginning of the workshop Sher's energy field was vibrant and quite expansive. It was filled with the colors of blue, violet, purple, and a touch of pink. Most participants had fields that were smaller, close to the body, and a variety of colors.

> At the end of the workshop all the participants were vibrating in tune with Sher's aura. Their auras expanded and also filled with the colors of blue, violet, purple,

and pink. It was as if Sher became a human tuning fork. As she sent out her vibrations the participants began to vibrate in sync with her energy field. We all resonated with her and with each other. It was the most amazing thing to watch.

LEARNING TO RECEIVE LOVE

Most people who think about loving are focused on sending out the energy of love to others. To keep ourselves balanced energetically we must also focus on receiving the energy of love.

A TURTLE WITHOUT ITS SHELL

"Love infuses life with meaning. It performs magic and miracles. It brings light to where there is darkness and hope where there was despair. It is your greatest teacher, and your most constant blessing."
— Barbara DeAngelis, *Real Moments*

I developed the theoretical concepts of Radiant Heart Therapy largely from my own experiences of receiving healing from various healers who worked with my energy field. I will never forget the day when I opened my own heart to receive. You must understand that I was unconscious (in denial) about having my heart closed to receiving. I had been doing energy work for years and was well into the process of developing Radiant Heart Therapy. My perception of myself was that my heart was very open to both giving and receiving. Little did I know. We often have blinders on when it comes to seeing ourselves.

I was working as the client with Ken Bentall, a healer from Chicago. Ken had the ability to see seven layers of energy in my aura. We had been doing two-hour weekly sessions for over a year. Each week I learned to be more sensitive and gained more abilities in perceiving the flow of subtle energies in my own energy field. I did these sessions knowing I was transforming myself as I worked with my field; I also knew I was improving my abilities to facilitate transformation with my clients.

This particular day I lay on my back on a massage table in Ken's office. We had finished meditating together and our minds were very attuned with each other. Ken placed his right hand over my heart chakra and began sending this very gentle energy from his hand. I remember feeling it warming the outside of my chest wall. Then my consciousness was gone somewhere—it was like being in an altered state. I was seeing colors and drifting deep into a trance state.

From what seemed very far away I heard Ken's voice say, "It's safe to let me in." I didn't understand why he was saying that because I didn't know I was blocking him out. He kept repeating things like, "You're safe. You can take down the wall now."

At some point I felt this opening in my energy field in the front of my chest. The image I saw in my inner screen of vision was of the earth with its shifting plates. Then I felt this warm energy flood the inside of my chest cavity. Indeed, I felt like saying, " My chest, my chest feels filled up for the first time in my life." I knew I was experiencing for myself what I had been giving to my clients for years. I was so moved I didn't want to talk for fear of breaking the feeling. Tears began flowing gently down my cheeks as I felt the energy of divine love being channeled into my heart. There are no words to describe how deeply moving this energy feels the first time one has the experience of opening and receiving.

Ken and I were both quiet for ten to fifteen minutes as I soaked up the energy and allowed it to move gently through my heart chakra. Words would have been an intrusion in the process of sensing the energy. Finally he asked, "How are you feeling, Sher?" I surprised myself as I answered, "I feel like a turtle without its shell."

Indeed, the protective shell was gone from the front of my heart. It was an invisible wall of energy that I had erected in childhood to protect myself from the pain of feeling unloved and abandoned. I learned I unconsciously started building the wall as a premature infant when it was a medical necessity that I remain in the hospital for six weeks after my birth. The emotional pain of separation from my parents was too much to comprehend, so I numbed myself by closing off my heart. As I took down this invisible wall, I felt extremely vulnerable. I had always had my heart open to give but this opening to receive felt much more vulnerable. While in this state I suddenly realized the difference in having a protective wall and taking down the wall. It was a totally different feeling having my energy field so open.

RECEIVING THE ENERGY OF LOVE

People must have an open heart to even experience receiving the energy of love. When people are able to sense the subtle sensations of receiving love, they report a wide variety of sensations. Below are descriptions from my clients as they participated in energy exercises designed to open the heart chakra to receiving:

I felt something shift in my chest. Like an opening of some sort.

I felt a lot of heat in my chest.

It feels like a waterbed. Like my chest is the waterbed and the energy is the water moving inside. I can feel the energy sloshing around inside my chest. It moves in waves.

My heart feels like it is growing—expanding.

My heart feels full—like all filled up.

My chest feels like it is expanding. It's like there's this invisible balloon getting blown up on the inside of me. I like the feel of it.

I feel a pressure inside my chest cavity. It's a nice warm pressure.

I feel like my chest just got bigger—like my shirt buttons might pop open.

My chest feels like a beehive. It is buzzing with energy inside. I've never felt anything like this before.

My chest swells so much I feel like a puffer pigeon.

I feel like my chest has been unzipped.

HEART SYMBOLS

In working with the healing power of love I must first help my clients become conscious of their own heart chakra. Using the heart symbols is an easy way to do this. I ask clients to imagine a symbol that represents their own emotional heart. People in pain have imagined symbols like an open wound, a huge boulder, a big open cavern, a valentine with a red gash across it. People in more peaceful states have imagined a fluffy cloud, a chest filled with jewels, a balloon filled with sparkles.

These symbols provide valuable information for diagnosing the state of a person's emotional heart. They can also be used to facilitate change at the emotional level and promote healing. I give these instructions to the client:

• Get in a comfortable position and relax your body.
• Close your eyes and focus inward.
• Breathe slowly and deeply to center yourself.
• Focus your attention on your heart chakra.
• Simply be with your emotional heart for a few moments.

- Notice how it feels in your chest.
- Notice any physical sensations or lack of physical sensations.
- Notice your emotions or lack of emotions.
- Imagine a big blank screen in front of you.
- Ask your Higher Self to give you a symbol that represents your emotional heart.
- Let the symbol appear on your screen without judgment.

These heart symbols provide important information from the unconscious mind of the client. People usually have an "Aha!" experience as they interpret the meaning of their symbols. Working with the symbols usually brings hidden emotional patterns to the surface of awareness and invites people to come out of denial about these patterns. Working with these simple heart symbols in therapy sessions can open the door to profound transformational experiences for the client.

A BULLETPROOF VEST

Jim and Martha came for counseling because Martha wanted to feel more connected with her husband. They had been together twenty years in a very distant relationship. Jim was a big burly man of German heritage who earned his living remodeling houses. He did not relate to his wife emotionally nor was he aware that there was a void in their emotional relationship. He seemed content in his everyday world, living closed off and emotionally distant from his wife and two children. I asked him to create a symbol for his heart.

Jim replied, "My heart has a bulletproof vest over the front of it. It's big and real thick. It protects me."

Jim proceeded to explain his reasons for protecting his heart. As a child his German family fled their homeland to escape the terrors of Hitler and the Third Reich. They came to America hoping to start over in a new land. He began first grade in the public schools of a small rural community. It was 1942 and the United States was fighting against Germany during World War II. Jim spoke broken English with a heavy German accent, so he could not hide his heritage.

He looked at me with tears in his eyes as he said, "The kids were so cruel teasing me. They pierced my heart over and over calling me Kraut and Nazi. I had to do something to shut them out. I guess that's when I put on the bulletproof vest. I did not realize I still have it on forty years later."

A BIG, HEAVY ROCK

A very shy Cambodian woman, Merle, attended one of my Radiant Heart workshops. She had just finished six hours of lessons and exercises designed to open peoples' hearts. As I gave her a farewell hug I felt this hot energy ball between our hearts. I said to her, "Wow. Your heart is very open."

She looked very puzzled and gave me a most interesting response, "If my heart is so open, how come it feels so heavy? Actually I feel like I have a big, heavy rock in there. I have never felt it before today. What's happening to me?"

I replied, "Your heavy heart is due to all the sadness you carry in your heart. You know you certainly have a lot to be sad about with your mom near death and your dad's death years ago."

Merle asked, "How come I never felt it before today?"

I answered, "Today you opened your heart so now you can feel it. Before your heart was closed and numb."

She asked, "What do I do with this rock?"

I probed, "Do you let yourself cry?"

Merle responded, "Sometimes I cry a little bit but only when I am by myself."

I comforted her by saying, "Good. Let yourself cry. Your tears will dissolve the rock."

This young woman was carrying an extremely heavy burden of emotional pain. Her symbolism of "a big heavy rock" perfectly represented her emotional state. The heaviness in her heart was caused by numerous great losses in her life and by her Cambodian cultural norms which required her to repress rather than release her feelings.

Merle had not allowed herself the luxury of crying during the workshop, nor had she cried as a child when her father was murdered in a concentration camp, nor when she left her homeland as a refugee at age twelve, nor while she cared for her mother who was fighting for her life against cancer. No wonder she felt that her heart was a big, heavy rock.

A BIG HOLE IN MY CHEST

A forty-six-year-old woman came for counseling because she was going through a divorce. She had difficulty sleeping, had lost her appetite, and could hardly function at work. She realized she needed professional help with her depression. She found this heart symbol:

I get this strange image. There's no heart—only a big hole in the center of my chest. This is fascinating. I have been saying for several months, my husband 'ripped my heart out' with his affair and this divorce.

A BLACK, OILY SPONGE

A nurse attended one of my Radiant Heart workshops. On the surface she was jolly, friendly, and carefree. She described herself as a light-hearted person who enjoys being a nurse. The symbol she received from her Higher Self presented her with a very different picture:

> The symbol that appeared on my screen is a big sponge filled with black, oily stuff. It's so yucky that I don't want to touch it. It's so full that I know I couldn't pick it up.

As she processed the meaning behind her symbol, she opened her heart and began to release her tears about all the suffering she witnessed in taking care of dying patients in a critical-care unit. The "black, oily stuff" was years of denied pain she had absorbed from her patients. She worked with her heart wide open, taking in the emotional pain of the dying. Her heart was indeed a very large sponge.

STEEL PRISON DOORS

Mike and Sylvia, married for thirty years, came for marital counseling to improve their relationship. Mike was a retired policeman who had worked two and three jobs to provide for their five children born over an eight-year period. When the children grew up, Mike and Sylvia realized they could not talk to each other as a couple once they were no longer in the roles of parents. His heart symbol provided the impetus for a profound breakthrough in their therapy. Mike said:

> I see these steel prison doors. They are solid, heavy, gray steel that slide together on automation. They are impossible to break open. Only the guard has the combination to open them.

As he pondered the meaning of his symbol, Mike got a look of pain on his face and tears welled up in his eyes. He proceeded to look at his wife with tears streaming down his face. Their eyes locked and their hearts connected in a moment of deep intimacy. It was so profound I was embarrassed to be present. I pulled in my energy in an effort to disappear and allow them their moment of deep sharing. Mike said through his tears:

> I have been locked away behind prison doors—away from you and the kids. I am so sorry. You must realize I didn't even know I was in the prison. I think I am ready to come out now, if you want me.

They both stood up. Sylvia opened her arms, they embraced, and no words needed to be said. She accepted him with her heart wide open and tears of joy in her eyes. The energy emitted by them was something to behold. I felt my own heart open in the deep joy of this sacred moment.

Their relationship changed dramatically after this session. They learned to share feelings, having many heart-to-heart talks. He began to share his repressed pain about past events during their thirty-year marriage. She discovered she was married to a man who had many deep feelings locked behind those steel prison doors.

They continued to attend weekly therapy sessions to sustain this deepening of their relationship. However, we all three fondly remember this one dramatic session on their healing journey.

CLIENT STORIES

The following client stories are examples of using the healing power of love in group therapy. Each of these clients could have described his or her own heart in the words from *My Heart Poem*, "I am hurting now way down beyond the frozen river around my heart." These stories show how the group members and I channel love energy to melt the frozen river.

THE TERROR OF AN EMPTY HEART

"Loneliness and the feeling of being unwanted is the most terrible poverty."
— Mother Teresa

Jeff, age thirty-seven, had been given up for adoption at birth. His adoptive parents were unloving and both physically and emotionally abusive. Jeff had closed his heart to protect against the pain of being abandoned by his biological parents and unloved by his adoptive parents. Jeff came to me for psychotherapy when his wife was diagnosed with cancer.

When I'm working closely with a client I tune in psychically to his or her energy field. As I sit listening to the client I go through a process of entrainment—meaning that the vibratory patterns in my energy field begin to move in synchrony with the vibratory patterns in the client's energy field. I feel the same physical sensations in my body. I often get the same thoughts and visual images as the client. I feel the same emotions and the movement of emotional energy. I sense the same energy blocks in my body. I also feel the same releases of energy in my body as the client does the emotional release work.

Jeff was doing a piece of work to release the pain of feeling unloved by his adopted parents. He lay on a mat on his back and I sat beside him with my hands on his heart chakra. I led him through a relaxation process and then asked him to focus his consciousness on the inside of his chest so he could begin to experience the heartache he held there. He had never felt it because he had so many defenses to deny his emotional pain. He had "thought about" his lack of love but he had never ever "felt it." He had not moved from his head to his heart. Jeff really did not know how to feel it because he had numbed himself. I felt sad for the little child in him who could not let himself feel because the truth would be so blatant and so terribly painful for him.

He was lying on the mat being very quiet. As I sat beside him I opened to the worst terror I had ever felt in my life. As I tuned into his heart space I felt like I was in this vast empty canyon. There was this feeling of vastness and absolute aching emptiness. My own chest turned to ice on the inside and I felt this ache in the very center of my being. I sensed in the moment that Jeff was experiencing the same sensations. Tears welled up in his eyes and he started to cry these deep, heartrending sobs saying, "I'm so alone. Nobody cares about me. I hurt . . . Oh, my God, I hurt so much." And he released the deep pain of his abandonment, sobbing uncontrollably for about five minutes.

Underneath the heartache was his terror of being alone and abandoned. Jeff moved from the pain to this deep fear that seemed to come from every cell of his body. I moved my right hand above his solar plexus and had him give the terror a color and visualize sending it out with his mind. A geyser of hot energy came up against my hand as he imagined releasing the color. His whole body shook as the fear energy left his body. I looked around the room and every group member was crying as they supported him in this release work. His pain and terror touched each of their hearts and they wept openly with him. Some were opening to their own pain and terror of abandonment. Others were weeping with compassion and empathy.

As we finished the release work, the whole group gathered around Jeff on the mat and filled him with the energy of universal love. All the members knew how to do the Radiant Heart visualizations. They grounded themselves, opened their crown chakras, pulled in the radiant healing energy, mixed the earth energy and the radiant energy in their hearts, and sent it down their right arms into their hand and into Jeff. His heart was wide open after releasing the heartache and the terror so he was able to receive the loving energy.

As Jeff received the energy of love he transformed right in front of us. He started smiling and his whole face brightened—he literally lit up like a Christmas tree. His whole body got hot from the flow of radiant energy moving through his entire being. His aura got bigger and brighter as we filled it with love and light. As I witnessed this transformation I remembered Dr. Richard Gerber's quotation, "Unconditional love is the most powerful healing force in the universe." And I thought quietly to myself, "Yes, it's really true and these group members have learned to pull in the energy of love from the universal source and send it to this fellow group member. They have really learned to channel the energy—pulling it through their own physical bodies and directing it to another human being in need of love."

There was no greater gift they could give to Jeff than the unconditional love he didn't get from his own parents as a tiny infant. Indeed, some of his cries during the release work sounded exactly like tiny baby cries. When I heard those cries I looked over at my assistant and our eyes met with a knowing look. We both knew that cry and we also knew it meant he had regressed to being an infant and was truly releasing the pain and the blocked energy from the emotional traumas experienced as an infant.

This was a dramatic, intense healing session for Jeff. He healed his closed heart chakra by moving into the pain within his heart and releasing it. He opened his heart and received the energy of love like he had never been able to do previously in this lifetime. He transformed easily after this session. He became less angry and more loving. His self-esteem improved greatly and he started taking much better care of his personal appearance. He bonded emotionally with his group members and began to experience heart connections with them.

BREAKING DOWN THE ENERGETIC WALL

Becky, age twenty, was in group therapy to heal her life-long depression. She came because she realized one day that she just never felt happy. One night she wanted to release a feeling of deep sadness about her childhood and the lack of love, abandonment, and rejection she felt from her mother.

I asked Becky to imagine her mother in front of her on the empty pillow and tell her about her heartache and feelings of being unloved. Becky turned to me repeatedly and talked about her mother in a detached kind of way. She was extremely good at rationalizing away her feelings and talking about lots of details and "whys." I would redirect her to talk to her mother and she would freeze, getting absolutely silent. In fact she seemed to turn to stone. Her whole body got rigid and she surrounded herself with a wall of energy. The expression *stonewalled* kept coming to mind as I watched her resist expressing her feelings to her mother.

For the third time I directed Becky to talk directly to her mother and she said, "It's no use. She never listens to me anyway." With that she withdrew her energy and retreated inside, walling herself off from her mother and everyone else in the room. She sat there like an impenetrable fortress—walled off and daring any of us to try and break through to reach her.

I remembered Becky's initial interview when I told her she reminded me of a beautiful princess who had locked herself inside a castle and put a moat around it with double stone walls so nobody could get near to her emotionally. I knew I was watching the results of her early childhood belief, "I won't let people get close to me." Throughout her life she had said, "I like animals better than people. Animals won't hurt you." Becky was very good at resisting so I said a silent prayer to my guides to help me find a way to break through her invisible, energetic wall.

I hesitantly put my left arm around her as I sat beside her on the couch and placed my right hand a few inches in the front of her chest. Her heart chakra was absolutely closed and as I tuned in psychically I felt the searing pain of her heartache flow through my own heart chakra. The pain of it was almost unbearable and I wondered how she could sit there immobilized and stonewalled with all that pain. And I realized in the moment that she wasn't even feeling it because she was a master at denying and detaching from her emotions. This is exactly what she did in childhood to cope with her pain of being unloved. She numbed herself, closed off her heart and put up an energetic shield to protect herself. The shield kept her pain inside so she didn't have to experience it. It also kept people at an emotional distance because they unconsciously felt the wall and stayed away from her. She felt safe but desperately lonely behind her invisible energetic wall.

I gently suggested that Becky give her heartache a color and release it with imagery, using her mind to send the painful energy out of her heart chakra and out of her entire energy field. She chose an "icky green" and began using imagery to send out the negative energy of her heartache. I felt this hot stream of energy pour against the palm of my right hand which was a few inches in front of her chest. It was a hot stream and it was very forceful. At the same time I experienced a lessening of the pressure inside my chest and I knew Becky must be feeling the same sensations.

As she released the energy she became less stonewalled and she started to feel her heartache. The rigid mask of repressed emotions broke, and tears of deep sadness flowed down her cheeks. Suddenly she curled up into my arms and started sobbing. She cried as if she would never stop and I knew she was releasing years of repressed pain from childhood. I gently rocked her as I held her and simply let her cry. In the moment I felt such great joy knowing she was clearing this old pain out of her heart. I was smiling to the other group members over the top of her head. They understood my joy and excitement because they had each done their own release work.

As we rocked together on the couch I felt this sudden burst of fiery energy explode across the front of my chest. Then the energy ballooned out in front of me like an airbag in a car about to have an accident. The balloon of energy was so strong I felt like I could actually palpate it with my hand. I quickly asked Becky, "What are feeling in your chest?" She answered, "My chest went from cold and numb to on fire. I felt this explosion in the front of my chest as I was sobbing. Something burst and all this really hot energy came rushing out! I never felt anything like this before. What's happening to me?"

I answered with such joy in my voice, "You just broke the energetic wall you put around your heart when you were three years old. You just transformed your energy field! Becky, you will never be the same walled-off human being. Now you can let people get close to you. You can let us in because the wall is gone."

Indeed, Becky looked transformed. She was radiant with light shining out of her sparkling eyes and her glowing face. She couldn't stop smiling and laughing. Using imagery I sent the energy of universal love from my heart down my right arm, out my hand and into her heart chakra. Her heart was so open she literally sucked up the energy, filling herself up with it. Her aura kept getting bigger and brighter.

After a few minutes she spontaneously jumped up and gave me a wonderful hug. Becky had never hugged like this before. She used to hug in a rather stiff way that said, "Let's get this over as quickly as possible." I could always feel her invisible, energetic wall when we hugged. It was like she had barbed wire around her heart. This time she held on in a bear hug and seemed to love it. I could feel the hot energy rushing inside her chest cavity. I could also feel a magnetic energy connection between us as our energies met between our heart chakras, and I could no longer feel her invisible wall!

These are the moments I patiently work and wait for with each of my clients. I wait for the transformation of the energy field because I know the field holds the pattern for the other levels of being: mental, emotional, and physical. I know when I facilitate this kind of energy field transformation the client will experience a spontaneous and lasting shift in consciousness at the mental level.

Indeed, Becky did shift from, "I won't let people close to me" to, "People are safe and I can take in love from them." She immediately hugged each of the group members with the same zest as she hugged me. They made comments like, "You feel so different. This is like hugging a different girl. Becky has never felt like this before." Her fellow group members could easily feel the difference in her energy field. They could feel the absence of the wall. And they could feel the magnetic connection that happens when two people hug with open loving hearts.

I know at these moments that I'm following my soul path doing the work I came here to do. I never know when such a deep transformational experience will take place but I know it is the most important work I can be doing. Helping other human beings open their hearts and experience the energy of unconditional love is still a thrill for me no matter how many hundreds of times I have done it in the past. I know deep in my being that I am facilitating growth and change at the soul level.

LAURA'S HEALING JOURNEY

At the human level Laura suffered from both depression and anxiety all her life. If the stress in her life got bad enough she would have panic attacks, which included a racing heart, feeling trapped, and a need to run away from the situation she was in at the time. She lived with a great deal of insecurity and fear, although she kept this a secret from her friends and family. She was able to function very well at work by keeping a protective facade for her coworkers at the office. As she explored her inner thoughts and feelings in the process of psychotherapy, she realized that she had a strong deathwish all her life. She never attempted suicide, but she had always had secret wishes for her life to be over. This deathwish did not become conscious until age thirty-two when she divorced. At that time in her life her favorite saying was, "I just want to crawl in a hole and die."

Laura's deathwish process is typical of a person who is going through life with a closed heart. She often felt lonely and unloved, which was the root cause of her depression and her wish to leave this life on earth. She was not conscious of her own connection to soul and therefore was disconnected from her spirituality. She was going through life with a very materialistic attitude, struggling with work and bills and the many problems of being a single parent. She had very little joy because she was mired down in her struggle to survive.

As she began treatment Laura had no awareness that she had her heart closed all her life. She came from a family with four children and they were all basically nontouching and unaffectionate with each other. There were no hugs and kisses as part of their family process. They were all very inexpressive about all feelings, including the positive feelings of joy and love. Though it was assumed they loved each other, no one actually said, "I love you" to anyone else. Laura's description of her family told me they were all good people who had closed hearts and were all suffering from being disconnected from their souls. Laura said:

> Growing up I didn't realize anything was missing. We showed no affection but I didn't know other families who did, so I didn't feel bad about it. I didn't know what was normal.

Laura's birthstory was a very important cornerstone of her deathwish and her disconnection from both her parents. As a child she had always felt unloved and unwanted by her parents. This was her perception of reality which probably differed substantially from her parents' perception of reality. However, these feelings were not unwarranted because she discovered as a teenager that her parents had had to get married because her mother was pregnant with her.

Laura did a very significant piece of healing work around her birthstory. We sat together on a couch in Thursday morning group. I had my left arm around her shoulders for protection and my right hand on her heart chakra. I induced a light hypnotic trance and asked Laura to go back into her memories of being a baby in the womb. She went back in time and tapped into her thoughts and feelings at that early time of consciousness. As we did the work her heart opened and deep pain poured forth. She actually felt the deep rejection of being an unwanted baby. She felt the pain of it in every cell of her body. She started to cry in deep sobs, and through her tears she said:

> My mother is ashamed that I'm here. She doesn't want to tell anyone she is pregnant. Her parents are very stern and judgmental people. She's afraid they will disown her. Both my parents are wishing I wasn't even here. I'm an embarrassment to them. Everyone is angry I'm here.

I felt the pain of her rejection in my own heart. As I glanced around the group I could see that everyone was deeply moved. Laura's pain was so real and so poignant that it touched the hearts of all of the group members. Next I asked her, "And what did you decide about yourself?" She answered:

> I don't want to be born. I want to go back where I feel loved. I don't want to come here. I have to find a way out of this. This is all a big mistake. I'm wrong for just being born. I want to die before I'm even born.

As she tapped into this knowingness, tears streamed down her face and hot energy poured out of her heart. She released hot energy all over her body as she let herself cry about being rejected from the moment her mother knew of her existence. I knew she was releasing the pain of her deathwish. It had been stored in her cells for forty-five years. I also knew this releasing would allow her to remove at least some of the energetic block in her heart chakra. She had formed the blocks when she closed off her heart to deaden this pain. Now, as she released the pain she could begin to open her heart. As she opened her heart she could experience the sensations of taking in loving energy.

After she finished releasing, I began sending the radiant universal energy from my heart through my arm and hand and into her heart. This was the loving energy she needed at the time of her birth. I mourned with her the fact that her parents did not have the experience of receiving it themselves. They did not know the feeling of this loving energy. I mourned with her the fact that they had their hearts closed to this beautiful new human being born into their care. We both mourned the fact that they knew how to care for her as a physical human being but not as a spiritual being. They knew how to care for her body but not her heart and not her soul. They fed her physical body with milk but they didn't know how to nourish her soul with the milk of human kindness—the energy of divine love.

This releasing process went on for about twenty minutes. Three group members were able to see energy fields and the changing patterns of our auras. As we finished all three described the very same picture. Laura's aura was very dull and small as we began the work. My aura was very big and bright white. As I sat beside her on the couch my aura surrounded hers like a big umbrella. As she released her pain her aura got bigger and brighter. As we finished the pain release, I sent healing energy into her heart chakra. I used my mind to create a channel of the radiant healing energy and filled her heart chakra with white light. As we did this her aura got even more brilliant. Her whole chest got as hot as fire and she described it as feeling full.

It was an incredibly beautiful moment for both of us. This work touched my own heart and I had tears gently flowing down my own face the whole time I did the release work. Laura and the other group members were used to seeing me cry as I did this kind of deep work. They understood that my tears were simply a sign that I was touched at the very core of my being. Throughout the work my own heart was wide open and flowing with the energy of unconditional love.

After we finished the work, the three group members who could perceive energy patterns of the higher frequencies started describing a most unusual happening in the energy field around me. Throughout this piece of work I was sitting with my arm around Laura and my back to an East window. About halfway through the process a shaft of bright white light came through the window and went directly into the back of my heart chakra. This shaft of light stayed present for a good ten minutes. Each of the three confirmed that they "saw" it. This made it more believable to me than if only one person had reported seeing it. The other seven group members without the gift of subtle energy perceptions were not able to tune into this reality.

Driving home that night I had time to reflect about the healing work of that morning. I had a sense of awe that I was involved with such deep spiritual work. I believed the three group members who described the shaft of light coming into my heart chakra. I remembered their animated conversation describing how it looked to each of them. It was punctuated with remarks like:

> Did you see it, too? Oh wow! It was so neat! I knew I saw it but I'm glad to have a confirmation because it is hard to trust my perceptions at this level.

I had often wondered how I could sustain such a high energy level while I did this heartwork. Perhaps this was the answer to my question. Perhaps I am often being filled with white light as I do this heartwork with my clients. At the heart level I believed and trusted that this was true. I found myself wondering what forces were sending and directing that shaft of light. I also wondered, "Why me?" Again I yearned for the expanded consciousness that would allow me to tune in to that level of knowing. I longed for the time when that would happen. I wondered to myself how long it would be.

And as I continued my drive I felt myself slip from this knowingness of the heart to the human level of doubting. I felt myself shift from the heart level to the mind level. I began questioning with my logical mind: "Is it really true? How could this be? Where's the evidence? Do you really believe there was a shaft of light coming in your clinic window? Maybe it was just the early morning sun? Maybe it has no significance at all? Maybe this is all make believe. But how did three people all see the same thing if they were just making it up? How can I make sense of this?"

After I allowed myself to be with these questions for a few minutes I shifted again to the heart level and listened for the whispering voice of my soul. The messages I received gave me great comfort: "Follow your guidance. Follow your heart. You know in your heart what is real. Trust your feelings. Trust the process of your journey. Each step of your journey is being guided. You are not alone."

"No attempt should be made to cure the body without the soul,..."

– Plato

CHAPTER 10

RADIANT HEART - RADIANT HEALTH

I GOT IT! SEVENTEEN YEARS LATER

t was a hot summer day seventeen years after my father's death. It was my day off from my clinic and I sat enjoying the sun as I wrote in my journal. I recorded my experiences of doing subtle energy work with the heart chakras of my clients. I also browsed through *Vibrational Medicine* by Dr. Richard Gerber. I was excited to find a medical doctor writing about physical diseases, subtle energy, and chakras. He believed heart disease was caused by energy blocks in the heart chakra. He also noted that heart disease could be alleviated or prevented by healing the energetic heart. I remember thinking that it was a very interesting theory and I kept on reading. Dr. Gerber states:

> The lessons of love are among the most critical that we must learn during our allotted time upon the physical plane. Difficulties in learning these lessons can manifest as abnormalities in the function of the heart chakra which, in turn, affects the physical heart. . . . It is ironic that most doctors and patients fail to recognize the significance of the energetic link between heart disease, the heart chakra, and one's inability to express love.

> One of the most important links between the heart chakra and a physical organ is seen in the association of the heart chakra with the thymus gland.

Finally, my brain tired of thinking, writing, and studying. I put down my books and took a long, hot shower. I was concentrating on the wonderful feel of the water pounding on my crown chakra when I got this flash of connection. The awareness popped out of my subconscious with such force that I lost my balance. I remember leaning against the shower wall for support. In that moment I finally became conscious of what I was really doing with Radiant Heart Therapy.

I knew in this flash of intuition:

> The Radiant Heart Therapy I'm doing daily with my
> clients is the work my father needed to heal or prevent
> his heart attack.

My own heart opened and I cried such tears of joy. I couldn't stop
crying. I stood in the shower, my hand over my own heart chakra, my
tears joined in the water from the shower, thinking:

> My God, I didn't know. I had no conscious plan to
> develop a method that would have healed my father.
> Oh, my God! It took me all these years to get it.

Making the connection had something to do with the water
pouring over my head and opening my crown chakra to my Higher
Self and divine inspiration. I can't predict or plan it, but I have had
many "psychic" kinds of experiences while taking a shower.

I always thought it was an interesting bit of synchronicity that I sat
in a class on psychotherapy at the very moment my father had his first
heart attack. When I think about it, I hear my Higher Self say,
"Remember, there are no accidents." The class was where I needed to
be to take my first step down my path to Radiant Heart Therapy.

I know my life is very guided. When I start doubting about divine
guidance I remind myself of the synchronicity of that moment. I also
remind myself that I developed Radiant Heart Therapy intuitively
without thinking about it with my logical left brain. It developed
outside my consciousness, from the inspiration that I now believe was
the whispering voice of my soul.

My life plan at the soul level had all the perfect ingredients for me
to evolve and do the work I came here to do. It had all the ingredients
for me to grow and evolve, becoming conscious of who I really am, a
soul with a physical body, a human with a radiant heart.

TRAVELING AND HEALING

Prior to 1992 I only worked with clients in ongoing psychotherapy
sessions, meeting with them weekly in individual and group sessions
and using the Radiant Heart techniques to facilitate in-depth
transformation over a fairly long period of time—one to five years.
Clients who decided only to solve the crisis that brought them into
therapy stayed six months to one year. Clients who desired to do the

deeper work of personality transformation and spiritual transformation stayed in the process longer. I explained to each of them that the journey of healing your life, your personality, and your connection back to soul is a lifelong journey. I expected to be only a part of that as they would continue growing and expanding their consciousness long after finishing their process with me.

In 1992 I began traveling and teaching workshops on Radiant Heart Therapy at international conferences on energy medicine and spiritual healing. Through these teaching experiences I connected with several holistic healing centers and began traveling to these centers to do one-time healing sessions with their clients. This was a totally different way for me to work because I was used to working with my clients in repeated sessions on a weekly basis over an extended period of time. I was also used to working in group sessions and using the energy of the entire group to facilitate the healings.

As I agreed to do this new process, my human self felt anxious and unsure of myself. I knew Radiant Heart Therapy was very successful in assisting my on-going weekly clients with their transformational processes. I knew this because I had been doing it for ten years and I had seen the consistent results. As I considered traveling to other centers, I felt unsure of myself because I had never done one-session healings before. In fact, I did not really believe in one-session healings.

My belief system at the time was that healing the damage from early childhood emotional traumas needed to be done over a period of time with consecutive sessions. I believed this process was necessary to give each client time to integrate the energy changes, make their many redecisions needed for healing their inner child, and learn the visualization techniques for keeping their vital life force energy flowing smoothly after completing their work with me. Yet, in spite of my belief system, I agreed to travel and do these one-session healings. A part of me was saying, "What am I doing?"

It must have been my inner guidance prompting me to agree in the moment when I was invited to travel and work in this way. After making the arrangements I had many moments of doubt and indecision. I wavered back and forth between believing these sessions could be productive and believing they would fail. I also worried I might stir up more than clients could comfortably handle in one session. I wavered back and forth between going ahead with the plan and calling to cancel.

I finally realized I was wavering back and forth between my human self and my Soul Self. My human self was saying, "This is not possible."

My Soul Self was saying, "Anything is possible with the help of spirit guidance." I decided on the human level to trust the universe and flow with the process of what Spirit was asking me to do. Obviously, I would not have been presented with this opportunity if Spirit did not want me to learn to do one-session healings.

A SIGNIFICANT DREAM

I awoke the morning of my first day at a new clinic in Oregon feeling rather strange. I had this vague sense of dreaming something important, but it was lost in the depths of my unconscious mind. As I lay awake in the first few moments of the day I was aware of feeling very emotional and my heart chakra felt wide open. My chest was all filled up with this wonderful hot energy. I felt so incredibly loved. I wondered what kind of dream could have opened my heart and filled it with so much loving energy. Suddenly the dream burst through from the depths of my unconscious mind and I burst into tears just remembering it.

These were tears of joy because I was remembering a wonderful experience of talking with my father on the other side. In my dream, he and I were standing facing each other and having a very deep serious conversation. We both had our human bodies and he looked like I remembered him before he transitioned to the other side twenty years earlier. I knew we were on the other side because we were both surrounded by this radiant light. The same light radiated from the core of my father's being, illuminating his body and his face.

We stood there sharing for a long time, and then he suddenly turned into this bright glistening energy ball. His body simply melted away and a big ball of energy flew towards me from his heart chakra. This ball of bright radiant energy moved forward with a meteor-like tail trailing behind it. The ball of energy swished towards me, brushed right against the center of my heart chakra, came up towards my face, and arched back over before it went zooming out into the universe. I watched it go with both joy and longing.

My father had just touched my heart in a very significant way. No wonder I awoke with my heart wide open and feeling so incredibly loved. This dream was such a gift. I will always treasure it. How perceptive of my father to know I needed him and his loving supportive energy as I felt so unsure beginning this new way to work. I remembered how he used to encourage me when I was fearful saying, "That's my girl. I know you can do it."

I kept this dream a secret from my coworkers and clients that day. I didn't want to dissipate any of the special feeling by sharing it. So I kept it inside my heart knowing that again the universe had sent me exactly what I needed so that I could do the healing work with an open, loving heart. I felt very taken care of. Again, I knew I was assisted greatly from the other side and I heard the message with my inner mind, "You are not alone."

HEALING THE HEART — HEALING THE SOUL

"For every physical body is a schoolroom and every disease is a lesson."
— Barbara Brennan, *Hands of Light*

My first client that day was a man who had been severely ill for the previous ten years. John was a retired paper mill worker. As we met I connected with him immediately through his intense blue eyes. I asked him to tell me his health history and what he wanted from this healing session. He was only sixty-two years old, but he had been forced into early retirement five years previously because of his physical condition. At that time he was so ill that he had spent two years unable to get out of bed.

My heart went out to him as he described a five-year history of getting sicker and sicker while doctors were unable to diagnosis his condition. Finally, he found his way to a holistic physician who diagnosed his condition as metal toxicity, severe food allergies, environmental allergies, and chronic fatigue syndrome. He had improved greatly but he could not seem to get totally well.

John also developed a heart condition and had just failed a stress test at his cardiologist's office the week before. His main focus for this session was to see if I could help him heal his heart problem. He was very scared about having a heart attack or dying from irregular heartbeats. Several years earlier his heart had started beating irregularly, skipping beats, and pounding in his chest. This problem seemed to be getting worse instead of improving, and John was frightened.

I briefly explained the Radiant Heart process to John and asked his permission to put my hands on his heart chakra so I could tune in to his energy field. He agreed without any hesitation. His heart chakra opened easily and within minutes I tuned in to a most incredible emotional pain, which resonated in my own heart chakra. Trusting that my body was attuning to his, I asked him if he was feeling the same thing. He nodded silently looking rather mystified by what was happening to him. I felt as if my heart would break with the pain in my chest. I intuitively asked John:

> Have you ever had some kind of heartbreak that you never got over?

He nodded his head, unable to speak for a few moments. I could feel the heartache filling his whole chest and the energy of it moving up into his face and his eyes. He burst into tears and related:

> Yes, my son was electrocuted on the job. He was operating a crane when it hit the high tension wires. I still remember the moment I got the call. The world seemed to just stop for a time. I don't think I ever got over it.

I instructed John to focus on the pain in his heart and simply be with it allowing it to get bigger. Then I asked him to give the pain a color. Within a few seconds he saw the pain as black. I gave him these directions:

• Visualize opening a spot in the front of your heart chakra.
• Give every cell in your body permission to release the stored negative energy of this emotional trauma.
• Release the negative energy from inside every cell and from the spaces between the cells.
• See black energy forming a geyser of gushing energy like an oil well.
• Send the geyser straight out of your chest into my hand. (My right hand is now about four inches in front of his chest.)
• Release all the old negative energy from your son's death.

As John entered this visualization, a cylinder of hot air flowed from his heart chakra to my hand. It felt like he had turned on a hair dryer that was blowing from inside his chest. Hot energy also flowed out the back of his heart chakra with equal force into my left hand. John's body heated up and the whole room became hot from the energy pouring out of his body. Tears flowed down his cheeks, though he is a man who claims he never cries.

After approximately ten minutes, John reported that the black geyser was changing to gray and then to a clear stream of energy in his mental pictures. At the same moment, I felt the stream of energy pouring from his chest begin to lessen in intensity and temperature. These spontaneous changes indicated we had finished the release work. The stored negative energy of his son's death was now released from his heart chakra. Next we visualized bringing the radiant healing energy into John's chest. His chest grew very hot. His face was glowing and he grew very peaceful.

I asked John what he did after his son's death. His response was significant:

> I started working sixteen-hour shifts and drinking real heavily. I knew I was trying to kill the pain. Nothing seemed to help. I just wanted to die.

My next question was an important one for John:

> After your son's death how long did it take before you started getting physically sick?

He responded immediately, "Just two years." I sat there quietly, allowing the truth to come to his consciousness. I saw the look on his face as he realized the connection between his buried emotions and the loss of his health. He kept shaking his head and repeating:

> I just never knew. I just never knew. I didn't know I was killing myself.

I felt very sad as we finished this session. I felt sad for all of humanity who are carrying grief and have had no training as to how to release it. I was sad for John that he did not know to ask for help with his emotions when his son died. Like most people, he coped in the only way he knew, which was to bury his feelings and carry on trying to deaden his pain.

I believed this emotional process was the real reason John became ill in the first place. I knew in my heart that doing the emotional release work immediately after his son's death would have prevented ten years of emotional pain and agony for John. I also knew in my heart that John could have prevented his physical illnesses if he had been able to release his emotions and avoid creating an energetic block in his heart chakra. Psychotherapy and healing for his grief was the real preventative medicine that John needed twelve years earlier.

John's physical health changed dramatically after this healing session. His chest pain ceased and the erratic heart rate cleared up significantly. Two weeks after our session he returned to his cardiologist and repeated the stress test he had failed a month earlier. He passed with flying colors and his cardiologist looked puzzled as he announced:

> You are clear. You have no evidence of heart disease. I don't know what you have been doing but keep it up. You don't have to come back unless you develop another problem.

This healing session also produced significant emotional changes for John. I interviewed him three months after the session and he described these results:

> The heaviness in my chest area is gone. I used to feel this sense of having a big weight on my chest. Now that is gone and I feel unrestricted. Physically, I feel lighter. I can't explain it any more than that.

> My heart doesn't hurt anymore about my son. I guess now I'm talking about my emotional heart rather than my physical heart. It's so strange. The facts haven't really changed but I've changed. My son is still dead, but now when I think of him I don't feel any emotional pain. I can't for the life of me explain to anyone how this change happened, but I know it is real for me.

As I listened to John, I felt very blessed that I had learned to be a channel of the healing energy. I felt very blessed to have guidance and help from the other side. I wished with all my heart that I had the ability to see into the other dimension so I could know what spirit beings were assisting me from the other side. I yearned for the day when my consciousness would open to that level of sophistication. I even found myself wondering if my father had been part of the spirit team guiding the work. My intuition said yes, but I had no real proof.

I reflected how much John was like my father. I had this sense of my father still being present from my dream. I felt this great sadness that he was on the other side and I could not use Radiant Heart Therapy to heal his heart chakra. I wondered what his heartache was about? What kind of emotional pain had he carried for years without sharing it with anyone? What was his inner process that created the energetic blocks in his heart chakra? I felt this deep sadness that we never shared at that intimate level. Had he been alive he probably would not have been able to tell me because he would have been in denial. Without someone to guide him as I had guided John, my father would not have been able to bring to consciousness the root causes of his illness.

My human self felt this yearning to have been able to heal my father. And yet my Divine Self also knew that it wasn't meant to be. At the human level I needed to trust that what was meant to be was exactly what was happening. I was meant to go through the pain of losing him so that my heartache would push me to search for answers for myself. My searching helped me to expand my consciousness and open to a whole new perspective about life. In that process I found the joy of my life—my work of learning psychotherapy, healing, and developing the Radiant Heart Therapy. And in that process I also found myself—my real self, which is my divine nature or my soul.

It was all part of some grand plan that sometimes seemed beyond the comprehension of my small human brain. I could feel myself switching from the human perspective to the spiritual perspective— moving back and forth in my consciousness. It was a bit like looking at one of those pictures where you can see two different realities by changing your perception—the old woman and the young woman or the vase and the faces. Indeed, life has two very different realities depending on whether you are viewing it from the human level or the soul level.

THE PAIN OF IT IS KILLING ME

On this same trip to Oregon the nutritionist asked me to do a healing session with Steve, who was a cancer client who had been making medical history just staying alive. This forty-five-year-old man had been fighting cancer for eight years. He had a growing type of melanoma with a very poor prognosis. The average patient lived only twelve to eighteen months with this diagnosis. The nutritionist attributed his success to a very strong will to live and his willingness to combine traditional treatments with alternative medicine procedures as he traveled along his healing journey. Steve would be in remission for months and then another tumor would appear. They desperately wanted to find the root cause of his illness so that he could heal it and finally stay clear of the cancer.

Of course I attributed the root cause to some emotional trauma that was causing a block in Steve's energy field. I had no idea what that might be but I trusted that we would find it as we did the healing work.

When I met Steve I was not prepared for what I saw. He certainly did not look like a cancer patient. He was a very large Italian man with a very big energy field and an incredible zest for life. Although he had been through numerous bouts with cancer, chemotherapy, and radiation, he had restored his physical body using healthy foods and megadoses of vitamins and minerals. He didn't even look sick, but his medical tests showed that his blood chemistry was still abnormal and his immune system was functioning far below a healthy level. He still lived with the fear of a major recurrence of the melanoma. His immunologist would not give him a clean bill of health until the blood tests reached specific levels.

The setting for this healing session was magnificent. We met at Steve's resort home on the Oregon coast. We could see the great Pacific Ocean as we took our places in his living room. It was Easter Sunday morning and I was greatly aware of the spiritual influence that might have on our session. For me Easter had come to signify a time of deep transformation through death and rebirth. My hope for Steve was that he would be able to attain a rebirth through this healing session. As we took our places I said a silent prayer, asking for spiritual assistance as I did the heartwork with Steve.

I directed Steve through the grounding exercises and opening his crown chakra to the radiant healing energy. Immediately, I could sense that he was very adept at visualizing because the energy started building intensely inside his heart chakra. His whole body got hot within several minutes. The heat started radiating out into the room. As I kept my hands on his heart chakra I could feel his emotional pain beginning to well up inside his chest. It seemed to come from the very core of his being. As it was building I had not a clue what it was about, but I knew it was a very deep, old emotional pain. I simply sat with Steve allowing and witnessing the process. At times I coached him to breathe into the pain so it would intensify and be easier to release. Suddenly Steve broke into deep sobs saying:

> I hate what this divorce is doing to my boys. The pain
> of it is killing me.

I was elated that this statement popped out of his consciousness at the very beginning of the work. I knew that Steve did not see the significance of what he had just said. However, I felt this incredible energy shift in myself as I heard it and I knew something very important had just happened. Intuitively, I knew we had just found the key to his deathwish, even though we had not explored the history and the details about this divorce. I knew this pain and the fact that he was blocking this pain were the very core factors that were causing his body to create the cancer. And I knew we needed to proceed with releasing this deep emotional pain in order to remove the root cause of his illness.

I asked Steve to give me a brief history of his family situation and this divorce. My heart grieved for him as he explained that he had been quite unhappily married to a woman who was very angry and quite unloving.

As Steve described his marriage the pain in his chest kept increasing and increasing. I could feel the same pain. I felt a stabbing pain in the center of my heart chakra at the front of my chest. It felt as if someone had plunged a knife in the center of my heart. I also had a deep ache in the back of my heart chakra between my shoulder blades. I asked Steve to describe his physical sensations in the moment and he described exactly the same pains. Suddenly he got a shocked look on his face and said:

> My first cancer tumor was right there where that pain is now. It was on my back right between my shoulder blades.

Steve appeared quite amazed about this coincidence of his present emotional heart pain and the site of his first tumor eight years earlier. As he thought about this, he realized that this first cancer tumor appeared about four years after he discovered his wife was having numerous affairs. No one had ever made any connection between his heartache and his cancer. I silently marveled at how the body is merely a reflection of what is going on at the deeper levels of consciousness— particularly at the heart level. And I silently thanked whatever forces allowed this connection to appear before us with such startling simplicity that we could not miss seeing it.

I explained to Steve that he needed to release all the stored negative emotions surrounding his ex-wife. I also explained to him that these buried emotions were stored as negative energy in the cells of his body. This negative energy was causing blocks in the flow of his vital life force energy, thus shutting down the normal process of healing in the body. To accomplish the release work, I had Steve imagine his wife's face directly in front of us and begin talking to her as if she were really there. As he talked to her he began releasing words, tears, old negative thoughts, and old buried feelings. He also released hot energy from all over his body.

This process continued for fifteen or twenty minutes. Within the first few minutes he was enraged and screaming at his wife. The feelings seem to come from the depths of his abdomen. I held my hand on his abdomen and felt this hot ball of energy stored there. He was literally "screaming his guts out" as he released years of stored anger over her betrayals. For the first time he vented his anger at her instead of at the men involved in the affairs. In the torrent of words that he released he said:

> I just hate you. I hate you for not loving me. I hate you.
> I hate you. I hate you for hurting our boys. I hate you
> for being so selfish.

Throughout this release work he sat on this chair with the energy pouring out of his body. It came off his face, his back, the whole front of his torso, his arms and legs, and even the top of his head. I sat beside him holding my right hand on his abdomen and pushing gently to facilitate the release of the stored negativity. I kept my left hand on the back of his heart chakra and I could feel hot energy releasing there the whole time. We both became incredibly hot and the room filled with this heat as if an oven had been turned on and left open. At times I wished I could "see" as well as feel the energy of his stored emotional pain. It must have looked like a fourth of July explosion happening in his energy field. At one point Steve said:

> I feel like the top of my head is going to fly right off. I
> can't believe I'm doing this. I can't believe I'm feeling all
> this. I finished this divorce three years ago.

After a few minutes, Steve's anger subsided and he moved into a deep sadness that filled his whole chest. I thought his heart might break with the pain of it. I had him pick a color and visualize sending it out of his heart chakra and into my hand. He saw the sadness as orange and in his inner mind he saw it spewing out of the front of his chest like a geyser of orange oil coming out of an oil well. The energy of it felt very different than the energy of his anger. This was thick and moving slowly where as the anger energy was hot and moving fast. He cried as if his heart might break as he released this deep sadness.

As the sadness subsided, he flowed into feeling guilt and remorse about his own part in contributing to the failure of his marriage. This energy of guilt and remorse had a different feel to it than the anger or the sadness. It is very difficult to put these subtle differences into words. Just as his tone of voice changed with each different feeling, the vibrations of the stored energy changed with each different feeling.

It was exciting for me to be able to sense the changing vibrational frequencies with my hands. I realized I was using my hands and my intuition to sense the changing vibrational frequencies of the different feelings. My process could be likened to a deaf person who has learned to "listen" to music by putting his or her hands on a piano and sensing the changing vibrations as the musical notes change in frequency. It is a process of "listening" with the hands and the inner ear instead of the physical ear.

This healing session continued for two full hours, with Steve flowing from one feeling to another as he released through words, tears, and visualizations. He spontaneously went back through his life and allowed his old stored hurts to surface one by one. They seemed to emerge effortlessly from a place deep within the center of his being. I had no history about Steve's life so it was impossible for me to guide him. I could only follow his lead and keep supporting him as we allowed the releases to continue. It seemed as if a dam had broken and the water kept pouring forth with such force that it was impossible to stop it or control it. In my mind I likened the dam to a thick wall Steve had always kept around his heart to protect himself from his emotional pain. And the gushing water was all Steve's repressed emotional pain from years of not expressing his feelings.

Near the end of the session Steve spontaneously saw himself walking through a green meadow with the sun shining brightly on him. He saw "things" flying out of the top of his head as he walked along in the sunshine. At the same time hot energy was pouring off the top of his head as I held my hand above his crown chakra. He was jubilant as he watched this video in his mind and kept seeing these "things" flying out of the top of his head. He was releasing so fast there was no time to even know or discuss exactly what he was releasing.

Suddenly Steve got very quiet and a look of awe came over his face. His eyes were closed but he started describing what he was seeing with the videos of his inner mind:

> Everything is swirling colors. I see waves of green and then waves of purple. The colors are magnificent!! I've never seen anything like it. Now God's face is appearing out of the purple. He's smiling at me and saying, "I love you, Steve." That's all—just I love you.

I still had my hands on Steve's heart chakra at the moment he saw God's face. I could feel this explosion of energy as he took in the message of God's unconditional love. The inside of his chest became burning hot and his heart chakra opened with a burst of energy. It was like a bomb exploding in the center of his heart chakra. The energy of the explosion sent shock waves of hot energy racing through his chest. I felt all this happening under my hands as I kept them lightly over Steve's heart chakra.

At the same exact second I felt the very same energy explosion in my own heart chakra. It was exciting for me to experience the energy explosion. It was also a definite confirmation of what my hands were sensing in Steve's heart chakra.

As we finished the healing session, Steve looked totally different than when we started. His energy field expanded and he became radiant—absolutely radiant. His eyes were lit up and energy poured off his face. The energy pouring off his whole body filled the room with the feeling of electricity. He was euphoric, and he couldn't stop laughing and crying at the same time. He exclaimed:

> I can't quit smiling. My face hurts from smiling so much. I feel like I love everybody. I'm in love with life. God loves me! And I love me! I've never felt so much love in my entire life. My heart is on fire.

Steve stood up and we hugged in a long heart-to-heart hug. Indeed his heart was on fire. I could feel it hot against the front of my chest as we stood there together sensing the healing energy of spiritual love. Within seconds a hot stream of energy began flowing back and forth between our heart chakras. There was no denying its presence. It was hot and it was both electric and magnetic. We both felt it and we both knew it was sacred. We stood there transfixed for a long time, not wanting to break the magic of the moment.

RESULTS OF THIS HEALING SESSION

"I am convinced that unconditional love is the most powerful known stimulant of the immune system."
— Bernie Siegel, *Love, Medicine & Miracles*

This two-hour healing session on Easter Sunday morning produced dramatic results. Psychologically, Steve became a very different person. He lost his fears about cancer returning and taking over his body. He healed his deathwish and his depression that he did not know that he had. He opened his heart and was able to keep it open for months after this healing. He seemed to be able to rise above the ordinary stress in his life and feel the spiritual love. He laughing described himself as "Teflon coated" because stress seemed to slide right off his back instead of upsetting him.

Steve had been working with an immunologist for several years. This doctor was using prescription drugs to stimulate Steve's immune system in an effort to produce more white blood cells, more lymphocytes, and more T cells. This would give Steve more power to eliminate the cancer cells with his own immune system. This doctor had been doing monthly blood studies and keeping exact records of Steve's statistics. Two weeks after our healing session Steve went for his usual monthly check-up. The doctor could not believe the dramatic changes in all of his blood statistics. All the important counts were dramatically improved.

This immunologist also checked all the former sites of melanoma on Steve's body. He was always happy if he could get three or four red pimples to appear on these sites using the prescription drugs. These red pimples were an indication that Steve's own immune system was fighting the cancer. The doctor was incredulous to see that every previous cancer site was covered with red healing pimples. He counted over fifty healing pimples and finally gave up trying to record the exact number.

Steve had not yet told his doctor about our healing session using Radiant Heart Therapy. Luckily, this doctor was very receptive and listened to Steve with an open mind and an open heart. He had never heard of the kinds of experiences Steve was reporting, but he believed in miracles and he believed in spontaneous remissions. This immunologist was very supportive of Steve and encouraged him to believe in the miracle he saw reflected in the blood statistics. His comment to Steve was, "I don't understand it but I have to believe something happened to you."

Each month for the next three months Steve's blood chemistry statistics continued to improve. We did not have any more contact and Steve did not do any other healing sessions. It seemed as if the healing energy was still in his system and was still "cooking". After four months the immunologist announced:

> All your blood statistics are above normal. Your lab
> tests show you no longer have cancer.

I sat alone in meditation after hearing Steve's medical report. I tuned into the joy in my heart. I heard my own voice in my head saying, "Follow your joy. Follow your bliss. That's how you know you are on your path. This work is part of your journey." Again, I had that wonderful satisfying feeling of knowing I was on my path doing the work I came here to do. I felt very fulfilled in my purpose in life and very blessed that I had opened to my own spiritual awakening. I was very aware that I could not lead Steve to this level of spiritual awakening if I had not already awakened myself. I silently thanked the universe for providing me these opportunities for awakening. The spiritual forces had indeed opened many doors for me over the years. I silently thanked myself for having the courage to walk through those doors. I felt such a feeling of peace and contentment in the moment. And I knew I was feeling my own conscious connection to soul.

I also had this deep knowingness in my heart that I had turned the "work" with Steve over to the spiritual forces in the universe. I didn't feel like I was even working during the session. The whole process was almost effortless on my part. At the human level I was bringing twenty years of clinical experience to the process but this healing session went far beyond my previous experiences. It went far beyond what I could conceive with my mind. I knew I had gone beyond the level of mind and was working at the level of heart and soul. I opened my own heart and asked for spiritual assistance and guidance as I did the work. Steve opened his heart and received the healing energies. I knew it was these heart openings that allowed the spiritual energies to flow through and produce the miracle of healing.

As I thought about my process of surrendering and turning the work over to the spiritual forces, I wondered how my life would be if I was really able to surrender not only in the healing sessions but on a much bigger scale. What would my life be like if I could surrender and trust my guidance all the time? What kind of assistance would I receive if I opened my heart and asked for all that I needed? I heard my own voice say, "Ask and you shall receive."

As I continued my meditation I reflected on Steve's role in the healing session. I was deeply thankful Steve had trusted me so much and participated so actively in the process. He had absolutely no resistance throughout the session. This was a very important piece of the formula for success in the healing session. I knew from past experience that I needed a client who had an open mind and a willingness to follow my lead as we proceeded in the process. At any point Steve could have blocked the process and blocked the healing energies and we could not have achieved these wonderful results.

I meditated on the definition of healing. Healing is awakening to that which already is. God's unconditional love already existed for Steve. As he opened his heart and released his old buried pain, he awakened to the awareness of his connection back to God. He awakened to the conscious knowing of spiritual love and spiritual healing. He awakened to a conscious connection to his soul. Steve already had everything he needed to heal himself. However, since he was not conscious of this fact he was not able to heal himself. All the pathways for healing already existed. The Radiant Heart process did not create new pathways for healing. It only opened and strengthened the already existing pathways. The Radiant Heart process removed the blocks from Steve's energy field and allowed the healing energies to flow through, as they naturally flow when humans are aligned with their soul.

I wondered to myself why this one healing session had produced such marvelous results. Why had I not been able to produce the same results in previous sessions with other cancer patients? Would I be able to produce these same results again in the future? I became aware that I was thinking from the human perspective of believing *I* had to do it. Actually I know *I* couldn't do it with this session and *I* couldn't do it in any future sessions.

I wondered to myself if the significant ingredient in Steve's session was my ability to surrender at the human level and shift to truly believing that the work would be done at the divine level. I wondered if the significant ingredient was shifting from the level of mind to the level of heart. I made a promise to myself to keep surrendering and keep asking for spiritual assistance as I continued on my healing journey. I also made a promise to myself to keep opening my heart and trusting with the faith of a child. I realized again at a deeper level that I was healing myself as I worked with healing my clients. With each step down my healing path I was more and more awakening to my own conscious connection to soul.

EMPOWERMENT FOR SELF-HEALING

"Our remedies in ourselves do lie
Which we ascribe to heaven."
– William Shakespeare

I returned from this trip to Oregon and focused my attention once again on my work at my clinic in Indiana. As I meditated one morning I was guided to begin teaching my clients to use the principles of Radiant Heart Therapy for self-healing. I knew this would give them a sense of empowerment over their lives and give each of them the tools to be in charge of their own health. The purpose was to help them both align their own energies with their soul and learn a process for transforming their own vibratory frequency to a higher vibration.

ANGIE'S SELF-HEALING

Angie came for psychotherapy because she was suffering with severe depression. Her grandmother had just committed suicide and Angie could not reconcile her grief. She was only nineteen yet she seemed to be carrying the weight of the world on her small shoulders. She looked at me with such sad eyes and said:

I just don't want to go on. I want to go be with my grandma. Life is just too much pain.

I explained to Angie that she had developed a deathwish which she could clear by releasing her grief and using her creative powers to envision a wonderful future for herself here on earth. She didn't really comprehend what I was saying but she agreed to follow my direction and learn a process for accomplishing this goal.

Angie was a very motivated client and she cleared both her psychological and physical health issues in fifteen months. At her young age she had already developed arthritis and a connective tissue disease that made her whole body ache. Angie discovered that her physical illnesses were due to holding onto the emotional trauma of being born with a cleft palate. She had had thirteen surgeries to reconstruct her mouth and upper lip. She went through all these procedures being "a brave little girl" which meant she didn't cry and didn't release her fear. Consequently, she was still carrying the negative energy of her repressed emotions.

Angie attended a weekly therapy group and learned to release her lower frequency feelings. She learned to meditate and became quite proficient at visualizing and bringing radiant healing energy into her body. Within a few months she opened to seeing auras around her fellow group members. She learned to feel energy blocks in her own body and release them using visualizations with color. Angie found she could do all the Radiant Heart techniques on her own and be just as effective as when I was doing the healing sessions with her. I realized how powerful she had become when she told me this story:

> Last week I felt a cold coming on. My sinus cavity filled up and my left ear filled with fluid. I was in a great deal of pain. I went to bed and as I lay there I decided to try a visualization to clear my head. I gave the pain the color red and imagined it flowing out of my ears and my sinus passages. Then I brought in the radiant healing energy.
>
> As I did this I felt this very hot energy move through my ear and all my sinus passages. Something burst energetically and I felt this sticky fluid flow out of my ear onto my pillow. The pain ceased and I went to sleep knowing somehow I had healed myself. The next morning I had no symptoms and I felt perfectly healthy. It was so easy and I feel so excited to know I am so powerful!

Angie's success with self-healing inspired me to make a meditation tape for my clients to use as an adjunct to our work in the office. I was guided to work with Jim Oliver, a wonderful musician, who uses sound frequency for healing. Together we developed a Radiant Heart meditation tape with his keyboard music and with my voice directing guided imagery to achieve the grounding, bringing in the radiant healing energy and merging these two energies in the heart chakra.

I began using this meditation tape as an adjunct to weekly sessions with my clients in Indiana. They found it very useful as a guide to remembering the visualizations that we did in the office. Numerous clients reported significant healing effects while using the tape.

One such client, Flora, a Filipino nurse in her thirties, came for psychotherapy to alleviate her depression. She had a great deal of anxiety and she was very stressed with her responsibilities as a critical care nurse and the mother of three small children. Three years earlier her doctor had detected a heart murmur and diagnosed her condition as mitral valve prolapse. This condition was causing her to experience severe chest pain and shortness of breath.

Within a month of starting treatment with me Flora came down with a severe case of the flu. She was so sick she stayed in bed for a full week. She had just purchased the meditation tape the week before so she started listening to it over and over. She recalls playing it four or five times a day for seven days. At the end of this time she returned to her doctor for a checkup concerning the flu. As he listened to her chest with his stethoscope he looked at her and said, "I don't understand this. I no longer hear your heart murmur. This is quite impossible. This mitral valve condition is not reversible."

Flora shrugged her shoulders and smiled inside. She knew her chest pains were gone and she felt great! She also knew intuitively she had healed her heart murmur and her mitral valve prolapse with her own mind using the visualizations on the tape.

And a woman who held a babe against
her bosom said, Speak to us of Children.
And he said:
Your children are not your children.
They are the sons and daughters of Life's
longing for itself.
They come through you but not from you,
And though they are with you yet they
belong not to you.

You may give them your love but not
your thoughts.
For they have their own thoughts.
You may house their bodies but not
their souls.
For their souls dwell in the house of
tomorrow, which you cannot visit, not even
in your dreams.
You may strive to be like them, but seek
not to make them like you.
For life goes not backward nor tarries
with yesterday.

– Gibran, Children

CHAPTER 11

BIRTHING RADIANT BEINGS

pirit has led me to so many places and given me so many gifts as I continue my journey doing the heartwork. The gift of birthing radiant beings has been one of my greatest treasures. It all began with one client named Marie.

Marie originally came into treatment to learn assertiveness skills. She felt she was having difficulty communicating with other professionals in her job as a hospital nurse. Indeed, she did need assertiveness training but we also uncovered a much deeper psychological trauma as her therapy proceeded.

The first thing I noticed about Marie was her extreme avoidance of being touched. My usual style is to hug my clients at the end of each session. Marie would not allow me to hug her nor did she allow anyone else to touch her in any way. After several months of individual sessions she participated in a weekly therapy group. She was careful to avoid being touched by anyone in the group and darted for the door when other group members exchanged good-bye hugs.

I thought this behavior was rather strange for a thirty-five-year-old woman. Of course, I immediately suspected sexual abuse as the core reason for her defensiveness; indeed, this is what eventually surfaced. Marie gradually became strong enough psychologically to allow the repressed memories of childhood sexual abuse to surface from the secret files of her unconscious. The memories that surfaced over a period of six months were the worst I'd heard in twenty years of practicing psychotherapy. She opened to the memory of her minister grandfather abusing her on the church altar at the age of three. Her adult body still carried the scars of being physically ripped and torn during this episode. Her heart still carried the emotional scars of this incredible abuse.

A major part of our work together was aimed at healing her heart. She had obviously closed it off to protect herself from the devastating emotional pain. I assured her this was a wise decision because these feelings were too much for any child to bear. Now that she was in therapy she could choose to open her heart and release the pain, hurt, and sadness of the betrayal by her grandfather. She did much deep work releasing the emotional pain she had carried for thirty years. The energy of it came out of the cells of her body releasing the energy blocks she created at the time of the abuse. She showed great courage in her willingness to do the release work. Her heart began to heal and she opened a tiny bit to connecting with other members of the therapy group.

As we were finishing this process, Marie discovered she was pregnant. Initially, she was shocked because she and her husband Dave had both agreed that they did not ever want to have a child. They had been married for sixteen years in a very stable but emotionally detached relationship.

Marie adapted rather quickly to the idea of being pregnant. Within the first weeks she even saw the baby as an unexpected blessing. However, her husband had much greater difficulty adjusting to this turn of events. He was extremely angry and seriously tried to convince Marie to have an abortion. He responded from his own woundedness although he was not conscious of the psychological issues preventing him from welcoming this new baby into the family. Marie resisted his pressures and decided to keep the baby. She knew in her heart that she couldn't allow any other choice. She had already bonded heart-to-heart with this new life she carried within her body.

Dave reluctantly entered therapy for himself to come to terms with the prospect of becoming a father. He expressed many deep feelings about the pregnancy, including rage at the prospect of raising a child. Actually his rage was covering deep fears and feelings of inadequacy regarding parenting this new human being. He had very negative memories of his own childhood in a severely dysfunctional family. He had developed a closed heart to hide the emotional pain he felt about feeling unloved and emotionally abused by his parents. He also felt deeply jealous about the prospect of sharing his wife's time and attention with a new baby. Gradually he came to understand that these feelings were the result of his own early childhood needs being unmet. He also came to realize that he could change his feelings by doing his own psychotherapy and making his own shifts in consciousness. I remember saying to both of them:

> This baby is going to be a little miracle baby. And the miracle will be the transformation of each of you.

Marie and Dave spent the last six months of the pregnancy preparing for the birth. They read books on parenting and child development, listened to tapes, took Lamaze classes, and reorganized the house to allow for a baby's room. Together they listened to an audio tape by Dawson Church entitled, *Communicating With the Soul of Your Unborn Child*. I found this tape "accidentally" in a metaphysical bookstore as I was doing routine Christmas shopping. It was my Christmas gift to them and the baby.

The tape contained a whole series of guided imagery exercises designed to bond the soul of the baby with the souls of the parents. It also had imagery designed to open the hearts of both parents and connect their hearts energetically with the baby's heart chakra. Both Dave and Marie enjoyed the process of following these exercises. They even took it with them to Hawaii practicing daily as they vacationed in this beautiful island paradise.

Dave had a transformational experience while he and Marie were listening to the tape in a beautiful garden setting in Hawaii. He described it with a look of wonder in his eye:

> It was a cloudy overcast day and we were sitting on the lawn of our vacation house. We were going through the process and were just at the part that says, "Put your hand on the fetus and send loving energy to this new soul." As I did this the clouds opened up and a stream of bright light poured forth shining right on the three of us. It was a very magical moment for me. Something shifted in me and I felt different about the baby from that moment on. I know I opened my heart in that moment and bonded with this unborn child that I had been rejecting.

This was the a transformational moment for Dave. I was so thankful to the universe for helping him achieve this shift in consciousness. Now he could truly be the father this baby needed in order to be born into love. Now he could open his heart to this infant and give the loving energy needed for a wonderful beginning. Without this shift in consciousness he would have only been going through the motions and the baby would sense he was faking it.

The last month before the birth Marie became quite agitated and fearful about the labor and delivery process. She began having recurring nightmares about the childhood sexual abuse scenes. The impending birth seemed to be stirring up the remains of the buried emotional pain from her childhood abuse. I became quite concerned for her psychological well-being during the painful process of labor and delivery. I actually feared she might experience a psychotic break if the labor and delivery pain was too reminiscent of the earlier pain of her abuse. She spent several weeks doing fear release work in an attempt to totally clear herself of the old trauma. My heart went out to her at the end of one particularly heavy session. I asked if she wanted me to assist her during the birth process. She burst into sobs and hugged me holding on like a very frightened child. She gave me an immediate yes.

At the time we thought we had three weeks until the birth. Marie's obstetrician listened to the circumstances and agreed to allow me in the labor and delivery room. We also scheduled an appointment that same afternoon for me to meet with Dave and Marie together. The three of us spent the hour discussing the preventative measures I felt were necessary for Marie's psychological well-being.

The very next night my home phone rang at 10 p.m. It was Dave saying that Marie was in labor and they were leaving for the hospital. He asked me to arrive at midnight. I agreed and promptly broke out in a cold sweat from a panic attack. Suddenly I realized I had no earthly idea what I needed to do to assist in this process. I had volunteered the day before from my heart. My mind had still not had time to formulate a plan of action. However, I trusted my intuition and my heart, knowing that I needed to be present.

I marveled at how everything had easily fallen into place the day before. I thought it was an interesting bit of synchronicity that Marie did her feeling release work in the morning, received her doctor's approval in the afternoon, and then found an empty hour on my schedule for their couple's session. It all flowed easily and without effort as if we all knew the birth was imminent. As I drove to the hospital I reminded myself, "You are not alone in this. You have a lot of guidance. Listen to your guides. They will help you know what to do."

When I arrived in the labor room Marie was doing very well. She had taped a picture on the wall next to her bed. My heart opened as I looked at this picture. It was a mother's hand reaching out to an infant who was grasping her thumb with precious little fingers. A white light streamed from the mother's hand into the hand of the baby. The light seemed to be connecting them and surrounding their hands in a wonderful glow.

Marie had intuitively found a wonderful symbol of all the energy work we had practiced over the previous months. The caption on the picture stated, "Touching: One of your baby's greatest needs." As I looked at that picture through the long night I silently thanked Marie for her inspiration to seek treatment several years before the birth of this baby. Now that she had made her shifts in consciousness she could truly touch this baby with her loving energy from an open heart. Though they had not yet touched on the physical level I knew somehow that she had already touched this baby's soul.

Dave and Marie had taken Lamaze childbirth training. As her labor pains increased Dave coached her in breathing through the pain. They were quite connected emotionally as they worked together to birth this baby. Dave stood at the side of her bed holding her hand and talking her through each contraction. I chose a place on the other side of Marie, being careful not to interfere in the bonding between them. I induced a light hypnosis trance and began giving Marie hypnotic suggestions designed to help her relax and flow with the process while reducing her fear and her physical pain. Dave followed my lead and repeated some of the same suggestions.

The labor lasted approximately six hours, which was very fast for a first delivery. I used the following imagery to assist Marie in relieving her labor pains:

- See yourself floating on a pink cloud.
- Allow your body to sink into the softness of the pink energy.
- Send any pain you have into the cloud. This wonderful cloud will take away all your pain.
- Allow your body to float above the pain as you relax easily and effortlessly on this wonderful cloud.

Without explaining to Marie, I was purposely using the color pink because it is the energetic color of unconditional love.

These suggestions seemed to help Marie rise above the pain. Several hours into the process I spontaneously added some new suggestions. These must have come from my guidance because I did not consciously plan to say them. It was as if I opened my mouth and suddenly heard myself saying these new hypnotic suggestions. They flowed easily and effortlessly as if I had written a script and rehearsed it. I heard myself saying:

- With each contraction your heart chakra opens to receive this baby in love.
- As your cervix opens for the delivery your heart opens to bond energetically with this baby.

- Your heart is more and more open to receive this baby in love.
- As your cervix dilates your heart chakra opens in equal proportions.
- Visualize opening your heart and sending love energy into this child as you hold him or her against your heart. Surround the two of you in a pink bubble of unconditional love.

As I continued through the night with these hypnotic suggestions Marie stayed rather calm and peaceful, rising above the pain and proceeding with the labor process without any psychological problems. At times through the night I placed my own hand on her chest and sent healing energy into her heart chakra. I found I could easily keep visualizing and sending healing energy into Marie's heart chakra while I verbally sent the hypnosis messages for pain relief and opening her heart chakra. I also felt my own heart opening and being filled with radiant energy as I worked as a channel for Marie.

As I channeled the energy I silently asked God to bless this mother, baby, and father. I silently asked that the radiant healing energy be guided to heal all their hearts so they would be open and clear for the heart bonding to happen easily and effortlessly.

Throughout the process Marie's doctor and nurses were very cooperative. They had no concept of what I was doing with the healing energy and Marie's heart chakra but they could see that Marie was very calm and doing extremely well both physically and psychologically. I felt assisted in that they allowed the process to continue and did not make any negative comments that might have interrupted the process.

The final moment of birth is a moment in time that will always remain as a peak experience for me in this lifetime. I felt so honored to be present and witness this wondrous event. At the moment of birth Marie cried with joy at finally seeing this baby she'd been communicating with for so many months. Her heart was so open that her feelings were flowing easily. She was laughing and crying and being absolutely jubilant. Tears flowed down her cheeks as the doctor placed their beautiful baby girl skin-to-skin on Marie's stomach. Marie began talking to this new human being so spontaneously saying:

> Welcome to the world, little one. I'm your mother and this is your father. We have talked to you for months already. Your name is going to be Katie. We have waited so long to see you and touch you. And now here you are!! We love you so much and we are so happy to have you.

Then Marie brought the baby to her open heart chakra. Dave placed his hand on the back of Katie's heart chakra and sent loving energy into her from his own heart. Marie place her hands on top of his and they both wrapped this baby in a blanket of love. They did this without any communication with each other or any instruction from me. It was as if they were guided by some unseen and unheard directions that were just perfect.

It was such a magical moment, touching everyone in the room. The doctor, the nurses, Dave, Marie, and I all cried with our hearts wide open as we witnessed the absolute beauty of this new soul being received into the world with such loving tenderness.

Then the most amazing thing happened as the nurses took the baby to the bassinet beside the bed. Marie, the woman who couldn't be touched, began spontaneously hugging and kissing her husband, the doctor, the nurses, and me. She threw her arms wide open, drew each one of us up against her heart chakra and hugged us each tightly. She even kissed each one of us, joyously calling out, "I love you."

Marie was so open and so loving that I could hardly believe her transformation. This was not the same woman who had begun treatment three years earlier. I felt like I had witnessed a double miracle. The first miracle was the birth of a new soul in this beautiful baby girl. The second miracle was Marie opening her heart chakra to this baby and then to everyone present in the room. Suddenly, I remembered my words of prophecy to Dave and Marie at the beginning of her pregnancy, "This baby will be a little miracle baby. And the miracle will be the transformation of each of you." I silently thanked all the unseen forces for being present and helping me to facilitate this transformational process.

FIVE YEARS LATER

It has been five years since the three of us created this wonderful birthing process using the suggestions for opening the heart chakra. As I predicted this baby was and is a miracle baby and she has indeed motivated her parents to advance on their individual healing journeys. They both continued in therapy with the goal of healing their relationship and becoming the best parents possible. They both understand at a very deep level that they are preventing the hereditary chain of negative messages from being passed on to another generation. They both understand that the work they are doing is healing future generations.

Dave recalls these feelings about the birth process:

> I had this moment of pure joy when our baby was born.
> I felt this exhilaration that I have never felt before or
> since. My own heart was wide open being in the
> presence of such a miracle. Katie is helping me heal my
> own heart. I'm learning how to love because she came
> into my life and into my heart. I am warmer and softer
> now that I have opened my heart. This is the first time
> in my life that I have felt anything in my heart. I guess
> I am beginning to experience loving with my heart
> rather than with my head.
>
> I am learning so much from parenting Katie. I have
> learned to accept another person and give
> unconditional love. She is also teaching me how to feel
> my feelings. Her feelings are so transparent. She's
> happy, sad, scared, mad and she shows it. In a way she
> is teaching me how to be open with my own feelings.

Marie says of her daughter:

> As a newborn infant Katie was extremely calm, content,
> and peaceful. She slept through the night at six weeks.
> She rarely cried unless she had a reason. As soon as we
> met her needs she would quit crying.
>
> She seems to have a special glow about her. People
> come up to us in restaurants and shopping malls and
> remark about how special she is. Often people say
> things like, "She is such a little angel." I think people
> pick up on her very bright aura.

BIRTHING THE SOULS OF INFANTS

Over the past six years I have worked with eight different mothers
who were in therapy with me before they became pregnant and stayed
in therapy throughout the pregnancy. They all worked with the
principles presented in Marie's story. They all worked with the
parenting techniques that include both energy work and feeling release
with little children. All eight of these babies (both boy and girl babies)
are peaceful, calm, angelic beings. All eight children are radiant with
large, bright auras and open hearts. All eight mothers report receiving

spontaneous compliments from strangers in restaurants and shopping malls:

> Your child is so special.
> I have never seen such a contented baby.
> This one is a little angel.
> Is this child always so good?
> I feel drawn to this baby.
> There's a special light around this child.

What I believe is happening is that these babies have their hearts wide open and their soul energy is radiating forth out into their energy field. The strangers are not conscious of the aura being brighter or bigger but they say things like, "I'm just drawn to this child" and, "This child is so special."

These children are simply wondrous examples of how humans beings are naturally supposed to be—radiant and alive and in touch with their soul energy. I wonder what the world would be like if all children were given the gift of bonding heart-to-heart with loving parents who have radiant hearts and are conscious of their own connection back to soul.

In our modern medicine we have become so focused on the body and the human level of existence that we have forgotten to attend to the soul. This is true in obstetrics as well as in other areas of medicine. To remedy this situation I envision birthing rooms with physicians or midwives who attend to delivering the physical body of the infant and spiritual healers who attend to delivering the soul of the infant.

I believe there is a solution to the current spiritual crisis on the planet and the solution is birthing our children with radiant hearts so they can live on this earth as human beings filled with divine love. Then they will be consciously aware of their soul and their purpose for coming to the earth. They will feel empowered to complete their spiritual lessons before returning to that place called eternity.

THE VISION I HOLD IN MY HEART

"A dream is a wish your heart makes when you're fast asleep."
— Walt Disney Records

My dream is to use Radiant Heart Therapy to introduce the true preventive medicine that I envision for the future. Since we know that a radiant heart results in radiant health the true preventive medicine must begin with teaching people a process for birthing radiant babies who are conscious of their soul connection from the moment of birth. Just imagine what the world would be like if all babies were brought into this world by healthy loving parents who understood the sacred responsibility of parenting this courageous soul who is venturing to our planet.

My dream is to move from healing the wounded hearts of adults to healing the wounded hearts of teenagers. Then they can become conscious, spiritual beings who are awake to their soul connection and create lives that truly integrate the human and the divine. They can heal their own wounds and develop radiant hearts before choosing life partners. Each will then be able to choose a healthy life partner who also has an open, radiant heart and create a partnership which includes a strong heart connection. This would be the ideal loving partnership for birthing radiant babies.

I imagine what the world might be like if prospective parents developed radiant hearts and a consciousness about energy fields and the heart chakra. Their babies would be surrounded with the energy of love from the moment of conception. They would be birthed in a manner that addressed the needs of their tiny human bodies and the needs of their souls. They would never have to experience the painful feelings of being unloved and unwanted. They would never have to feel the pain of disconnection from their spiritual nature.

Imagine what the world would be like if these radiant babies were taught how to honor their humanness and honor their souls. They would know from birth how to integrate the human and the divine. They would be radiantly alive, flowing with the whole range of human feelings. They would know from childhood how to experience and release the emotions of fear, anger, hurt, and sadness. They would know how to think positively and create positive feelings. They would be grounded to the earth and conscious of their soul connection. They would never feel alone because they would be multisensory human beings who are conscious of their spirit guides and guardian angels. They would be conscious of their purpose for this lifetime and have a strong lifewish.

As spiritual beings without a physical body we once swam in a sea of unconditional love energy. We existed in a state of pure light, pure love, and pure health. Imagine that we could be born into this physical world and be surrounded with the exact same sea of unconditional love energy. This would be possible if both parents were conscious of their soul connection and had the ability to open their hearts and transfer the energy of unconditional love from their own radiant hearts into the heart chakra of the newborn infant. Imagine spiritual beings with physical bodies being able to exist on the earth plane in a state of pure light, pure love, pure health, and pure radiance. Just imagine.

This is my dream for the planet. This is the vision I hold in my heart. This is the true preventive medicine of the future.

"To me it is odd that so many people regard their interests and careers as ends in themselves, rather than as scaffolds for the development, balancing, or expression of faculties of consciousness."

— Richard Moss, M.D.,
The Black Butterfly

EPILOGUE

DISCOVERING MY TRUE PURPOSE
IN LIFE

The process of writing this book has been a transformational journey in itself. Like the rest of my life, it has been a journey filled with emotional moments. I live my life with such passion, and I have also written this book with the same passion. I have felt the incredible joy of being with my Soul Self and flowing with the creative energies that can only come from connecting with that divine part of my being. And at other times I have felt the total frustration of not being able to make the connection and struggling to write from the human level of personality. I had many moments of despair when I felt like giving up. And I had many moments of excitement, laughter, joy, and love. And, of course, I had many touching moments when I wrote about my father and felt his presence guiding and encouraging me still. It has truly been a journey filled with the agony and the ecstasy of the creative process.

Throughout my journey I have felt the frustration of "not enough time" as I struggled with my evolutionary process of becoming an author, while still devoting time to my psychotherapy practice. At times I felt I must choose one or the other, and then I realized the two were complementing each other in a very special way. Spirit had again given me all that I needed to fulfill my purpose.

As I wrote, I had to become more clear about my own theories. And as I taught these theories to my clients, they were able to do deeper work and transform at deeper levels. So, as I wrote the book, I observed this deepening of the heartwork and a deeper honing of my skills as a psychotherapist and a spiritual healer.

As I continued to do sessions with clients, I also received more inspiration for the book. Many, many times I would be struggling with a concept in the book, and a client would speak the answer in a session. I often had the experience of "knowing" that Spirit was speaking through a client and giving me the key for solving the theoretical mystery of the moment. And many times I would finish a session and write detailed notes, knowing we had just created another story for the book.

Throughout my journey I have asked the question, "What is my purpose in life?" Over the years my answer keeps changing. I often wonder when I'll find the true answer. And how can I be sure it is truth? During adolescence and my twenties I never even considered the question. In my thirties I began the process of therapy and I began to think about my purpose in life for the first time. Then I believed my purpose in life was to be a mother and take care of my children in the best way possible. Next I came to believe my purpose was to become a psychotherapist and assist other people with their personal growth. In my early forties I believed that my purpose was to study holistic medicine and create a holistic center. In my late forties I believed that my purpose was to develop the heartwork.

In the process of writing this book I went to Sedona, Arizona, and had a reading with a trance channel named Eileen Rota. She channeled some information from one of my spirit guides that was most helpful in redirecting my thinking about my life purpose. My guide said to me:

> The heartwork is not your purpose. It is only a tool in your true purpose in life which is to develop yourself and discover who you really are.

> Your true purpose in life is the birthing of your spiritual nature. It is finding the connection with your own soul.

Through this reading I became aware that my only true purpose is to open my own heart and reclaim my own radiance. My only true purpose is to align myself with the flowing of spiritual energies so that I can easily develop and expand my own radiant heart. As I opened my mind to these new ideas I thought to myself, "We teach what we need to learn."

This trip produced an interesting shift in consciousness for me. I discovered that none of my original ideas were ever really my purpose in life. The heartwork is only a tool in my true purpose which is to develop myself and discover who I really am. My true purpose in life is the birthing of my spiritual nature—finding my connection to my own soul.

Imagine my surprise in discovering this. Actually it was a tremendous shock to my whole being. It was a major shift in consciousness. It was a shift that required me to look inward at myself rather than outward at my work. I suddenly realized that I had always thought of my work as my purpose. Instead the work is only a means to an end. And the end is me—becoming the best me I can become, becoming aware of the spiritual me. And so I discovered at a very personal level about spiritual evolution and evolving to higher levels of consciousness.

The process of writing this book has taken three years. As I look back I can see that it has been another step on my journey to heal myself. The very process of writing has led me to higher levels of consciousness. It has also led me to continue on my transformational journey to heal my own heart and heal my own soul.

In the process of writing this book, I realized all my life experiences had a purpose. These were situations my soul planned for me to experience so that I might evolve. Some were painful and some were filled with wonder, joy, and love. And they all served a purpose for my growth.

My journey through this lifetime has been filled with much human pain and heartache. I have had the grief and heartache surrounding the loss of my loved ones—my father and my mother-in-law. I have had the heartache of supporting my twin as she struggled with her illness. I have gone through the pain and sadness of divorce and loss of family. At the human level all this pain makes very little sense to me. I ask myself, "What is the purpose of this pain? Why is this happening in my life?"

As I journeyed along my path I often had no answers to these questions about my human pain. I often felt lost in the pain and could not rise above it. And, of course, I often thought I should be able to rise above it. As I look back at my journey I realize that I did not need to rise above it. I realize that my human pain pushed me to begin the journey of transformation. My pain was my great motivator. Without the pain I doubt I would have even begun the transformational journey—the journey inward to the center of my heart. Without the pain I might not have opened my heart and gone through the doorway to connect with my soul.

My journey has also been a journey filled with much joy and love. I have had the joy of watching my clients connect with the beauty of their souls and bring that beauty into their lives. I have had the joy of teaching so many to open their hearts and learn how to love. And I have had the joy of learning so much from each one of these beautiful souls as they share their life stories with me.

While writing this book over the past three years I have evolved so much that I look back at the old me and see her as a shadow of my current self. She is a shadow because I now have more of my soul light shining through my physical being and my own heart has become more radiant. And to that shadow I say:

> Bless you for having the curiosity, the spirit of adventure, the urge to discover, and the will to keep taking one more step on our journey of transformation. For you are a wonderful part of who I have become. And I love you for who you were then.

BIBLIOGRAPHY

Atwater, P. M. H. *Coming Back to Life*. New York: Ballentine Books, 1988.

Beckley, Timothy Green, and Crockett, Arthur. *Angels of the Lord*. New Brunswick: Inner Light Publications, 1993.

Benor, Daniel, M.D. *Healing Research*, Vol. I. United Kingdom: Helix Editions, Ltd., 1993.

Benor, Daniel, M.D. *Healing Research*, Vol. II. United Kingdom: Helix Editions, Ltd., 1993.

Brennan, Barbara Ann. *Hands of Light, A Guide to Healing through the Human Energy Field*. New York: Bantam Books, 1988.

Church, Dawson. *Communicating With the Spirit of Your Unborn Child*. Boulder Creek, CA: Aslan Publishing, 1988.

DeAngelis, Barbara, Ph.D. *Real Moments*. New York: Delacorte Press, Bantam Doubleday, 1994.

Dossey, Larry, M.D. *Space, Time & Medicine*. Boulder: Shambhala, 1982.

Dyer, Dr. Wayne W. *Real Magic*. New York: HarperCollins Publishers, 1992.

Eadie, Betty J. *Embraced By the Light*. Placerville, CA: Gold Leaf Press, 1992.

Gerber, Richard, M.D. *Vibrational Medicine: New Choices for Healing Ourselves*. Sante Fe: Bear & Company, 1988.

Gibran, Khalil. *The Prophet*. New York: Knopf, 1993.

Goulding, Mary McClure. *Changing Lives through Redecision Therapy*. Menlo Park, CA: Shea Books, 1982.

Hay, Louise L. *You Can Heal Your Life*. Santa Monica: Hay House, 1985.

Huffington, Arianna. *The Fourth Instinct, The Call of the Soul*. New York: Simon & Schuster, 1994.

Janov, Arthur, M.D. *The New Primal Scream*. Wilmington: Enterprise Publishing, Inc., 1991.

Johnson, Elizabeth A. *As Someone Dies*. Santa Monica: Hay House, 1987.

Kübler-Ross, Elisabeth. *To Live Until We Say Goodbye*. Englewood Cliffs: Prentice Hall, 1978.

Kunz, Dora Van Gelder. *The Chakras and the Human Energy Field*. Wheaton, IL: The Theosophical Publishing House, 1989.

Laskow, Leonard, M.D. *Healing With Love.* San Francisco: Harper & Row, 1987.

Leadbetter, C. W. *The Chakras.* London: Theosophical Publishing House, 1974.

Levine, Stephen. *Who Dies? An Investigation of Conscious Living and Conscious Dying.* Garden City: Anchor Press/Doubleday, 1984.

Meek, George W. *After We Die, What Then?* Franklin, NC: Metascience Corporation, 1980.

Moody, Raymond A. *Life After Life.* New York: Bantam, 1976.

Moody, Raymond A. *Reflections on Life After Life.* New York: Bantam, 1977.

Moore, Thomas. *Care of the Soul.* New York: HarperCollins Publishers, 1992.

Morgan, Marla. *Mutant Message Down Under.* New York: HarperCollins, Publishers, 1994.

Morter, Dr. M. T., Jr. *The Healing Field, Restoring the Positive Energy of Health.* Rogers, AR: Best Research, Inc., 1991.

Moss, Richard, M.D. *The Black Butterfly, An Invitation to Radical Aliveness.* Berkley: Celestial Arts, 1986.

Pierrakos, Eva. *Guide Lectures, 1-258.* New York: Center for the Living Force, 1956-1979.

Roth, Gabrielle. *Maps to Ecstasy.* San Rafael: New World Library, 1989.

Siegel, Bernie. *Love, Medicine & Miracles.* New York: Harper & Row, 1986.

Tansley, David. *Subtle Body.* New York: Fames & Hudson, 1984.

Verny, Thomas, and Kelly, John. *The Secret Life of the Unborn Child.* New York: Dell, 1986.

Viney, Geoff. Surviving Death, *Evidence of the Afterlife.* New York: St. Martin's Press, 1993.

Whitton, Joel, L. M.D., Ph.D., and Fisher, Joe. *Life Between Life.* New York: Warner Books, 1986.

Zukav, Gary. *The Seat of the Soul.* New York: Simon & Schuster, 1989.

ORDER FORM

If you know someone who would benefit from *The Radiant Heart*, you can order additional copies of this book by filling out the following information:

(Please Print)

Name: _____ Phone: (   )   —

Address: _____

City: _____ State: _____ Zip: _____

Please send me further information on:

     _____ Individual Healing Sessions
     _____ Radiant Heart Seminars
     _____ Professional Training Programs
     _____ Radiant Heart Therapy Retreats
          _____ weekends
          _____ full week

	__Book__	__2 Tapes__
Cost:	$16.95	$20.00
Shipping & handling:	2.00	2.00
Total:	$18.95	$22.00

(Indiana residents include 5% state sales tax.)

Please send check or money order to:

       Radiant Heart Press
       520 Ridge Road
       Munster, IN 46321

Dr. Wendt is available for lectures, workshops, and conferences. Dr. Wendt is also offering a professional training program for healers and psychotherapists. Call 219-836-5109 for details.